STEPPENWOLF THEATRE COMPANY

OF CHICAGO

STEPPENWOLF THEATRE COMPANY
OF CHICAGO

In Their Own Words

John Mayer

Bloomsbury Methuen Drama
An imprint of Bloomsbury Publishing Plc

B L O O M S B U R Y
LONDON · OXFORD · NEW YORK · NEW DELHI · SYDNEY

Bloomsbury Methuen Drama
An imprint of Bloomsbury Publishing Plc
Imprint previously known as Methuen Drama

50 Bedford Square	1385 Broadway
London	New York
WC1B 3DP	NY 10018
UK	USA

www.bloomsbury.com
BLOOMSBURY, METHUEN DRAMA and the Diana logo are trademarks
of Bloomsbury Publishing Plc

First published 2016
Reprinted 2016

© John Mayer, 2016

British Library Cataloguing-in-Publication Data
A catalogue record for this book is available from the British Library

ISBN:	HB:	978-1-4742-3944-8
	PB:	978-1-4742-3945-5
	ePDF:	978-1-4742-3946-2
	ePub:	978-1-4742-3947-9

Library of Congress Cataloging-in-Publication Data
A catalog record for this book is available from the Library of Congress

Series: Theatre Makers

Cover: Jeff Perry, Amy Morton, Francis Guinan © Ian Barford

Typeset by RefineCatch Limited, Bungay, Suffolk
Printed and bound in the United States of America

For my mom

CONTENTS

LIST OF ILLUSTRATIONS

Cover: Jeff Perry, Amy Morton, Francis Guinan © Ian Barford

Chapter 2

Chapter 3

Chapter 4

FOREWORD

by Jeff Perry, Co-Founder of Steppenwolf
Theatre Company of Chicago

At the University of Chicago in the 1950s, Paul Sills, Mike Nichols, Elaine May, and Sheldon Patinkin were among a group of supremely gifted classmates who arguably invented the ensemble culture of theatre and comedy in Chicago. Together they shaped a Chicago environment of self-deprecation, meritocracy, and artistic self-determination that would become the famed Second City. Both that environment and the remarkable ensemble-based films and TV shows of the 1970s helped shape our worldview when Gary Sinise, Terry Kinney, and I gathered six other theatre-addicted classmates from Illinois State University and started the Steppenwolf Theatre Company.

We instinctively made god and goddess out of "ensemble," out of our chemistry, out of the form and pressure of our connection to each other. Deeply reverent of the written word, we simultaneously believed that the quality and texture of how we interacted was where the story lived—it was the space between each other that defined our story telling.

Going into our fortieth season with an ensemble of forty-four actors, directors and writers, I suppose we continue to be one of America's longer-running theatrical examples of "the inmates running the asylum." The level of communal democracy in the early days that forever shaped us was both laughable and inspiring. We would argue equally and for hours about who was going to clean the theatre toilet in the same way we would argue about what play we should do next. It was the most ridiculous way to try and run a theatre organization, but the familial chaos that defined the particular crazy of our group was its greatest joy.

To me the deepest, most compelling work we've done is in response to what William Saroyan called "the shame and terror of the world." Steppenwolf's first resident playwright Dan Ursini, speaking of this quality, wrote, "There is a tension in the work that to me defined the core of Steppenwolf's signature accomplishment. Time and again they produced plays with characters who were deeply alienated and hopeless; and they presented them in a way clarifying the moments of redeeming intimacy and connection which yet occur, even in the most desolate circumstances."

John Mayer has chosen to capture this ongoing theatrical experiment by using the voices of his subjects in a way that echoes the work of the legendary Chicago journalist Studs Terkel. He has created an "insider's" chorus that takes the reader through large swaths of Steppenwolf Theatre's history from the point of view of its artists, board members, designers, directors, writers, and critics. As someone who has loved and lived Steppenwolf from the beginning, I found myself continually amazed and moved by the myriad of events and feelings I had either never witnessed, or had only partially understood.

If you love theatre, and particularly ensemble theatre, whether you have seen every show or are curious to climb aboard for the first time, you are about to get the "First Time Ever VIP Tour" into everything Steppenwolf.

Figure 1. Steppenwolf Ensemble 2016, courtesy of Steppenwolf Theatre Company.

ACKNOWLEDGMENTS

In September of 2014, I received an email from Anna Brewer, Senior Commissioning Editor at Methuen Drama in London. Anna was inquiring to see if I wanted to write a book on Steppenwolf, and although her email was a complete surprise, it set me on the path to completing something that I had considered since I wrote my dissertation about the early history of Steppenwolf twenty-five years ago. I am eternally grateful to Anna for reigniting the fire of my passion to complete this task.

None of what is contained in the book would have been possible without the full support of Steppenwolf Theatre Company. Although a few decades have passed since I had been a presence at the theatre, everyone I encountered along this journey treated me with the utmost respect and support from the very beginning of my work. Each time I sat down with an ensemble, staff, or board member, I was treated like an old friend—and this was even the case with the people I had never met before. Gary, Jeff, and all the others with whom I had history were easy, but the time with everyone else felt the same—relaxed and natural. Thank you to everyone associated with Steppenwolf for your kindness, generosity, and support—I hope you are pleased with the fruits of my joyful labor.

INTRODUCTION

I grew up in Highland Park, Illinois in suburban Chicago, the birthplace of Steppenwolf Theatre Company, where I was a high-school classmate and close friend of Gary Sinise and Jeff Perry, who with Terry Kinney were the original founders of Steppenwolf Theatre Company. Our career paths have taken us in somewhat different directions, but my connection to them and Steppenwolf has never waned. I became a theatre professor and believe that in many ways I was destined to write this book. The Steppenwolf story, however, started quite a bit earlier than our theatre days in high school.

It was 1941, and twelve-year-old Barbara June Fluhrer made a telephone call that in many ways would metaphorically represent the philosophy that shaped the lives of many of her high-school students at Highland Park High School (HPHS)—students who would reimagine the American theatre. She recalled,

> I called the acting studio where my mother worked and said, "Momma, Sally set fire to the house and there's water everywhere." Said my mother, "Well, then, get the mop." And she hung up.

The self-empowering "do-it-yourself" principle implied in this simple story would become the backbone for the entrepreneurial approach that Sinise and Perry, together with Kinney, would use to launch Steppenwolf in 1974. Perry said of his/our mentor Mrs. Greener (née Barbara June Fluhrer):

> At the heart of it always was Barbara June. With her giant industrial flamethrower of life-loving, theatre-loving knowledge and practice she revealed what became the seeds of our passion.

Gary Sinise adds:

> Barbara was a tour de force. She would blow down the hall like she was a spinning tornado. She would entertain us at the same time she

was teaching. Barbara recognized that people needed different things to bring out the best in them. She didn't teach or direct every single person in the same way. A good director does that and I didn't realize how much that was implanted in me until I started directing more later on. All the fundamentals I learned started with her. She saw that I was a do-it-yourself sort—an intuitive kind of person. I had trouble reading and studying, but she gave me confidence and courage. I learned at an early age to just rely on my instincts. When I started directing in the early days of the theatre, I didn't know what I was doing, so I just had to go with my gut. Barbara planted the seeds that eventually led me to pursue it.

I sat transfixed by this very force, myself, in directing class alongside Gary Sinise and Jeff Perry in 1973, as Mrs. Greener preached the gospel of ensemble performance, collaborative spirit, discipline, hard work, and fun. Her philosophy was summed up in two words: "Balls out!" Imagine the sheer audacity of having a directing class for high-school students in which their final project was to direct a one-act or full-length play.

High-school theatre for Gary, Jeff, and me was a religion. We lived and breathed theatre twenty-four hours a day, seven days a week. With all the directing class projects going on, as well as our regular school shows, it was as though we were in a stock company during high school, often rehearsing multiple plays at one time, while simultaneously performing in other shows in the evenings. We were typically at school well into the night, rehearsing and feverishly developing our artistic souls.

Simultaneously, the other early members of the ensemble, including Terry Kinney, John Malkovich, Al Wilder, Laurie Metcalf, Moira Harris, Joan Allen, Rondi Reed, Randy Arney, Francis Guinan, Nancy Evans, Tom Irwin, and H.E. Baccus—many from small Midwestern towns— were learning from a variety of influential mentors at Illinois State (ISU) and Eastern Illinois University and shaping their artistic view of the world. One young professor at ISU, Gail Cronauer, who many mentioned as an inspirational force, shared her perceptions:

> I was young and passionate with boundless energy. I did dinner theatre in the area, because I was so hungry to act. The place [ISU] was very established at the time and I think my coming in began to signal a bit of a shake up.

Cronauer's energy clearly meshed well with the company members she encountered who were not looking for "established." They wanted energy. They wanted passion to match their own; the same passion we had gotten from our mentor, Mrs. Greener, at Highland Park High School.

Steppenwolf literary mainstay John Steinbeck, in his preface to the nonfictional masterpiece *Travels With Charley*, penned my favorite quote from literature, which underscores my philosophy of life:

> A trip, a safari, an exploration, is an entity, different from all other journeys. It has personality, temperament, individuality, uniqueness. A journey is a person in itself; no two are alike. And all plans, safeguards, policing, and coercion are fruitless. We find after years of struggle that we do not take a trip; a trip takes us.

This has certainly been true of the Steppenwolf Theatre journey and of my responsibility to write this book.

My professional experiences over the years set me on a path to engage with the Steppenwolf story in a capacity other than as an ensemble member. I was in the cast of *Grease*, the second "unofficial" Steppenwolf Theatre production ever, back in 1974, which was directed and produced by Gary Sinise inside the gymnasium at his former grammar school, Indian Trail in Highland Park, Illinois. We blissfully did *Grease* nine times to full houses, all of whom had heard about the show through word of mouth, because there was no advertising. The show was free, but Gary boldly passed a hubcap soliciting donations, many of which went into funding the next show later that summer.

I was cast in Tom Stoppard's *Rosencrantz and Guildenstern are Dead*, the third Steppenwolf production, which featured Gary, Jeff, and Terry together for the first time. Jeff had gone to school at ISU and had become fast friends with Terry, and, at Gary's urging, decided to bring him up to Highland Park to work with all of us—but, I have no doubt, particularly Gary. There are so many stories in the history of Steppenwolf that suggest that many of the ensemble members have been somewhat omniscient, because moments such as this occurred with seemingly no sense of what the future held, but led to such good fortune and further synchronicity. In *Rosencrantz and Guildenstern are Dead*, Gary and Jeff were the two title characters, Terry was the Player King, I was scheduled to play Hamlet, and my girlfriend, my first true love, was cast as Ophelia. She and I began to have some highly emotional teenage relationship issues and the pressure of working with her was too much, so I dropped out of the show. The first "misstep" on my pathway to the writing of this book.

In the earliest days of Steppenwolf, in the original eighty-eight-seat basement theatre in Highland Park, we all hung out together. I helped with the move in early 1980 into Chicago as a designated driver of sorts, because I had a V W bus (awash in plush shag carpet and funky paisley curtains) that we used to haul stuff. I was also a sometime procurer of the requisite "pot." After settling into the famed Hull House Theatre, which had previously housed improvisational legend Viola Spolin and Chicago theatre impresario Bob Sickinger, Steppenwolf was ready to become a member of the Chicago theatre community.

One day Gary handed me a script of Lanford Wilson's *Balm in Gilead* and said, "Man, I think there might be something in this for you." I immediately took it home to read it. The first six or seven pages of the script were like nothing I'd ever seen, unintelligible to me, and I struggled mightily to decipher the play—ultimately opting out. I returned the script to Gary and, as they say, the rest is history, because *Balm in Gilead* remains, arguably, the most defining production in the theatre's history. Sitting in the audience at the Hull House Theatre, watching *Balm in Gilead* in production, I marveled at what I witnessed, seeing it at least ten times—mesmerized each time. There is not a single show among the many I have experienced over the last thirty-five years that has continued to resonate with me so clearly.

Shortly after I missed the boat on *Balm in Gilead*, John Malkovich directed Christopher Hampton's *Savages*, a play about the exploitation and extermination of Brazilian native Indians. The political and religious officials who oversaw the extermination were played by ensemble members, whereas I was a member of the tribe of twenty naked Brazilian Indians, which also included longtime Steppenwolf artistic directors Martha Lavey and Randy Arney, in their first and second Steppenwolf shows, respectively. The tribe went through intensive rehearsals developing complex rituals through the process of improvisation, all led by our fearless director. Our hard work was to little avail in the critics' eyes and the production failed commercially. *The Threepenny Opera*, co-directed by Sheldon Patinkin and Jeff Perry, provided the next opportunity for me to perform with Steppenwolf. Sadly, the show was canceled after a week of rehearsal due to the inability of the theatre to weather the financial risk. So, it has been an unusual connection to Steppenwolf for me all these years, but a supremely meaningful one nonetheless.

My doctoral dissertation twenty-five years ago brought me back to my roots and the company, and the result was an early history of Steppenwolf. My mentor Barbara Greener's passion; the Steppenwolf ensemble approach, style, and philosophy; and my training with Chicago improvisational gurus Del Close, Paul Sills, and Sheldon Patinkin remain the backbone of my approach to teaching theatre students. Additionally, for many summers over the past fourteen years, Jeff Perry and I, with Steppenwolf Classes West, have created intensive training seminars as part of CSU (California State University) Summer Arts. I've been fortunate enough to work in Fresno and Monterey with ensemble members Rick Snyder, Al Wilder, Gary Sinise, Laurie Metcalf, and Jeff Perry, as well as Steppenwolf teachers Sheldon Patinkin, Kim Rubinstein, Alex Billings, Monica Payne, Dave Razowsky, Eric Hunicutt, Evelyn Carol Case, and others. I am proud to say we have positively impacted the lives of countless students who learn valuable lessons about working together in a collective environment of trust and generosity. We teach them how to collaborate and, when necessary to "Get the mop."

Writing this book brought with it a daunting responsibility, which at times overwhelmed me. My anxiety was eased by a comment from ensemble member Frank Galati, professor emeritus of Northwestern University, when at the end of our first interview he stood up, walked over to me, gave me a hug, and said, "John, you are just the right person to write this book." With that comment from a man for whom I have such deep respect, my reservations subsided and I did not look back.

Interestingly, there are four individuals that have been instrumental in the success of Steppenwolf over the years, and they were born within one year of one another in 1929 or 1930: Barbara June Patterson; Bruce Sagan and Margie Marcus, powerful and creative board members; and ensemble member Lois Smith. This generational sharing of information has been a large part of the story of Steppenwolf Theatre, and the current ensemble will benefit from the contributions of these individuals as they grow and develop the company—just as the founders benefited from their wisdom in the company's beginning.

It was important to me to write the book with the full support of Steppenwolf, and my goal as I proceeded forward was to interview all the ensemble members. I knew this objective was probably impossible to achieve, given the fact that there are now forty-four ensemble members; however, I did interview almost 90 percent of the ensemble, as well as staff and board members and Chicago theatre illuminati spanning all forty years of the theatre's existence. The entire process has been one of the most gratifying experiences of my life, because everyone who stepped forward was lucid, candid, and open in the interview process, and because the leadership and staff at

Steppenwolf Theatre Company could not have been more supportive of my efforts.

Good fortune has followed me on this journey from the outset. I was in Chicago when my flight for my first trip to Europe was delayed twelve hours. On a whim, I decided to send Tracy Letts an email to see if he might be free during the day for an interview. We had tried over the past months to get together, but it had never worked out. About ten minutes after I sent the email I got a response back from Tracy telling me he would be home all day and that I should come by. I drove to Tracy's home, or as he described it, "the house that *August* built." He was so generous and honest, and for me, the conversation could not have gone better. At one point, Tracy shared this:

> You seem like a very positive man and your spin on all this material is positive, as I think it should be, and I think that for the most part, you are going to portray, either for you or for themselves, a sense of family that we feel in this company. And, the truth is there is so much to see in this company that's admirable and there's so much good work and good will associated with this company. It's absolutely true. But, I remember once, we had to give a speech, I think it was a gala night, and we had to give a written presentation and I actually got up and said, "You know, some of these people up here on the stage don't like each other. Let's just tell the truth." Frank Galati came up to me later that night, and said, "That's why you're a playwright—you're a truth teller. You just can't resist it."

As with any family, there have been challenges, but Steppenwolf throughout the years has continued to flourish by finding common ground in the collaborative process.

Today, we literally hold all the knowledge of the world in our hand on smartphones with far too much information to weed through. When the founders of the theatre and I grew up, we essentially had four TV networks to choose from. We obsessively went to the movies at a time when far fewer films were released, so our influences were very similar. That kind of shared experience is a great deal more challenging today, so when Gary Sinise, Jeff Perry, Terry Kinney, and the others got together in the mid-seventies, they were tracking on a much more common set of artistic identifiers. All three mentioned the profound influence of films such as *The Godfather*, which came out in 1972, and one year later, Scorsese's *Mean Streets* which utilized rock and roll music to build the cinematic narrative, and particularly independent film pioneers John

Cassavetes and Ingmar Bergman. *Saturday Night Live* debuted in 1975 and people in our generation never missed an episode; we couldn't, because we did not have VCRs or DVRs. These were the inspirations that moved Gary, Jeff, and Terry; and from this fiber Steppenwolf Theatre Company erupted. The younger more diverse ensemble members of the company, added over the past decade, bring forth a whole new cultural experience that will continue to allow the theatre to change and grow.

When I go to the theatre I want to be "blown away," transported to places I have never been before. I want to feel emotional highs and lows. This is a majestic goal, which happens rarely, but it is no small coincidence that many of the times that it has happened to me have been while watching shows produced by Steppenwolf Theatre Company of Chicago. Gary Sinise and Jeff Perry acknowledge one of their first moments of being overwhelmed in the theatre occurring when they traveled to the Guthrie Theatre in Minneapolis during high school to see *Of Mice and Men*. Gary recalls his emotions during the curtain call:

> There was Peter Michael Goetz and the others. We wanted to stand up and scream something to the actors—with tears running down our faces—nothing would come out. We were clapping and applauding—so completely choked up. It was one of the first memories of having a live theatrical experience kick my butt.

The chance to have those types of moments—that's what keeps bringing me, Gary, Jeff, and all the others back to the theatre.

The Steppenwolf story demonstrates what the impact of a group working together with a common purpose can accomplish. Nelson Algren, writing with his particular Chicago vernacular, said of his beloved, adopted hometown, "Loving Chicago is like loving a beautiful woman with a broken nose." The bumps and grinds of the Steppenwolf journey have not always been pretty, as Tracy Letts intimated, but the company's lasting impact has been profound and is no less amazing in scope than the humble narrative of Microsoft's early beginnings in a garage. Steppenwolf Theatre Company was started by a group of teenagers in high school who just wanted to do plays because they loved the process of collaborative creation. And now, forty years later, they are internationally recognized for the excellence of their work with sights set on a plan for continued innovation.

To date, Steppenwolf Theatre Company has produced over 300 different productions. I have decided to focus on the early years of the company in the 1970s; three benchmark productions of Steppenwolf that are representative of their dedication and methodology: 1980's

Balm in Gilead, 1988's *The Grapes of Wrath*, and 2007's *August: Osage County*; and finally, a view to the future.

That somehow it has fallen upon me to write this book is an honor and a privilege, and has filled me to capacity with deep emotion. I hope that reading it will stir memories for fellow travelers who have witnessed this extraordinary journey, and inspire a feeling of connection with Steppenwolf for those of you who are coming to the company for the first time.[1]

1. One addition to this book is a music playlist located in an appendix. Music has provided an ongoing background to the Steppenwolf story and this playlist can help you, the reader, to recall specific production moments, understand the mood of particular moments in the company's history, and help create a texture for the overall narrative.

Figure 2. Alana Arenas © Sandro Miller.

Figure 3. Amy Morton © Sandro Miller.

Figure 4. Frank Galati, John Mahoney © Sandro Miller.

Figure 5. Gary Sinise © Sandro Miller.

Figure 6. Ian Barford, Alan Wilder, Francis Guinan © Sandro Miller.

Figure 7. James Vincent Meredith © Sandro Miller.

Figure 8. Joan Allen © Sandro Miller.

Figure 9. Yasen Peyankov, Jon Michael Hill © Sandro Miller.

Chapter 1

THE EARLY YEARS: THE SEVENTIES

All you really need to have a theatre is the actors. You can have a
theatre without a script. You can have a theatre without a theatre.
You can do it out in the street. But, without the performers, without
the interpreters, you don't have a theatre.

—Gary Sinise

The 1960s represented a pivotal period in American history: a virtual
social revolution that composed a dynamic spiritual and philosophical
liberation. That reform generated progressive new agendas, expanded the
horizons for alternative lifestyle choices, awakened a heightened political
awareness, and incited passionate appeals for social transformation. The
relative complacency and indifference that characterized much of
the suburban youth culture of the 1950s was gradually replaced by a more
politically and intellectually aware generation. Steppenwolf Theatre
Company's early members' formative, highly impressionable teen years
coexisted with this turbulent period. Affluent liberal bastions, such as
suburban Highland Park, twenty-five miles north of Chicago, loudly
sounded this newly developing progressive ideal. It was here, amidst this
enlightened and impassioned political and social awareness, that the
roots of one of America's finest ensemble theatres first began to take hold.

The seeds of Steppenwolf were originally planted in the theatre classes
and plays at Highland Park High School in 1970. Gary Sinise and Jeff
Perry, as students in these classes and actors in the productions, were not
merely exposed to theoretical ideas pertaining to the art of performance,
but they also traveled into Chicago and beyond to witness many
professional productions. Chicago was alive with theatre during this
period, from the venerable Goodman Theatre, improvisational giant
The Second City, the non-traditional Organic Theatre, the roots of
St. Nicholas Theatre Company where David Mamet and William H. Macy
began to cultivate their craft, to major touring houses including the
Studebaker, Shubert, and Blackstone Theatres. Academy Festival Theatre,

an intimate 500-seat theatre, housed at Barat College in Lake Forest, Illinois, a mere ten-minute drive from Highland Park High School, provided students the opportunity to witness a diversity of high-level professional productions including Jason Robards and Colleen Dewhurst in the pre-Broadway run of Eugene O'Neill's *A Moon for the Misbegotten*, directed by Jose Quintero; Irene Worth and Christopher Walken in Tennessee Williams's *Sweet Bird of Youth*; Lynn Redgrave in Shaw's *Misalliance*; Cicely Tyson in an all-black revival of *Desire Under the Elms*; and Geraldine Page and Rip Torn in Lillian Hellman's *The Little Foxes*.

Highland Park High School's theatre program headed by Equity actress and teacher Barbara June Patterson was one of the first of its kind in the nation. In addition to the frequent field trips, a broad range of theatre courses were offered, including a directing class, which generated many student-directed plays. School-sponsored productions occurred frequently and Highland Park High School annually participated in Illinois statewide theatre competitions. In Sinise and Perry's junior and senior years, two productions respectively, Dylan Thomas's *Under Milk Wood* and Bertolt Brecht's *The Caucasian Chalk Circle*, made it to the statewide final. Both Sinise and Perry received further acknowledgment as members of the all-state acting team for their work in *The Caucasian Chalk Circle*. The opportunity to work with such intellectually challenging scripts as these taught the future co-founders of Steppenwolf Theatre the intrinsic value of quality scripts in terms of play selection and performance.

Patterson's classes offered students a broad theoretical vision of acting, directing, and script analysis, but also provided ample hands-on opportunities to apply the newfound knowledge. Jeff Perry fondly recollects this period:

> I was captivated by Barbara's passionate energy and theatricality. I was immediately struck by the sheer enjoyment of acting, which seemed to me more interesting in some ways than daily life, and that's still what I get a kick out of, the empathy and imagination employed to inhabit numerous lives. And early on too, I became addicted to the camaraderie and tradition of theatre, that and being exposed to great stories from great writers. Barbara was exposing us to Miller and Brecht and Williams and Shakespeare at an early age.

Sinise and Perry immediately put their classroom experiences to work in a collaborative final directing class project, Brian Friel's *Philadelphia, Here I Come!*

This 1973 production provided a preview of the innovative style that would eventually bring Steppenwolf international renown. Sinise and Perry, their cast, and various friends transformed a seldom-used portion of the school cafeteria into a black box theatre for their production, an inventiveness facilitated in part by the necessity to adapt and break free from the institutional regulations of the high-school setting. Sinise fondly remembered his first foray into directing in an interview with former Steppenwolf artistic director Martha Lavey:

> Everybody had to find a place to do their final project, so we did productions in hallways, in the parking lot, everywhere. I went to the principal and asked if we could turn the cafeteria into a theatre on the weekend. We wanted our own theatre lighting, because the cafeteria just had fluorescent lighting. Our friend Gordon Kapes, an electronics wizard at the school, and Bobby Newman, a great technical director type, put floodlights in coffee cans and some guy's dad had a wire store and we got all the wires and cables, and somebody else's dad had a conduit or hardware store, so we got all this conduit. We hung the coffee cans from the conduit we'd attached to the ceiling. To top the lights off and to make for a wider or narrower spread we took cardboard and wrapped it around in different focal lengths on the coffee cans. We hung twenty-four lights and Gordon made a little lightboard. We had six dining-room dimmers on this little lightboard and you could plug four lights into each one, then if we needed a special, someone would unplug three of the lights and we'd just have one up there. We used the school's risers and cafeteria chairs and made a theatre-in-the-round.

Highland Park teacher Sherry Rubel had been augmenting Patterson's performance studies classes with a curriculum of basic technical theatre courses. Ms. Rubel also began directing shows at the high school, including Molière's *Tartuffe*, which, in featuring Sinise as the title character, afforded him his first major role in a play. Classmate Kevin Rigdon[2] trained in Rubel's stagecraft classes and participated in pulling off the transformation of the cafeteria theatre space with classmates Sinise, tech wiz Bobby Newman, Joan Channick (Associate Dean of the Yale School of Drama), Alisa Solomon (Director of the MA Arts

2. Rigdon would eventually become Steppenwolf's first resident set and lighting designer and, more importantly, an integral member of the design team for the new $9,000,000 Steppenwolf theatre building completed in 1991.

and Culture Program at Columbia University, School of Journalism), and others.

The first performance of *Philadelphia, Here I Come!* burst to life in the little performance space carved from the high-school cafeteria; and a few years after the production, the high school turned the space permanently into a theatre. Co-directors Sinise and Perry also acted in the show, because both believed that working together as actors and directors would achieve the highest performance result. This decision foreshadowed what would become a Steppenwolf trademark, free crossover between actor and director. This flexibility came to form an essential aspect of the unique charm of the Steppenwolf ensemble. The focus was always on "the work," and how the best possible results could be achieved.

After the success of *Philadelphia, Here I Come!* a veritable barrage of student-directed plays ensued at Highland Park High School. In January, 1974, Paul Zindel's *And Miss Reardon Drinks a Little* directed by classmate Ricky Argosh was performed at the Unitarian Church in nearby Deerfield, Illinois. This became the first occasion for the use of the name, Steppenwolf Theatre Company. Argosh had been reading *Steppenwolf*, Hermann Hesse's classic anti-war saga at the time and, as Sinise remembers,

> We were going to have a program made for the show and we were sitting around the church before or after rehearsal one night discussing the idea of putting a company name on the program. That's when Rick held up the book and we agreed to put Steppenwolf Theatre Company on the program.

Barbara Patterson further recalls:

> Gary hurried out with his few remaining coins and bought a rubber stamp with the name Steppenwolf inscribed. He put that name everywhere and said that was the name of the theatre.

The first three plays of Steppenwolf Theatre in 1974—*And Miss Reardon Drinks a Little*, *Grease*, and *Rosencrantz and Guildenstern are Dead*—all went into production as "class projects", and played to ample audiences. There was no admission charge for the plays or to the original performances of *Grease* either, but the entrepreneurial Sinise made a strategic appeal for support during the show's breaks. He remembers:

I literally held the audience hostage, and sent ushers around with hubcaps to collect money. I recouped my original investment, and took in an additional $300 or $400, which went into the budget for *Rosencrantz.*

Philadelphia, Here I Come! had established what would become an element of the Steppenwolf methodology, crossover between actor and director. *And Miss Reardon Drinks a Little* had given the company its name, while *Grease* helped to set the tone for what would become Steppenwolf's early signature: rock and roll theatre. *Grease* also displayed to audiences the company's boundless energy and unrestrained commitment.

During this 1974 season, Perry enrolled in Illinois State University to study theatre, but he continued to support the goal of starting a theatre, spearheaded by Sinise back home in Highland Park. Meanwhile, following closely on the heels of *Grease* in the early summer of 1974, came Tom Stoppard's *Rosencrantz and Guildenstern are Dead.* Terry Kinney, Perry's classmate from ISU, gave his first Steppenwolf acting performance in this show. Perry recalls Kinney's initial impressions of Sinise:

> Terry and I had been talking; we had become very tight, great friends. I had been telling him what a great actor Gary was, and that he was going to love doing *Rosencrantz.* We saw *Grease* and really liked it. Terry thought Gary was great, but we laughed because he joked that it was really appalling that Gary was so shameless by asking people for money about three or four times during the show.

Highland Park provided the young Steppenwolf Company with a suburban audience ready to experience the arts and eager to support its local artists. The liberal community wanted to establish a strong cultural base and gave free rein and impassioned support to the youthful innovators. The three founders of the Steppenwolf Theatre Company, Sinise, Perry and Kinney, had, even at this early stage, a deep sense of their future possibilities. As Perry expresses quite simply:

> I don't know how many performances of *Rosencrantz* we did, probably two weekends or something like that and I headed off to Minneapolis to my girlfriend. Terry headed back to school and Gary traveled with bands and stuff. Anyway, we made an emotional pact with each other that we had to work together again.

In the winter of 1975 Sinise produced *The Glass Menagerie* under the name of Steppenwolf, with mentor Barbara Patterson as Amanda and himself as Tom. Despite this endeavor, the idea for starting a permanent theatre was put on temporary hold when Perry reentered the ISU program. Much like the program at Highland Park High School, ISU encouraged active student participation in performance. Many of ISU's students had been actively recruited, and subsequently given scholarships, because of their excellence in speech and drama in high school. The seminal experience of Sinise and Perry, studying with Barbara June Patterson as their singular influence, differed greatly from their ISU counterparts. Although faculty members Ralph Lane, Jean Scharfenberg, Cal Pritner, and particularly acting instructor Gail Cronauer were mentioned as prominent mentors, many members of the company related that a divisive factionalism, perhaps bred by the multiple performance approaches of ISU's tenured faculty, limited the department's impact. Al Wilder summed up these years simply, "The main thing about ISU was just that it was a place where we got together."

The Steppenwolf founders had high regard for two earlier theatre ensembles, The Group Theatre and the Moscow Art Theatre (MAT). Vladimir Nemirovitch-Dantchenko, one of the two co-founders along with Constantin Stanislavsky of the MAT, writing in *My Life in the Russian Theatre* had this to say about their theatre's early days:

> I have said, it will be remembered, that to the slightest questions of theatrical organization we had a positive answer. But of course afterwards, in practice, we came in collision with such an endless number of unexpected things! And such shattering unexpected things! It was very good in its way that we did not know everything and had not foreseen everything. Because if we had foreseen everything, then if you please, we would not have decided to go on with the undertaking. The important thing was that we were, in a sense, possessed. Thus, we at least seemed, one to the other, but each to himself appeared fully in his right mind. Actually we were "in blinkers." We suffered no doubts, we did not question the adequacy of our powers, we might accomplish anything! Anything! We knew everything that was necessary to know, and how to accomplish things!

Without the inclusion of the preceding passage's lofty prose or prior to reading the name at the start of the quote, it would have been easy to assume that Harold Clurman might have written this in relation to the Group Theatre, or that an early Steppenwolf ensemble member might have written it about their origins. One point is clear: from Nemirovitch-Dantchenko's point of view, the Moscow Art Theatre, one of the most influential contemporary ensemble theatres, started from youthful, often naïve beginnings. The precedents established by the MAT, founded in 1898, and the Group Theatre, founded in New York by Harold Clurman, Cheryl Crawford, and Lee Strasberg in 1931, and their impact on the development of American ensemble companies that followed them were considerable; however, the impact of these two companies on Steppenwolf seems to be more general than specific. Just as the Group members idealized the credos of the MAT as they perceived them and modeled their company upon those perceptions, so did Steppenwolf model their company upon their general perceptions of their two famed predecessors.

With the idea of forming an ensemble-based theatre in mind, a group of ISU actors proposed an off-campus project at ISU of Pinter's *The Homecoming* featuring Kinney, Perry, Wilder, and Sinise. It failed to reach fruition, but provided further spark to start an independent theatre company. The *Homecoming* proposal was opposed by the departmental administration, which frowned upon a number of scholarship students committing themselves to a production that would render them unavailable for performing in the department productions. Although the cast was disheartened by the turn of events, it unified them in their commitment to one another. They decided to look for a venture that would give them more complete artistic control. Discussions about starting a theatre were launched by the beginning of the spring semester in 1976. Classmate at ISU Nancy Evans, an original member of the company, remembers:

> Terry and Jeff invited John (Malkovich) and me to a meeting. A friend of theirs, Gary Sinise, was going to be there, and wanted to talk with us, so I said "sure." Literally everybody in the theatre department that I had respect for was there. There were maybe fifteen of us altogether and Gary was sitting in the corner off to the side. They started to talk to us about how Steppenwolf was a germ in their minds when they were in high school and they wanted to put this company together and be the best theatre in the world.

Subsequently, a series of organizational meetings took place over the next couple of months. Influenced by the films of John Cassavetes and Ingmar Bergman, the fledgling group made one objective clear from the start: ensemble work focusing on the actor would be the heart and soul of the company. Perry points out the simplicity of this approach in the beginning:

> I'm fairly sure that in those first meetings that when we talked about material, it wasn't highly intellectual or real coherent philosophically as much as it was the practicality of it. We were going to find good roles for each other and we were going to direct each other.

The actor-centered idealism espoused by Perry, even in its relative innocence, would ultimately become the backbone of the Steppenwolf ethos. Al Wilder speaks of his first recollections of these meetings:

> Over the school year of '75/'76, we had meetings at ISU, where different combinations of people came together and said, "Let's form a company that is an acting ensemble along the lines of the Group, and Moscow Art." It seems to me that things were very haphazard. It has all been trial and error.

Nancy Evans echoed these feelings:

> Moira Harris and I lived together. We literally sat in our living room, the nine of us, and tried to write a statement of artistic purpose for hours. We couldn't write one. We kept saying, "We want to do this, or we want to do that," but then we'd say, "This sounds so definite, we don't want to limit ourselves to that kind of thing."

Their commentaries affirm the youthful enthusiasm and general naïveté igniting the earliest ideals of the ensemble, but from the start the company seemed to understand implicitly the following quote from Harold Clurman's *The Fervent Years*:

> There were to be no stars in our theatre, not for the negative purpose of avoiding distinction, but because all distinction—and we would strive to attain the highest—was to be embodied in the production as a whole.

Attrition of participants over the course of the ISU meetings left a company of nine: Sinise, and the ISU classmates Laurie Metcalf, John Malkovich, Al Wilder, Moira Harris, H.E. Baccus, Perry, Kinney and Evans. They decided to start a theatre in Highland Park, and plans for Steppenwolf's summer season were set in motion. Although the company had produced plays since 1974, this expanded ensemble and fresh moment marked the "official" beginning of Steppenwolf Theatre. Sinise located a basement space in Highland Park in which to house the theatre at Immaculate Conception church and elementary school. The church was eager to support the efforts of the young group, graciously arranging a rental price of $1.00 per year. The layout of the space was designed and set up by Kevin Rigdon with the assistance of Sinise and Scott Peters, another Highland Park High School classmate. The rest of the company aided in the development when they arrived at the end of the semester. Chairs were salvaged from the remains of Chicago's McCormick Place fire. Rigdon had continued to hone his technical skills following 1974's *Rosencrantz and Guildenstern* by working at the Great America theme park in nearby Gurnee, Illinois, which came in handy in the design and implementation of the new space.

Malkovich, Metcalf, Kinney, Harris, and Baccus had all been raised in central and southern Illinois, so the pilgrimage north to their new home in Highland Park was quite an adventure. Baccus describes his rocky trip up with girlfriend and future wife Jan, and Malkovich:

> We picked up one of my dad's trucks, which was open air, and we didn't tie the mattresses on well enough, because we got a little way up the road, and they blew off and smashed into smithereens. John sort of had momentary insanity from laughing too hard. He was almost uncontrollable. Other things fell off too. We saved what we could, got in the truck, and it began to rain. We had no money on the way and realized that there were tolls. There were no tolls in southern Illinois, so we threw in bobby pins.

The relative inexperience and adventurous nature of the contingent from southern and central Illinois, coupled with the suburban experiences of Perry, Sinise, Wilder, and Evans, created an excellent blend of homegrown pragmatism, cultural awareness, and entrepreneurial inventiveness. All of the original Steppenwolf members were hungry for what the future held.

The members of the company found jobs to sustain themselves while they developed their theatre in the school basement. These jobs were never anything more than a way to earn a living, because the sustaining energy of everyone's life was the theatre and the company. Speaking of this period, Laurie Metcalf reflected,

> It was definitely like *Peyton Place*. We were very cloistered. We'd do our temp jobs during the day and then we'd do plays at night, and then party with each other after the shows—not really socializing with

anybody else. We never went into Chicago. We were stuck in the suburbs and saw only each other for three years. Different couples would form and break up. The good thing about being so isolated was that we'd get over things quicker if there were problems. We just had to.

Perry added:

I always thought this time was vital for the group to find its own character. We fed off that isolation a bit—in a way we were free of other theatrical influence, which rather forced us to figure out what we wanted to be.

Some in the company refer to this period of isolation as "the incubator period," but there is no question that it further bred the style that would come to characterize Steppenwolf.

Fred Plattner, a music instructor at Highland Park High School, became business manager at this time. Plattner became acquainted with Sinise and Perry during a production of *West Side Story* at HPHS.[3] For summer employment, Plattner worked with the prominent Ravinia Festival, as director of development, so he brought the company much-needed professional expertise in promotion and business. The company also officially became a not-for-profit theatre during his tenure, which allowed them to solicit donations and opened doors to federal and state grant support. Additionally, Plattner helped find employment at the Ravinia Festival for many of the newly transplanted ensemble members. With jobs secured, the Steppenwolf Company concentrated on the task at hand: the first summer season of one-acts in Highland Park.

The support of individual donors and a $500 grant from the Illinois Arts Council got the summer season going with a revolving repertory of twin bills of four one-acts. *The Lover* and *Birdbath* opened on Thursday, July 22, 1976, and played to an audience of thirty-five in the

3. Who and where are the members of the cast of the 1972 production of *West Side Story* at Highland Park High School today? For starters, Perry played Tony and Sinise played Pepe, one of the Sharks. Other cast members included: Jeff Melvoin, Hollywood television producer/writer with credits including *Hill Street Blues*, *Remington Steele*, and *Northern Exposure*; Katherine Borowitz, wife of actor John Turturro, and featured on Broadway in *Cloud Nine* and in films such as *Internal Affairs* and *Men of Respect*; Jack Reuler, artistic director of Minneapolis's Mixed Blood Theatre; Derin Altay, wife of Paul Gemignani, played Evita on Broadway; and Bob Greenebaum, longtime board member at Steppenwolf among others.

eighty-eight-seat space in the basement theatre at 70 Deerfield Road in Highland Park. *The Lesson* and *The Indian Wants the Bronx* played the following night, and the two sets of shows flip-flopped nights on a Thursday through Saturday schedule until the end of August. Tickets were $3 on Thursday and $3.50 on Fridays and Saturdays.

Perry, Kinney, and Sinise selected the plays primarily because of the roles they offered to various company members. These first four plays give a small hint about the type of material the company would pursue over the next few years. Their choice of plays by Harold Pinter, and 1960s alternative playwrights Leonard Melfi and Israel Horovitz, provided a blend of social comedy and intense physical drama.

With their choice of *The Lover*, the company selected a play by a playwright with whom they would develop a long-term relationship. The company's work with Pinter's scripts, which would be integral to their success, culminated with a Broadway run of their third restaging of *The Caretaker* in 1986. The production of *The Lover* demonstrated from the start the young company's ability to work with difficult literary matter.

The Indian Wants the Bronx became the most important play of the four to the future of Steppenwolf from a visibility standpoint. Featuring highly charged portrayals by Kinney and Sinise as tough street punks who terrorize an Indian in a phone booth played by H.E. Baccus, the play demonstrated the all-out physical, highly emotional and instinctual style that came to characterize the company's acting. Diana Diamond's review of the shows in the local Lerner Life Newspaper on July 29, 1976 was the very first review of a Steppenwolf production and was prophetic:

> Steppenwolf Theatre opened its doors last weekend in Highland Park—and if the caliber of the plays and acting continues to be as fine as what occurred at the premiere performance—this theater should have a fine life ahead of it.

Richard Christiansen, a powerful critic with the *Chicago Daily News* and later with the *Chicago Tribune*, took Kennedy's comments one step further in his memory of the play.

> One of my favorite stories, which I repeat every occasion I get, is about the early days of Steppenwolf when I went to see *The Indian Wants the Bronx*. There's this scene where the two street punks attack the Indian who's lost in the Bronx, and Terry and Gary were the two punks. They were so intense, so convincing in their portrayals, that for the first time I lost the suspension of disbelief. I really thought

they were going to come after people in the audience once they got through with the Indian. I just got caught up in the illusion of danger and menace and fear that they created.

Christiansen's future reviews of Steppenwolf shows, good and bad, were a primary factor in their gaining acceptance in the Chicago theatre world and proved particularly vital to their growth. Michael Unger (Mikey),[4] Steppenwolf's first ever intern, added to Christiansen's recollection:

> I wandered into the basement of the Immaculate Conception church and said, "Can I help?" I think I was fourteen, definitely before I drove, and from the moment I walked down those stairs, I was at Steppenwolf every day of my life until I graduated high school. I would assist Kevin Rigdon building sets and setting lights. I did everything. I got high with them. I watched every rehearsal I could. Before *The Indian Wants the Bronx*, Terry and Gary would playfully "beat me up" by the dumpster to get themselves revved up before storming onstage through the exit door full of testosterone and adrenaline.

Observations by Tim Evans, former Steppenwolf marketing and audience development director, sheds even further light on the early acting methodology of the young actors:

> They just went on stage and did it to their own feelings and instincts. It was always cool to watch because it was real honest. It wasn't flowered up or it wasn't stuck with all sorts of background about a particular character they were playing. In *The Indian Wants the Bronx*, while the audience is clearing their throats getting ready for the curtain to go up, they're in back running around in circles and then they come screaming into the theatre, sweating and the whole bit, because that is how they prepared. It wasn't that they intellectualized it; they went out and physicalized it. That's how they approached everything in the early days.

Though the members of the company have differing approaches to acting and character development, the earthiness and commitment implied

---

4. Unger is now Artistic Director of the NewArts: Newtown Musicals—a division of the 12.14 Foundation in Newtown, Connecticut, which brings high-level performing arts to the community that suffered the horrible Sandy Hook Elementary School shooting tragedy.

in Evans's anecdote seem to be consistent with early accounts of the Steppenwolf acting style. Kevin Rigdon's design work on the four one-acts, limited by a lack of funding, may have forced him into the minimalistic style that would come to be his signature in scenic design. His deft artistic style was often sparse and provided little more than a locale for the Steppenwolf actors, but his work was almost always highly praised.

Steppenwolf's 1976 summer season came at a time when Chicago critics could still find time to attend plays at new small theatres. The Chicago theatre community was undergoing a major growth spurt that would ultimately make it difficult for critics to see all the work being offered, but at this time a trip to Highland Park to see a small company such as Steppenwolf was still possible for the critics of the major newspapers. This brought attention to Steppenwolf and also gave the company members a sense of accomplishment. Jeff Perry said of the newspaper response to *Birdbath* and *The Indian Wants the Bronx*:

> They got really good press and that was a sustaining thing for us, particularly when we were playing to audiences of eight or twenty and it looked as though economically we couldn't go on.

In addition to the Highland Park performances, *Birdbath* and *The Indian Wants the Bronx* played a special one-evening benefit at Chicago's Off-Loop St. Nicholas Theatre on August 24, 1976, of America's bicentennial year. John Kennedy's review of *The Indian Wants the Bronx* for *The Reader* vividly captured Steppenwolf's first official trip into Chicago:

> The cast is superb and ought to be seen. Terry Kinney as Murphy and Gary Sinise as Joey turn in performances that make you want to punch those two sweaty fuckers right out of their garbage can kingdom, while at the same time you wish you could forgive them. These guys have what this play takes: physical dynamics, from their panicky boxing bouts to their panicky eyes and snapping fingertips. Kinney and Sinise are seamlessly choreographed by director John Malkovich into a fluid torrent of nervous energy and hyper-malice that makes the visual spectacle just as explosive as the language.

This account not only points up the intensity of the portrayals, but also suggests a sensitive vulnerability in actors Kinney and Sinise. This delicate balancing of emotions in performance, an indication of layered multi-dimensional acting, would become another one of the defining traits of the company's work. This brief introduction to the Chicago theatre, coupled with the positive feedback for their first summer season, encouraged the Steppenwolf ensemble to set up a six-show regular season to begin in October of 1976.

By a consensus of company members, H.E. Baccus was appointed to be the artistic director succeeding Jeff Perry, who had informally held that role from the start of the summer season. Perry comments on why the company decided to institute the role of artistic director:

> People knew that it was kind of a *Lord of the Flies* situation and that the only way the theatre would work was once there was a higher power and letting that person, the artistic director, make decisions.

Baccus's role as artistic director included play selection and casting, although the company members were still very much a part of all decision making. Baccus remembers how he was selected:

> Jeff didn't want to do it anymore at the end of the summer, so I was elected artistic director. I think they elected me because I seemed mature; I was on my way to marriage and I was someone that they could mutually trust. I seemed least partial of any of the other people.

With the new artistic director in place, the company moved on to their first official season. The opening play of the 1976 season selected by Baccus was *Look: We've Come Through* by Hugh Wheeler, a play that had originally premiered in New York in 1961 at Circle in the Square, but closed after four performances. Baccus tells how he decided on the play:

> I got this play out of a book called *Broadway's Wonderful Flops*. I read this play and thought, it concerns young people and a growing and maturing process, and Jeff would be great in it, so we chose to do it. It was horrible. It just didn't work out. The characters were pretty flimsy and two-dimensional and we just couldn't get serious about it.

Wheeler's comedy/drama featured Jeff Perry, Terry Kinney, John Malkovich, Nancy Evans, and Moira Harris and has been retrospectively referred to by company members as *Look: We're So Sad* or *Look: We've Been Had*. Despite the jokes, this show proved the company's staying power and their ability to survive a flop. Nancy Evans paraphrased one review of *Look: We've Come Through*: "This is a sterling silver company, why are they choosing to use flatware?"

One of the more memorable events from the first season occurred at the opening of *The Sea Horse* by Edward J. Moore and directed by John Malkovich. The play featured Gary Sinise and future wife Moira Harris, but just prior to opening night, Harris was unable to go on. Rondi Reed, Jeff and Terry's classmate from ISU and future ensemble member, had just completed the play at ISU and was recruited to come up to replace Harris for the opening. Reed recalls her first introduction to Steppenwolf:

> My first meeting with Gary Sinise was in Highland Park when they were doing *The Sea Horse*. They had a bunch of grant people coming for a donor night and I got a call saying that Moira had a blood clot in her leg and couldn't go on. So, Steve (Eich) and I got into the car; it rained all the way up from Bloomington Normal to Highland Park. I arrived about fifteen minutes before curtain. They threw some clothes on me; Malkovich said, "We have made these cuts and these cuts— and, by the way here's Gary Sinise, and it's a two-person play and you are going to be on stage with him." I'd never met him before in my life. I'd heard about him, but we'd never met.
> This was year one of Highland Park and he comes sauntering in and says, "Hey how you doing?" I said, "Hi. Now, there's a lot of physical violence in this show. Do you guys have it choreographed?" Gary said, "No we just kind of wail on each other." With about five minutes to go, Malkovich stepped out in front of the curtain and said, "Thank you very much for coming. We know we have a lot of donors here tonight and we want to thank you so much for your consideration. Unfortunately, one of our lead actresses is sick, but a good friend of ours who we went to school with is going to do the play." The lights went down and came up. I basically remember being on stage with Gary and then I remember being off stage. Once we got done, somebody handed me a fifty-dollar bill and a bottle of Scotch. I got in the car and Steve and I drove back to Bloomington. It was like a dream. That was my introduction to the Highland Park space, Gary, and what everybody was doing. We flew by the seat of our pants.

The exchange between Sinise and Reed about fight choreography is another indicator of the no-holds-barred methods ingrained from the earliest roots of the company. Laurie Metcalf replaced Reed and continued in the role until Harris recuperated. Perry's view of the production has much to say about the Steppenwolf's approach:

The Sea Horse epitomized a certain strain in the company's work in that it was, if not a great play, it offered the actors a great vehicle to express a relationship. I think we often picked things that "played" well.

In an article by Christine Koyama in *Chicago Magazine* Kinney stated, "We never felt we'd succeeded unless we tore people's evenings apart," which frames this attitude quite succinctly. Larry Kart writing for the *Chicago Tribune* on June 24, 1977 must have felt the essence as well:

The trip out to Highland Park puts you in a condescending mood. The Second City syndrome and a suburb to boot! The oldest actor in the company is twenty-four. Probably, a group of amateurs having harmless fun. You spot the sign that says "Steppenwolf Theater," park the car, and descend a flight of steps to a place that looks like what it is—the basement of a grade school. Rows of seats crowd the stage on three sides. The space left open hardly seems enough for a game of shuffleboard. Then the play begins and preconceptions vanish. The acting is thoughtful, intense. Afterwards you're hard put to recall another theater experience that worked so well.

The bleak financial state of the theatre prompted an attempt to improve the situation by returning to the successful one-acts of the first summer. *Birdbath* and *The Indian Wants the Bronx* replaced the previously scheduled plays: *Great Jones Street*, an original musical adapted by H.E. Baccus from the novel by Don DeLillo, and Brian Friel's *Philadelphia, Here I Come!* The change in schedule not only served a financial purpose and brought increased recognition, but also generated demand for additional performances. This prompted the company to rent space at Chicago's Hull House for a short run lasting through the fall. The Chicago performances garnered favorable reviews in *The Reader* and showed the company that they could possibly survive in the city.[5]

Our Late Night, a dark comedy by Wallace Shawn, was Steppenwolf's next Chicago effort. Replete with scatological ramblings and overt sexuality, Shawn's play provided a shocking vehicle for Steppenwolf's

---

5. Shortly after the Highland Park performances, Nancy Evans left the company to pursue a dance career in Minneapolis, so Laurie Metcalf took her place as Velma in *Birdbath* for the Hull House run.

return to the city. The poster for *Our Late Night* featured a silhouetted high-rise apartment stylized as a phallic symbol, and one put up for the show in the nearby suburb of Glencoe resulted in the first obscenity seizure in the history of the town; however, no charges were filed. Originally staged by the Manhattan Theatre Project in 1974, *Our Late Night* exemplified Shawn's outrageous style and provided the cast of Malkovich, Kinney, Wilder, Harris, Baccus, Metcalf, and newcomer Joan Allen with a variety of engaging characters. Allen had been a classmate of Malkovich at Eastern Illinois University, the school he attended before transferring to ISU.

Our Late Night was directed by respected Chicago director Gary Houston and marked the first time that someone from outside of the company directed a Steppenwolf show. Perry recalls how the company selected him:

> We saw a production of *The Local Stigmatic*, the Heathcote Williams one-act, very Pinter-like about a couple of guys sitting around like *The Dumb Waiter*. We really loved it and there was an accompanying one-act which we didn't like as much. Gary Houston directed the one-act we didn't like as much, but we thought he directed *Local Stigmatic* and so we asked him to direct *Our Late Night*. A third to three-quarters of the audience would walk out nightly, because it was so puerile and had this violent, sexual, and bathroom imagery all over the place.

Once again the material selection was questioned in the reviews, which were less than favorable, but the company's acting style was nevertheless applauded. Glenna Syse's review for the *Chicago Sun-Times* was particularly scathing.

> Wallace Shawn's *Our Late Night* is one of the most unattractive plays I've witnessed in a long time. No, I don't need my drama pretty, but I don't need it pointless. An hour and thirty-five minutes spent with seven characters engaged in or talking about their sick sexual misadventures is my definition of pointless.

Despite the poor critical reception of *Our Late Night*, the experience of performing a full run in a Chicago theatre, as opposed to the suburban church basement, gave the company a taste of what lay ahead. Money remained a concern and the actors were still not getting paid, so the ensemble members realized that a move into a larger Chicago theatre would be a necessity if they were to survive. Joan Allen joined the company permanently after her Hull House debut, replacing Nancy Evans.[6]

The company had been looking for performance space in Chicago, but since none had yet surfaced, the 1977 season saw the return of the company to the space in the Highland Park church basement. The show that opened the season *Mack, Anything Goes over the Rainbow*, a revue conceived by H.E. Baccus, which included works by Kurt Weill (*Mack the Knife*), Cole Porter (*Anything Goes*), and Harold Arlen (*Over the Rainbow*), was Steppenwolf's first and only attempt at a musical. The overt sexual content of *Our Late Night*, although performed in Chicago, and the general content of some of Steppenwolf's prior shows (i.e. profanity and violence), had raised serious questions about Steppenwolf's future in Highland Park. *Mack, Anything Goes over the Rainbow* was staged as a response to pressures that had been building from their landlord and various Steppenwolf supporters and served to temporarily appease their potential detractors. The local community audiences preferred lighter fare and were put off by such controversial or abrasive style as that exhibited by the work of Shawn and Horovitz. No doubt this attitude would also play a role in the company's permanent move into the city later on. Company members confirm that musicals were not considered a strong suit for the company despite the musical talents of many, nor were they a desired medium for the future. Sinise summed up these feelings:

> That was the last time we said let's do something because we think it will make somebody else happy. After that, we just did what we wanted to make us happy.

During the run of *Mack, Anything Goes Over the Rainbow*, John Malkovich became the first member of the company to perform elsewhere by joining the St. Nicholas production of *Ashes*, in which he gained great acclaim. Joan Allen also briefly left the company in order to return to school to finish her degree, although she returned for a role in *Fifth of July* in September of 1978. These experiences foreshadowed the

---

6. Of the original nine members, Nancy Evans and H.E. Baccus are the only ones who are no longer with the company forty years later, which is remarkable evidence of the company members' loyalty and commitment to the ideals established at the outset. This connection has allowed the company to survive and not fall prey to the traps of defection that had befallen other companies, most notably the Group Theatre.

type of movement in and out of the company that would become commonplace.

A restaged version of *Rosencrantz and Guildenstern are Dead* directed by former ISU professor Ralph Lane with Sinise, Perry, and Kinney reprising the roles they had played in the 1974 summer production was next. The importance of this show was due in large part to Kevin Rigdon's setting, which when coupled with costumes rented from the Guthrie Theatre made for one of the most technically realized productions to date, but the critical comments again focused on the acting style of the company. Christiansen wrote:

> This magical play is an especially tricky work, and the raw talent of the Steppenwolf troupe is enough to bring the drama through to clarity.

Rosencrantz and Guildenstern are Dead represented the company's first commercially successful show. Because of the show's popularity, additional performances were added at the end of the announced run and played repeatedly to full houses. The run culminated with a sold-out New Year's Eve performance and party, which welcomed 1978.

The world premiere of the comedy *Sandbar Flatland*, written by Dan Ursini and directed by John Malkovich, premiered on March 10, 1978 and was Steppenwolf's first work with a new script. *Sandbar Flatland* originated in a playwriting workshop at ISU, where Ursini had been a fellow student with many Steppenwolf members. The play is a series of monologues and playlets presented by the eccentric inhabitants of Sandbar Flatland who compromise that community's theatre group, the Corn Cob Players. Terry Kinney played Sandbar Flatlander Timmy Bough, the stuttering narrator for the piece, and was described in the opening stage directions, as "dressed in his flashiest K Mart outfit." Kinney introduced the offbeat cast of characters, including Laurie Metcalf, who presented a slide show of a striptease for Jesus, and Perry and Sinise, in each leg of a pair of overalls portraying Thick Jack Crack, the enormous town slob. Lines from Kinney's opening monologue seem to describe the way some audience members felt the first time they visited the Steppenwolf Company:

> Weird dimensions to our personalities grow like violet tentacles from our foreheads. Lots and lots of 'em. More than one visitor to our town has remarked that we, taken as a group, resemble a depressingly grim freak show. They're never invited back. But it's a pretty accurate

description. We <u>are</u> curious, and I'm pretty proud of that. Another
thing that we have in common is that we're energetic.

This speech could also have been written about the way the members
of the ensemble viewed themselves, because they obviously enjoyed
their autonomy. This independence allowed them to develop the
unusual characters in Ursini's *Sandbar Flatland* and demonstrated
their willingness to take substantial risks in their acting choices;
further perpetuating the exciting brand of theatre that the critics were
continuing to praise.

Ursini's outrageously playful yet occasionally melancholic script
played a pivotal role for Steppenwolf in the development of its tightly
knit ensemble with its attention to creating a show specifically for the
group. The opportunity to imprint an original play with the company's
own unique identity made *Sandbar Flatland* an important moment in
Steppenwolf's history and a harbinger of the type of work that would be
indicative of the new works presented under the leadership of artistic
director Martha Lavey in the 1990s and beyond; works such as Tracy
Letts's *August: Osage County*, Bruce Norris's *Clybourne Park*, Tarell
Alvin McCraney's *Brother/Sister* plays, and many others.

The business side of the theatre, although improving, remained
unstable. Plattner had moved on, but some sense of balance was
achieved with the arrival of Tim Evans as director of audience
development. Company members Perry, Malkovich, Kinney, and Wilder
all worked as extras on Robert Altman's *A Wedding*, filmed in nearby
Lake Bluff in 1976, and met Evans,[7] who was doing a story for a local
paper. Evans's journalism background proved invaluable and he became
the first fully salaried employee of the company, made possible by
funding from CETA, the Comprehensive Employment and Training
Act, a federal grant program for non-profit groups that was designed to
provide professional office support. Robert Biggs, another CETA
funded employee, joined the business staff as executive director soon
after and his responsibilities included fundraising and coordination of
the Steppenwolf board of directors.

---

7. Evans remained with the company for two years and was instrumental in
helping plan their permanent move to Chicago in 1980. He would later return to
the company in 1992 as director of marketing, audience development and
communications until moving on to become the executive director of Northlight
Theatre Company in Skokie, Illinois in 2007.

Harold Pinter's acclaimed 1961 tragic comedy masterpiece, *The Caretaker*, featured Al Wilder, Jeff Perry, and Gary Sinise, was directed by John Malkovich and concluded Steppenwolf's second season. Perry's remarks on Pinter's work and its impact on acting have much to say about the Steppenwolf style:

> One moment doesn't always tie to the next. Whereas in almost every other writing I had worked on you are piecing together a story out of moments, with Pinter the moment was king. His art comes out of a belief that we are ultimately unknowable to each other, and the sometimes confusing amount of detail and verification that people give about themselves or their history is at one time both really telling about themselves and at other times pure disguise. Pinter has said that his dialogue is often a smokescreen to hide what is really going on in his world. When I began to realize as an actor that there was a kind of life in Pinter that had nothing to do with linear or understandable or justifiable motivation in the ways I had understood motivation up to that point, it was a gigantic eye-opener for me; I felt liberated from the need to convey a conclusion of justification or of ultimate understanding, for myself or for the audience.

His comments not only reflect on the production of *The Caretaker* specifically, but also point up the importance of "the moment" to the acting technique of Steppenwolf actors.

The Caretaker was particularly meaningful to the ensemble because it gave Sheldon Patinkin, a vital and longtime mentor, his first glimpse of the company's work. Patinkin enthusiastically remembered, "I went to the theatre expecting very little from a group of kids doing a play that wasn't written for kids to do and I was knocked out."

The program for 1978's *The Caretaker* was crumpled before being given to audience members, symbolizing the clutter in the play, and listed Terry Kinney as electrical technician, Moira Harris as assistant director with set construction by Gary Sinise. The involvement of company members in all aspects of production both as actor/directors and as technical support staff occurred regularly. Joan Allen's personal memory gives a fair idea of the difficulty of getting a company going:

> We were getting ready to open a show and everybody was just beat. It was the day before. We were rushing to finish and so we painted the floor. There was a big rolling paintbrush that we had rolled on the floor, which I was going to clean. I was so tired that I just ran it under

water. I started squeezing out what turned out to be an oil-based paint and there was no way I could get it off my hands. We didn't have any paint remover at the theatre. We were always out of stuff. We never had toilet paper or paper towels or anything. It was two in the morning and I remember just sitting there sobbing, because I had this terra-cotta paint up to my arms. There was no way to get it off. Everybody was exhausted. John (Malkovich) came over, taking paper towels and gently wiping my hands for me.

Laurie Metcalf summed up the all-encompassing involvement this way:

We voted on everything by committee. We had to vote whether we were going to charge $3 for a ticket, who was going to clean the bathroom, who had to work the box office and who got to be onstage. We had to fight over who had to direct because nobody wanted to. Everybody just wanted to act, so directing was like drawing the short end of the stick.

The involvement of company members in even the most menial tasks helped to generate the intense interpersonal relationships that helped build the ensemble's deep connection.

By the beginning of the 1978 season the Steppenwolf Company was starting to get a strong sense of its identity and potential. H.E. Baccus had temporarily stepped aside as artistic director and Jeff Perry assumed that role. Perry's remarks in the Season 3 subscription brochure reflect the company's renewed sense of self:

It started with a small group of actors who shared a passionate, persistent dream. It was the dream of a theatre, a meaningful, affecting theatre. And with youthful idealism and nourishment by truly talented and gifted friends, Steppenwolf Theatre stumbled into existence on a warm summer evening two years ago. Between then and now, we have experienced the pains of a young growing child. Today, however, Steppenwolf Theatre is a child no more. With each season—in fact with each production—the family of Steppenwolf actors have developed a strong, consistent acting style that is unlike any other in the Chicago area. As a group, we have chosen to perform theatre that is often jarring, always engaging and enlightening. In all of our dramatic endeavors we have consciously decided to create the best possible theatre experience for the audience and the resident ensemble. I believe we have succeeded. Season 3 is evidence of our growth.

Critical acceptance and improving audience support placed the confidence level of the company at a high level. The Chicago Off-Loop theatre was booming and everything appeared finally to be in place for a successful move into the city.

Although their official home was still the basement theatre in Highland Park, their adopted home of Chicago was where they now produced more frequently. David Elliot in his *Chicago Sun-Times* review jokingly called Steppenwolf "The Highland Park company that lately seems to be almost a road show." The company members were anxious to end this nomadic period and move permanently into the city. Unfortunately, the ensemble's desire to establish a home in Chicago outweighed the financial and logistical realities for such a move.

The first play in Steppenwolf's third season was the Midwest premiere of one of Lanford Wilson's most successful plays *Fifth of July*, but was produced by, and performed at, the well-established St. Nicholas Theatre in Chicago's growing north side theatre district.[8] *Fifth of July* provided the Chicago theatre community an extremely positive experience with the company, and the co-billing with the more prestigious St. Nicholas enhanced Steppenwolf's visibility and gave them a crack at a hot new theatrical property.

The two main characters in the play are Ken Talley, a Vietnam vet, played by John Malkovich, and his caring lover, Jed, played by Jeff Perry; the same roles originated by William Hurt and Jeff Daniels in its premiere at New York's Circle Repertory Company three months earlier. In addition to Malkovich and Perry, *Fifth of July* featured Steppenwolf Theatre actors Gary Sinise, Joan Allen, Moira Harris, H.E. Baccus, and Laurie Metcalf. Malkovich had become a member of Equity during his earlier work at St. Nicholas on *Ashes*, and Perry, too, had gained his Equity membership with outside work, but for the others, this production marked the first time that they were paid for their services ($100.00 per week).

Fifth of July was the third show directed by a company outsider, Steven Schacter, artistic director of St. Nicholas. Although the play received immense praise from the critical community and helped Steppenwolf gain respect, many members of the company were uncomfortable about being produced by people from "outside." H.E. Baccus captured these feelings when he said,

---

8. The production was noteworthy because it introduced the company to the St. Nicholas location at 2851 N. Halsted, which would become Steppenwolf's second theatre space in Chicago after a move from the Hull House in 1982.

> We were shortchanged in many ways. We were all offended somehow
> that St. Nick didn't come out and say this is a Steppenwolf show. It was
> always: "this is Steven Schacter directing the Steppenwolf Theatre."

This was the price to be paid for being the young untested company in town: relinquishing artistic control in exchange for the benefits of working with the successful St. Nicholas Company. The *Fifth of July* experience added to the company's increasing desire to find a permanent Chicago home in which they could have total control over their productions. With this in mind, negotiations were soon initiated to secure the Hull House theatre space on Belmont and Broadway, a space with a storied theatrical history in Chicago. Wilson's quote from *Fifth of July* metaphorically captured this moment in time, "They were very happy, because then they knew it was up to them to become all the things they had imagined they would find."

A restaging of Sinise's and Perry's high-school directing project, *Philadelphia, Here I Come!*, directed by H.E. Baccus, closed out Steppenwolf's third season. The large number of roles precipitated the need to cast actors from outside the company in numbers greater than any production that had preceded it; among these outsiders were future ensemble members John Mahoney and Gary Cole. Mahoney had become acquainted with the company through Malkovich, whom he had met during the St. Nicholas Theatre production of *Ashes*. Bury St. Edmund's comments in the *Chicago Reader* review of *Philadelphia, Here I Come!* reveal the growing anticipation in the Chicago critical community of the company's work:

> They are the Children's Crusade of the Chicago theater scene. Their
> theater is in the basement of a Highland Park elementary school.
> Their budgets are strictly milk and cookie money. If they were to be
> typecast by their faces, none of them would play anyone older than
> Dobie Gillis. They have little or no professional performing experience
> outside their own company. Yet they regularly storm scripts ten times
> their size and somehow make them their own ... The production is
> another milepost on the Children's Crusade leading to ... where? I
> don't know. But I'm convinced it's well worth following.

His somewhat condescending commentary on the company was typical, because at this time some critics and audience members never seemed to take the company completely seriously; however, this attitude merely made the ensembles hungrier to prove themselves.

The final performance of *Philadelphia, Here I Come!* on New Year's Eve, 1978, was memorable for more than the nostalgia associated with closing a show. The performance had been a sell-out, but early in the day snow started to fall, beginning what would become known as "The Blizzard of '79"; only five audience members braved their way to the theatre that night, and money had to be refunded to the ticket holders unable to attend. Massive snows may have closed the year 1978 on a bad note, but the time period beginning with the 1976 summer of one-acts and ending with the Highland Park production of *Philadelphia, Here I Come!* represents in many ways the developmental and formative years for the company.

The weather didn't help their next effort either. January of 1979 started where December of 1978 had left off, and Chicago was still trying to dig out from what had been one of the greatest recorded snowfalls in the history of the Windy City. Drawing an audience to any theatre was not an easy task at this time; nonetheless, plans had already been made for Steppenwolf's return to the Hull House for their next show, a production of Eugène Ionesco's *Exit the King*. Ionesco's absurdist tragedy was a perfect example of the type of play that had not satisfied Highland Park audiences, but Chicago theatergoers were more open to this type of experimental work. Chicago's critical community again spoke of the intense, committed acting style of the Steppenwolf Company, and although Steppenwolf's production of *Exit the King* gained generally positive critical notices, sagging attendance taught the company a valuable lesson about the business of running a theatre. Tim Evans spoke of this difficult transitional period in Steppenwolf's history:

> There were a couple of spots that we really didn't think we were going to make it. *Exit the King* was one of them. I think it was one of the lowest points that I can ever remember. We were out of money and just couldn't go on. We had produced the show in the city on our own, thinking audiences would just flock to us and they didn't. Of course, the weather didn't help, the play didn't help, and the director didn't help. Everything that could have gone wrong went wrong.

The problems intimated by Evans regarding the director pinpoint the ongoing dilemma of the ensemble's troubled work with outside directors, in this case their former ISU instructor Ralph Lane. In truth, the problem rested not so much with the directors, but with the company's inability to subvert their own ideals to the desires of their guest directors, especially those of a former mentor. This was exacerbated by the fact that the company was still developing a methodology for producing plays. As a result, they turned inward in trying to answer the production questions they faced.

Money invested to give the Hull House space a facelift, coupled with the poor attendance to *Exit the King*, put increasing financial pressure on the company. These financial problems forced another upheaval on the business side. Tim Evans remained with the company as director of audience development, but executive director Robert Biggs was replaced by Tim Ansett. According to Evans, Ansett was brought in to help stabilize the financial situation at the theatre, but his appointment was brief. The ensemble members were forced to assert their own control of company matters, as Evans humorously recalls:

> Ansett sat down with the accountant who was donating his time. They had gone over the books and all this garbage for this theatre company that had absolutely no projected cash flow. It was day-to-day. We were struggling every day just to get the ensemble members a little money for food. The accountant made the recommendation that the theatre wasn't a viable business. Ansett then called a company meeting in the office one afternoon where he sat everybody down and said, "I think we ought to go out of business." It was pretty much that blunt. Gary looked at Jeff, Jeff looked at John, and John looked at Terry. They all looked at each other and then left. Everybody went back to John's apartment and sat down and they basically said, "What are we going to do about this?" They all said, "We're going to have to fire this guy," so they fired Ansett and decided the only way to survive was to get out of Highland Park.

This experience helped bond the company members in their common resolve to establish a Chicago home, but also made them face the reality of the company's financial situation and forced a delay to their much-anticipated move to the city.

As a way to right the damaged economic state of the theatre, in the early spring of 1979, another restaging of an earlier success, *The Caretaker*, replaced a previously scheduled show. John Malkovich took over the role of the younger brother Mick, because Gary Sinise, who had played Mick the first time, had taken a self-imposed leave of absence to test the waters of Hollywood. Malkovich still helmed the show and when asked by a local critic what it was like to handle the double duty of directing and playing a role, Malkovich responded, "I figure if Ricky Ricardo can do it, so can I." While in California on his temporary hiatus,

Sinise was featured in the Los Angeles premiere of Sam Shepard's *Curse of the Starving Class*.[9] Sinise's LA experiment did not go particularly well, as this recollection captures:

> I came into *Curse of the Starving Class* in LA as a replacement for somebody who had been there from the start. I played Wesley. Sally Kirkland was the mother. We started rehearsing. I did one little thing differently from the kid who'd done it before and she started complaining to the director. He said, "Come on. Just go with it. He's different." She said, "Ah, fuck it," and she quit. Then the girl and almost the whole cast quit, so they replaced everybody my first day. That was my first experience in Hollywood.

This restaging of *The Caretaker* succeeded by helping to temporarily ease the financial pressures on the company, and allowed the company some much-needed time to regroup and plan their future. Russ Smith, a college roommate of Malkovich, joined the business staff at this time, and together with Evans was instrumental in coordinating the final move into the city at the beginning of 1980. At the same time, the Steppenwolf board of directors, established during the first summer season, began to take a more active role in helping to raise the money needed for the anticipated move.

Tennessee Williams's American classic *The Glass Menagerie* directed by H.E. Baccus was the final show to be performed at the basement theatre in Highland Park and ran from May 10 to June 24, 1979. This production was repeatedly singled out by early ensemble members as one of the most memorable in the theatre's history due to its original and unique interpretation. Director Baccus remained true to the directions of playwright Williams by incorporating the original Magic Lantern scene headings and projections in Steppenwolf's interpretation. Excerpts from Williams's writings, and *Portrait of a Girl in Glass*, a short story about his institutionalized sister Rose, were strong reference points utilized by Baccus in the development of his production concept. This cast included guest artist Anne Edwards as Amanda Wingfield, and John Malkovich as

9. Earlier ensemble members Malkovich and Glenne Headly had met while working on the Chicago premiere of *Curse of the Starving Class* at the Goodman Studio 2 during the Blizzard of '79. This play was both Malkovich's and Sinise's first work with a Shepard piece, which foreshadows their more renowned work on another Shepard play, *True West*.

her son Tom, Laurie Metcalf as his sister Laura, and Terry Kinney as the gentleman caller. Though the individual performances, particularly Metcalf's Laura, received great critical notice, it was Steppenwolf's creative interpretation of the play that gained the most attention.

The challenge of doing an American classic for any company rests in putting a unique stamp on the production. Steppenwolf's *The Glass Menagerie* responded to this challenge by redirecting the focus of the play back to the character of Laura, as had been Williams's original intent. Metcalf remarks on her interpretation:

> The part that I played, Laura, was not some girl, that if she just changed clothes and combed her hair a different way, then she could have a boyfriend. This time she was on the verge of getting a lobotomy and there was no hope.

Jeff Perry further elaborates:

> H.E.'s take on the play presented a Laura more damaged and even closer to Williams's sister's situation. It went past someone who was a social recluse to someone who was destined to psychiatric hospitalization. John played overtly the fact of Tom's homosexuality, and going to the movies became clearly a euphemism for liaisons that he could never talk about with his mother. Terry's "gentleman caller" was a sublime mix of empathy and self-serving ambition; Anne Edwards's Amanda was infused with a grasping desperation. The production avoided any and all easy sentimentality. That the play sprung from a tortured grieving was not new, but for us that was a bit lost historically. In the original, Laurette Taylor's luminescence made it about Amanda, because her performance was so celebrated, much in the same way that Marlon Brando's brilliance had made *Streetcar* about Stanley for a time. H.E. put the play and its conditions back in Laura's hands. For our theatre it was a seminal moment. *Menagerie* became a benchmark and a guide for us in the ways it revealed an American classic that we felt had become momentarily hidden.

Once again, the acting choices of the Steppenwolf players, arrived at through intensive director/actor collaboration, made for an exciting and special retelling of this often-done Williams's masterpiece, and the critics responded enthusiastically to the inventiveness of Steppenwolf's interpretation. The opening line in David Elliott's review captured the excitement, "Heavens, does drama ever get much better than

Steppenwolf Theater's new production of *The Glass Menagerie*?" Richard Christiansen's review added to the accolades.

> This is not a gentle, wispy interpretation. It is jagged and harsh in many scenes, spooky and quirky in others. Yet, it strikingly illuminates the poetry of the play by casting it in a different light, re-examining its humanity, and dispelling some of the false illusions that have surrounded it in past presentations.

Not only did this production enhance Steppenwolf's reputation, it also proved that the company was capable of doing a contemporary classic with the same power and grace that it had brought to its previous productions.

The production became Steppenwolf's first to gain prestigious Joseph Jefferson Award nominations (Jeffs), given annually to the best of Chicago theatre. The nominations included Best Production, Best Ensemble, Best Actress (Edwards), and Best Supporting Actor (Kinney). Metcalf won the Jeff for Best Supporting Actress. H.E. Baccus discussed the importance of the Jeff recognition:

> To us, artistically, it didn't matter a bit, but suddenly the Chicago theatrical community said, "Oh yeah they're good. They can do something." People were suddenly more interested in us.

This increase in stature would help with audience development after the move to Chicago later in the year.

An article by Larry Kart in the *Chicago Tribune* during the run of *The Glass Menagerie* focused on Steppenwolf's growing stature and the strength of the character work in the play, Kart wrote:

> As is the norm at Steppenwolf, these interpretations were arrived at through collaborative work in which much room was left for give and take between the director and cast. "I think we do approach things differently here," Baccus says, "and part of that difference comes from our commitment to the actor. Often, at other theatres, the actor does his job, the director does his, and sometimes they come together. But because our goal, first and foremost, is to get fully founded characters onstage, it's very important for us that each actor understands the character as the director does." That approach, in which the "why" of acting takes precedence over and determines the "what," can be a risky business. The parties involved must know how to talk to each

other, and it's easy to imagine productions that remain mired in the discussion stage.

The Glass Menagerie provided an unforgettable finale for Steppenwolf in the tiny eighty-eight-seat basement theatre that had given birth to their work. *The Glass Menagerie* marked the first time that all of the ensemble members were compensated financially for their work in a Steppenwolf-produced show. Although their $100 salaries may not seem like a windfall, after three years of doing theatre for nothing it signified the beginning of a new era in Steppenwolf's history. Moreover, as a result of their work with Steppenwolf as well as work on shows in the Chicago community, more members of the ensemble began to join Actors' Equity, the stage actors' union. Equity had helped the growth of many of the small Chicago theatres, including Steppenwolf, by allowing them to produce professionally while gradually adding actors to the union. If these small companies had been forced from the beginning to pay all of their actors Equity wages, their growth and survival would have been substantially limited.

During the 1970s, Chicago theatre was in a growth mode, and in the years just prior to Steppenwolf's permanent move into the city, important Off-Loop theatres such as Victory Gardens, Wisdom Bridge, the Evanston Theatre Company (later Northlight), Travel Light, Goodman Stage 2, and St. Nicholas Theatre had all commenced operations; in so doing, they laid the groundwork for Steppenwolf's arrival. St. Nicholas became the business model to which Steppenwolf aspired. The operating budget of the theatre at its inception in 1974 was $12,000 and grew to over $1,000,000 by 1979. Started by David Mamet and others, the St. Nicholas Theatre not only launched the career of one of America's finest contemporary playwrights, but also established an audience development methodology for contemporary non-profit theatres. Jeff Perry remembers:

> Our art [Steppenwolf's] always outstripped our business sense, whereas St. Nicholas was really a wonderful marriage between art and business. They were amazing. They literally rewrote how to get an audience in Chicago's Off-Loop theatre with their commitment to a season of five new plays every year. Patricia Cox and Peter Schneider at St. Nick were the very first ones outside of the Loop, and the Shuberts, to build a subscription audience, and it was massive. They had 14,000 in a couple of years. It took us fifteen years to get 18,000 in our subscription base. It was really a remarkable achievement that happened alongside us.

Ensemble member Amy Morton remembers her first encounter with Steppenwolf Theatre as a student at St. Nicholas:

> Steven Schacter brought them in to do *Fifth of July* and that was the first thing I ever saw them do. I remember very clearly being at a party at Steven's house and him going on and on about these people he found in Highland Park who were some of the most brilliant actors he had ever seen. It was all very exciting.

When the Steppenwolf Company first performed in the city in 1978, ensemble member Laurie Metcalf worked as a secretary at St. Nicholas. In this position, she saw firsthand the St. Nicholas approach to audience development, and, perhaps more importantly, her access to St. Nicholas mailing lists and other business support (i.e. copy machine, press memos, ticketing information, etc.) aided the young Steppenwolf Company as they prepared for their permanent move into the Chicago marketplace.

After a nine-month absence from Chicago and after lengthy negotiations, Steppenwolf returned to the city in the fall of 1979 in an Apollo Theatre production of *Waiting for Lefty* directed by Sheldon Patinkin.[10] Odets' landmark play is comprised of a series of scenes that take place at a meeting of union taxi drivers who wait in futility for their leader, Lefty, to help them decide whether or not to strike. When the Group Theatre premiered the play in 1935, it created a minor sensation and it is safe to say that few plays capture the emotion of an era as did *Waiting for Lefty* in its original incarnation. The play seemed a perfect vehicle for the Steppenwolf Company and their philosophy of ensemble performance as John Kennedy's review captured: "There's no point singling anyone out in this show; it's truly an ensemble creation."

---

10. Early in 1978, Jason Brett and Stuart Oken built the 330-seat Apollo, a for-profit theatre at 2540 N. Lincoln Avenue. According to Richard Christensen, the Apollo became "an important landmark in the history of Chicago Theatre" by being the first brand new auditorium built as part of the Off-Loop theatre movement. Prior to building the Apollo Theatre, Brett and Oken had staged a highly praised production of Michael Weller's *Moonchildren*, directed by University of Illinois classmate Robert Falls at the St. Nicholas space. This production proved meaningful because it introduced the work of Falls, who would become a leader in the Chicago theatre, first as artistic director of Wisdom Bridge, and finally as artistic director of the Goodman, as well as a friend and colleague to many in the Steppenwolf ensemble.

Stuart Oken and Jason Brett, owners of the Apollo Theatre, had been encouraged by director Sheldon Patinkin to see Steppenwolf's production of *The Glass Menagerie* earlier in the year; impressed with what they had seen they decided to invite the company to perform at their Lincoln Avenue theatre. The opportunity to make money with a show in Chicago and the chance to work with Chicago veteran Patinkin made the project very appealing for Steppenwolf. Evans and Smith negotiated the deal and, after a short period of indecision regarding whether to produce *Waiting for Lefty* or an updated version of *A Streetcar Named Desire*, plans were made for the Apollo production of Odets' play. The production opened on September 5, 1979, with a cast comprised of most of the ensemble, including newly installed members Glenne Headly, John Mahoney, Francis Guinan, Tom Irwin, Michael Sassone, and Mary Copple. Gary Sinise and Moira Harris were still pursuing other interests in LA at this time, but would return in 1980 and 1981 respectively.[11]

The growing success of Steppenwolf and the impending move into the city necessitated an enlargement of the ensemble, and the original members hoped the new blood would stimulate continued artistic growth for the company. Patinkin's background in ensemble work and improvisation, resulting from his association with The Compass/Second City, enabled him to play a pivotal role in the molding of the new, larger ensemble into a cohesive unit. The improvisational aspects of *Waiting for Lefty* provided a perfect opportunity for Patinkin to use a variety of exercises developed by Viola Spolin for group dynamics, all of which were part of his teaching repertoire. Although company members expressed varying opinions as to the value of this work, new member Francis Guinan had no doubt that the exercises were much needed:

> Sheldon was very important to the company at that time. He was instrumental in molding us into a single group. He did lots of Spolin and Second City exercises for weeks. It was absolutely invaluable. I had thought all of that stuff was nonsense when I was in school, but somehow working with Sheldon and all of those people in the same

11. Mahoney, Copple, and Sassone had worked with the company once before in *Philadelphia, Here I Come!* Headly had worked with Malkovich at the Goodman Studio 2 on *Curse of the Starving Class* and Francis Guinan had recently become acquainted with the company members through connections at ISU. With the exception of Copple and Sassone, and many years later Headly, all of the others have remained members of the ensemble.

room—it just crystallized us. *Waiting for Lefty* in many ways set a pattern for our work later on. *Balm in Gilead* is considered our signature production, but I think the whole thing started with Sheldon's production of *Waiting for Lefty*.

Rondi Reed echoes Guinan's impressions and puts them into an even greater historical context:

I remember doing improvs with Jeff and Terry in college and we just humiliated ourselves totally. We weren't very good at it and felt it was the antithesis to the kind of acting that we wanted to do. Sheldon said, "You know what you do is not so different, it's just applied differently." He very kindly started out with simple things, basically Spolin and Paul Sills's theatre games, which usually would make most of us retch and spit up at the mere mention of it, but they were sort of disguised as drama exercises. They were exercises with a point.

At that time, we were very much an "American Stew" of acting techniques. We all had different styles and techniques; so, Sheldon was laying in some groundwork and flexibility that was really good for us at the time. A lot of us were resistant to it off and on. The things that were fun were fun, and the things that were hard were hard, and we didn't really want to do things that were hard. It forced us to work together, and then, of course, we came out trying desperately to amuse each other all the time. That was a big factor. "What can I do to amuse and harass you and just basically goof around?"

In many ways, the new company members needed the Spolin work more than the original members, because it helped them feel as though they were an important part of the ensemble. This assimilation process between old and new members would continue to evolve over an extended period. Perry commented on the blending of old and new:

There was a big feeling at the three-year mark for new members of a sense of being second-class citizens. There were original company members and there were new company members. I heard this all the time and I remember very vehemently saying that we weren't going to continue without new people. It just wasn't going to be. They had to know that they were important, because they were experiencing the full weight of three years of work and history and interchange that can make it hard to get into a group of people.

Patinkin not only brought the company a solid background in improvisation, but he also encouraged more technical approaches to acting as well. Patinkin remembers a particular moment in the rehearsal process for *Waiting for Lefty* that illustrates this point:

> It was a new experience for them working with so many people in one show, especially since they were spread out all over the house during the union meeting parts. There was one rehearsal that just completely bewildered them. It was right before we started previews. I did a pacing rehearsal. I was sitting in front and the ones in the audience were behind and I started pointing. I would just point with my finger when they weren't coming in soon enough. They were astonished at that kind of simple technical approach to doing a show. Nobody had ever done that with them before. I actually said, "You're doing it fine, but now let's make it move." They got excited about that.

The work with Patinkin, the company's first truly positive experience with a director from outside the company, gave them confidence to work with more outside directors in the future. The Steppenwolf production of *Waiting for Lefty* received a Jeff nomination for Best Ensemble, which is evidence that Patinkin's work with the company paid dividends. During the run of *Waiting for Lefty*, as part of the contract agreement with Oken and Brett, the ensemble staged benefit performances at the Apollo called *The Best of Steppenwolf* every other week on Mondays and Tuesdays when the theatre was dark. These benefit performances, showcasing past Steppenwolf successes with the original casts and directors, generated cash flow that helped pay for the company's later move into the city. *The Real Inspector Hound* by Tom Stoppard was the only play newly staged for the series and that cast included many of the new members, which furthered their involvement with the ensemble.

Reminiscent of their successful productions of *Fifth of July* and *Waiting for Lefty*, the Midwest premiere of their next show, Ralph Pape's *Say Goodnight, Gracie*, featured Steppenwolf actors, but was produced by another group. Michael Cullen of Travel Light Theatre produced the play at the Theatre Building in Chicago, where it ran for three months. He brought in the play's original New York director, Austin Pendleton, to do the staging and add the credibility of an outside "name" to the production. The success of the initial three-month run brought on an extension, and the show was moved to the larger Ruth Page Auditorium, which was close to Chicago's Loop. There the play ran an additional five months, making it the most financially successful production with which the company had ever been associated. Unfortunately, Cullen's Travel Light Theatre reaped most of the financial benefits. Nevertheless, the show offered sustained employment for a number of Steppenwolf actors, who took turns in the cast over the course of the lengthy run.

Never before had a show provided the company with a vehicle that so completely matched its talents with the commercial desire of the theatre-going public as did *Say Goodnight, Gracie*. Pape's story looks at three men and two of the women in their lives on the night of their high school's ten-year reunion. This was the first production in which every single character in the play was almost the exact same age as the company member who was playing the role. Moreover, the backgrounds and lifestyles of the characters in the play were somewhat similar to those of the ensemble. Director Pendleton's description of the play could just as well have described the Steppenwolf actors themselves:

> There's no plot at all. Pape puts a bunch of people together in a room for one specific occasion and lets things happen. They sit around smoking pot and doing riffs on one another. The dynamics of a pot party and all that free association fit exactly with the combination of drift and paralysis that are the characters' lives. *Gracie* is about a bunch of people caught in a very particular moment of history; the overriding reality they share is their friendship. It's a very difficult thing to dramatize—it's been the challenge of *Gracie* from the beginning.

Steppenwolf caught this particular moment in their developing trajectory perfectly. The deep friendships of the ensemble members helped them catapult their theatre to heights of unimagined recognition with this show, and Pendleton's work with Steppenwolf on *Say Goodnight, Gracie* helped cement the company's popularity, making this production especially significant to their forward progress. The original cast included Malkovich, Headly, Allen, Guinan, and former executive director Robert Biggs, and over the course of the run many ensemble members rotated in and out of the cast. Malkovich's line as the idealistic dreamer Steve in *Say Goodnight, Gracie* magically sums up the company's sense of their own potential at that time:

> I mean: I firmly believe the time is ripe for something like this: it cannot miss! Do you see what I'm getting at? You'll never have to work in an office again.

Pendleton had directed the original New York production of the play, but also spent considerable time working with Pape on preparing the script. That he had already spent so much time on the piece made him reticent to work on it again, and besides, he really had loved the New York production. Also, Pendleton had a young daughter and did not want to leave his home in New York for an extended period of time; however, after relentless prodding by Wayne Adams, the New York producer of *Say Goodnight, Gracie*, Pendleton relented and came to Chicago. The reluctant Pendleton had this to say upon his introduction to the company:

> My first encounter with Steppenwolf was extraordinary. I mean, you come into a room and there are John Malkovich, Joan Allen, Glenne Headly, Laurie Metcalf—all of those people—and Terry Kinney and Gary Sinise. It was endless. It was like opening a broom closet and there stood the future of the American Theatre. I didn't expect anything like that.

He continues on about the early rehearsals:

> I thought these people are very talented, but I'm going to come out for two weeks, and in effect I'm going to teach them the New York production and then I'm going to go home. We read through the play a couple of times. Then at our next rehearsal I was essentially going to present them the blocking from the New York production. Within about an hour, I just threw away the book and started all over again. I was so excited. They were so unique.

In many ways, what *Waiting for Lefty* said about the Group Theatre and the 1930s, *Say Goodnight, Gracie* said about Steppenwolf and its generation. Whereas the 1930s were a time of heightened political and social awareness and activism, the 1970s were a time more focused on a search for self, the "me generation." The reevaluation of society that took place in the 1930s came in response to the excesses of the 1920s that ultimately resulted in the depression, whereas the personal introspection of the 1970s grew out of disillusionment with the failures of the activism of the 1960s. Similar themes had been addressed before in the company's collaboration with St. Nicholas on *Fifth of July*. This time the issues were dealt with in a more comic fashion. Michael Cullen's Travel Light Theatre promoted the show heavily and audiences flocked to see it. Glowing reviews helped. Richard Christiansen's review included words that might very well have been written by a Steppenwolf publicist:

Ralph Pape's *Say Goodnight, Gracie,* is an almost perfect and completely joyous Production ... The acting is by five members of the Steppenwolf Acting Ensemble, an extraordinary group of young players who richly deserve the title of "ensemble." The staging is by Austin Pendleton ... who has forged the unique talents of the Steppenwolf people into a fresh, absorbing wonder of theater ... This is ensemble acting so generous, understanding and committed that it can bring tears of joy to our eyes.

This was the beginning of what would be a vital artistic relationship between future ensemble member Pendleton and the Steppenwolf Company.[12] Once again, the Jeff committee acknowledged the company's work with awards going to the company for Best Ensemble and to Glenne Headly for Best Supporting Actress. John Malkovich also received a nomination for Best Actor. The play was subsequently taped in 1982 for WTTW, the local public broadcasting station, with Jeff Perry taking over the role created by Biggs.

Despite the unbridled success of *Say Goodnight, Gracie,* an outside group had once again produced the show, leaving many in the ensemble dissatisfied. This would be the last time that outside producers would finance a Steppenwolf show until the company's first productions in New York. Ironically, it seems that each time the Steppenwolf ensemble looked to conquer a new horizon, they needed first to enlist the support of independent producers; but having learned the lessons from these excursions, they were then equipped to do it on their own.

With *Say Goodnight, Gracie* still in production at the Ruth Page Auditorium, and the Chicago success of *Waiting for Lefty* a recent memory, Steppenwolf's visibility was at a high level and the company finally completed the long-awaited permanent move into Chicago. In the newly renovated Hull House Theatre at the corner of Belmont and Broadway they opened their premiere Chicago season in February 1980 with Canadian playwright Michael Tremblay's family drama, *Bonjour, Là, Bonjour.* Ticket prices for this show were $6.50 for the Friday and Saturday shows, $5.50 for Wednesday, Thursday and Sunday shows. Critical reaction was mixed, but most of the blame was placed on a troubling script. Christiansen chided:

12. It was also producer Wayne Adams' first association with the company and he would play a major role in later bringing Steppenwolf shows to New York—most importantly *True West.*

If there were at least a few gleams of insight amid the banality, the play might have provided some precious moments of honest emotion. But no. Despite the heated passions, the situations are phony and the emotions counterfeit ... Steppenwolf has given the play its best shot. The production, in the freshly painted and carpeted small theater, has been carefully orchestrated by Baccus, and the actors, through sheer dint of sincere involvement, keep the drama from falling apart. But the show isn't worth it, and they probably should have known it.

Once again a less than memorable script had produced a less than enthusiastic reaction from the critics. But this time, audiences were so eager to see Steppenwolf in their new home that they came to the theatre anyway, resulting in a one-week extension. The acting of the company continued to be praised. Newcomer Rondi Reed, their friend from ISU, who had helped out during *The Sea Horse*, was in the cast of *Bonjour, Là, Bonjour* and became a continuing member of the company. Her tenure began at the same time the company became firmly established in their new Chicago performing space. Jeff Perry talked about the importance of Steppenwolf's permanent move into Chicago:

> It was a question of the company hitting its stride. People thought that it was our "shot" as a group. We went from Triple A to the major leagues, as far as we were concerned, in that we went from eighty-eight seats and the ability to sometimes get eight people and sometimes fill the house to a bigger theatre in a major city. We had watched the material well-being of the Organic, St. Nick, or the Goodman or whatever, and I'd been hawking egg rolls, and Al had been driving a bus and doing all this shit, and we were really sick of it. We felt our work was as good as these others, but we weren't getting paid, so it was a big motivator.

Francis Guinan added:

> Another really galvanizing experience for all of us was the move into Hull House and literally building that place. The fact that we were all in there ten to twelve hours a day had a real solidifying effect on the group.

The ambitious company now set its sights on becoming Chicago's preeminent theatre.

During the run of *Bonjour, Là, Bonjour*, the theatre began the "Almost Midnight" series in an attempt to give members of the ensemble, which now numbered sixteen, more acting and directing opportunities and to increase company visibility. The series became a forum for lesser-known works. Over the course of a little over a year, four plays were produced as part of the Almost Midnight series. These plays provided interesting theatre for both audience and performer because of the experimental nature of the productions. *Action* by Sam Shepard was of particular note because it provided Sinise his first opportunity to direct, as well as his initial directorial connection to Shepard, which would take on great meaning for the company in the not-too-distant future. *Big Mother* was Metcalf's first and only directing assignment. Stephen B. Eich also directed, leading to a more prominent role with the company when he became managing director in 1982. In this position, Eich was instrumental in guiding the company during one of its greatest periods of expansion. The Almost Midnight series was successful from both a business and an artistic standpoint. Actors were kept busy, and extended runs for both *Action* and *The Collection* helped the company's finances. The series finally came to an end because of increased participation by ensemble members in other Chicago-based projects, leaving them unavailable for the opportunities created by the Almost Midnight series.

For the next mainstage production of its fourth season, Steppenwolf again collaborated with director Sheldon Patinkin, on Arthur Miller's modern American classic *Death of a Salesman* about Willy Loman and his struggle to attain the American dream. Now somewhat comfortably ensconced in the city, Steppenwolf enlisted the services of popular Chicago actor Mike Nussbaum for the role of Willy in the hope of increasing their chances for an audience. Unfortunately, critical response to the production was indifferent. Lloyd Sachs' review in the *Chicago Sun-Times* was representative of the less than enthusiastic critical comment:

> If anyone should have tackled a revival of *Salesman*, it is the Steppenwolf Theater Company, which has, over the course of the last two years, delivered the most consistently fine ensemble performances this city has seen ... the production, which is blessed with some clean, thoughtful staging by director Sheldon Patinkin, never manages to sell us on one of the play's key sentiments, voiced by Mrs. Loman in the first act, that "attention must be paid" to her husband. To do that, a presentation of *Salesman* has to strike a lot more sparks than this one does; this is a conservative, almost reverent interpretation that never really allows Loman's plea to resonate.

Clearly, audiences had come to expect intense high-energy performances from Steppenwolf actors.[13] When a Steppenwolf production could be described as conservative, surely something was amiss. The program for *Death of a Salesman* included these brief comments about the company's purpose, giving the audience a chance to understand what might be in store in the next few years:

> Committed to the presentation of ensemble theatre, Steppenwolf has garnered high acclaim from audiences and critics alike for its strong acting style. The primary element that sets Steppenwolf apart from other Chicago theatres is the existence of the resident acting ensemble. The concept of a resident ensemble is not a new one. Historically, the "resident company" has been the great developer of the theatre arts. Groups such as the Moscow Art Theatre, England's Royal Shakespeare Company and America's Group Theatre forever changed dramatic art through a collective approach … The artistic vision of Steppenwolf, conceived and pursued by the ensemble, stresses the presentation of new works, neglected works, self-generated works and those works that promote the growth of the ensemble.

The administration's promotional skills were evolving, and the business side of the theatre continued to be streamlined and improved during this period. Russ Smith exercised firm control as the company's executive director, and a small full-time staff was in place to handle day-to-day operations. Steppenwolf had begun to take on all the trappings of a regional professional theatre. The company was exceedingly busy. The Almost Midnight series was going strong, performance classes were being offered by the actors, during the day and on weekends, and Steppenwolf ensemble members were among the most sought after in town for work at other Chicago area theatres.

In the blistering heat of a particularly humid Chicago July, the third play in Steppenwolf's fourth season opened. *Quiet Jeannie Green*, an unusual fantasy comedy by Steppenwolf's anointed "resident" playwright Dan Ursini, was a world premiere. Ursini had previously written *Sandbar Flatland*, which the company performed in March of 1978, but this would be the last play of Ursini's to be performed by the company; however, it did further establish Steppenwolf's desire to perform new works. The critics unanimously found fault with the challenging script,

13. Malkovich would reprise the role of Biff in a memorable Broadway production in 1984, which featured Dustin Hoffman as Willy Loman.

but once again they all praised the sincerity of the performances and the visual beauty of the show. Linda Winer's *Chicago Tribune* comments are typical:

> I just spent 90 enchanting minutes with the Steppenwolf Theater Company's world premiere of *Quiet Jeannie Green* and, to be honest, I don't have the vaguest idea what it meant.

Bury St. Edmund's review in the *Chicago Reader* goes one step further:

> I hate reviewing shows like this one. The author's done some fine writing, but the play's a mess. The directing, acting, and design work are excellent, but beside the point. Write an encouraging review that sends a lot of people to the theater and I lose credibility. Write a negative review and some talented people who've done some very hard work might get discouraged. So here's what: *Quiet Jeannie Green* provides more than a few moments of first-class verbal and visual whimsy, more than its share of dull, self-indulgent passages, and the air conditioning works.

Steppenwolf seemed to be enjoying a period in which they could do no wrong. The critics and their audience were supportive even in less than satisfying efforts. *Quiet Jeannie Green* remains a positive memory of many in the ensemble for being one of the most visually striking productions Steppenwolf has ever mounted. Tom Irwin provides insight to the process that brought *Quiet Jeannie Green* to fruition:

> I remember after some run-throughs and during previews, when we were still working with the script, there would be three or four people huddled in a corner with the director—members of the company who weren't in the show—everyone with legal pads—all trying to take the production to the next level. Directors had a lot of support if they wanted it. It was exciting.

A year and a half separated *Exit the King*, performed at the Hull House in the middle of the famed blizzard of '79, and *Quiet Jeannie Green*, also performed at the Hull House, this time in the midst of a searing Chicago summer. The change in temperature in some ways mirrored the change in stature of the Steppenwolf Company. The addition of new actors to the company, repeated commercial and critical successes, collaboration with experienced outside directors, alternative performance opportunities, and better promotional efforts made this one of the most energized times in the history of Steppenwolf. During this period, a collection of raw college students molded themselves into a tightly knit ensemble, a group worthy of the acclaim and attention they had begun to receive. With indomitable spirit and drive, the ensemble withstood ups and downs and focused their energies on the future. Despite initial problems with script selection, the company was able to craft an individual style that raised their performances above the occasional limitations of their playwrights' works. Writing for *Chicago Magazine*, Anthony Adler called this "The period of nasty bruises won in the course of brutal hand-to-hand acting ... an almost folkloric period." Laurie Metcalf fondly recalls:

> I remember long, drawn-out meetings when we thought, at different times, we needed a manifesto or something. I don't know that we ever got anything written. I think we all just understood that it was an actors' theatre. We got very lucky in that we had some future directors in the company who at the time didn't even know that they were good directors. But somebody always had to direct. Somebody always had to play the older or younger roles. We tried to take turns directing and playing these parts we weren't suited for and I think it stretched us in ways that we wouldn't have experienced had we gone about a more normal acting route.

Gary Sinise further reminisced:

> The fact that we started as an isolated group of young kids in a basement twenty-five miles from Chicago—where there wasn't any other alternative theatre experience for anybody—where there wasn't a casting director for twenty-five miles looking for the next Warren Beatty—and there weren't movies presenting the possibility of paying work helped us to create an incubator of sorts. The fact that we were isolated in this small space without a care for what anyone else was doing, bonded us in a way. If we would have started in Los Angeles or New York, I think we would have broken up. The fact that we were just an isolated group with a big chip on our shoulder gave us a sense of strength and commonality that is vital in the success of any ensemble theatre group. Having strong leaders that eventually were really respected by the other members also gave us strength. I've talked to a lot of young theatre groups that have tried to get their shit together and find a way of working and have tried to model

themselves after Steppenwolf. I just have to say that a lot of it was good fortune, luck and fate and persistence.

The twenty-one and twenty-two-year-olds that started Steppenwolf were no different from their peers; they partied, hung out with their friends, got in and out of relationships, and struggled to make ends meet. But their story had one difference: they had a laser-like vision to achieve their dreams in acting and the theatre. Their miraculous one-of-a-kind ascension from a church basement in suburban Chicago to international acclaim is truly legendary; the foundation had been built in these early years and their reputation was broadening as they moved into Chicago. The time had come to tackle the next level. The groundwork was in place for something special to occur; something that would catapult them to levels of success they had never imagined.

Figure 10. Barbara June Patterson and Gary Sinise, 2015, courtesy of Steppenwolf Theatre Company.

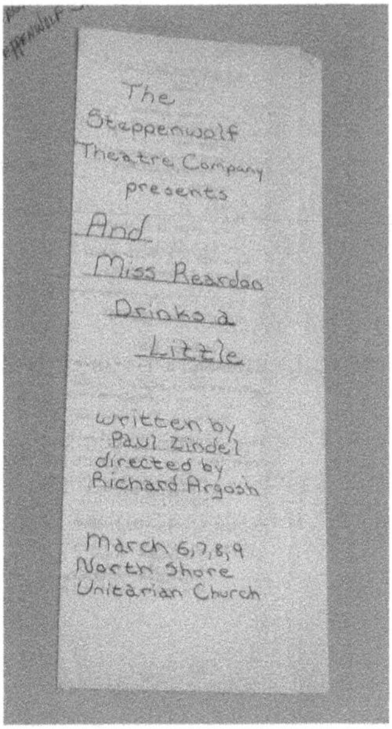

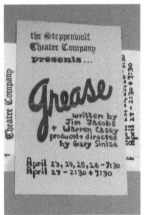

Figure 11. First Steppenwolf program, 1974, courtesy of Gary Sinise.

Figure 12. *Grease* program, courtesy of Gary Sinise.

Figure 13. *Grease* cast, 1974, courtesy of Gary Sinise.

Figure 14. Gary Sinise, first sign, Highland Park, 1976, courtesy of Steppenwolf Theatre Company.

Figure 15. Gary Sinise and Terry Kinney, promo for *The Indian Wants the Bronx*, 1976, courtesy of Gary Sinise.

Figure 16. John Malkovich and Laurie Metcalf, *The Glass Menagerie*, 1979 © Lisa Ebright-Howe.

Figure 17. Steppenwolf at St. Nicholas Theatre, 1978, courtesy of Steppenwolf Theatre Company.

Figure 18. Early ensemble photo, 1977 © Lisa Ebright-Howe.

Back: John Malkovich, Gary Sinise, Laurie Metcalf, Joan Allen, non-ensemble member Gregg Winters, Alan Wilder

Front: Moira Harris, H.E. Baccus, Jeff Perry

Figure 19. Jeff Perry, Alan Wilder, Laurie Metcalf, Moira Harris, Terry Kinney, Gary Sinise, *Mack, Anything Goes Over the Rainbow*, 1977 © Lisa Ebright-Howe.

IN THEIR OWN WORDS: ON GROWING UP

Joan Allen:
I was born in 1956 in a small town directly west of Chicago called Rochelle. It's basically about 8,000 people—pretty much a farm community. We lived in town. My father had this gas station where I used to hang out when I was a kid. It was sort of like the *The Andy Griffith Show*. Growing up—very small town, quiet, peaceful, riding your bike around in the summer—that kind of existence.

Jeff Perry:
I was in junior high and my sister and my dad had planned this family trip to something I've still never seen, the Black Hills, South Dakota. In the *Highland Park News*, our hometown newspaper, there was an audition notice that the American Conservatory Theater (ACT) was holding local auditions for non-speaking parts in Pirandello's *Six Characters in Search of an Author*. They were doing maybe three plays that summer in the Murray Theatre at Ravinia, which is mainly a music festival like Tanglewood on the East Coast, or the Hollywood Bowl in California, but they do a little bit of theatre here and there. My eldest sister Jo took me to the audition. It was some kind of simple little improvisatory premise of looking for someone and then being scared and running somewhere—something very simple and physical. I was eleven or thirteen, something. I got the part. I ruined the family vacation. We all had to stay home. I would find out years later that Steppenwolf member Austin Pendleton was at ACT at the time and was part of that show.

That was one of the very first moments. Then an eighth-grade moment, where our English teacher adapted part of Herman Wouk's novel *City Boy*, and I felt like I had had such a puzzled, not unhappy but meandering school life up to that time. I loved wasting time walking home with my friends, but suddenly there was this little play practice, and I loved it. I'd gotten such loving attention, which most actors will tell you is one of the addictive principles of why they ever got into it. However many little rehearsals we had, there was something about it that felt so great—so comfortable. And, finally, in the assembly that was the single performance of *City Boy* and I got on stage and started my lines. I froze. I went up. I don't know how I got off stage, but I've got this memory of somehow stumbling offstage and just crying in shame. What a funny beginning for someone who would end up loving doing this as a life's work. So, one of my first steps was a big fearful stumble.

My mom and dad were always incredibly supportive of the whole thing. My dad was an English teacher. They wanted their kids to find out what it was that they wanted to do and then do it and enjoy it. They didn't really try to push us in one direction or another, but they really did get a kick out of theatre. My mom was a great armchair critic. I can't tell you the number of times that we talked about how rehearsals were going good or bad. She knew all of the plays. She read all of the plays. Pinter was her favorite.

H.E. Baccus:

I was born in Herrin, Illinois, in the southern part of the state. It's very close to Benton, Illinois where John Malkovich was born. I lived in a very prosperous family. We had a fifteen-room house in Marion. It was a hundred years old or more at the time. A nanny, an African-American lady who lived across this stream, raised me. It was very segregated, and we lived in an area which was close to the black section. In the back of our property was a stream. I thought it was a huge thing, but it was just a stream, and Lilly Mae lived across the way.

Alana Arenas:

I went to a performing arts high school that I did not want to go to. I never grew up thinking I wanted to be an actor. I didn't have like a life-transforming experience in the theatre, but I had a drama teacher in middle school that saw the dramatic flair in me and told my mom to have me audition for a performing arts school in downtown Miami. I didn't want to go. I wasn't interested. My mom was really adamant about me auditioning and so I made a deal with her. I said, "Well, if I audition and I get in, can I have a bunny rabbit?" And she said, "Yeah, sure." I got into the school, but I didn't get my bunny rabbit.

I had just made the Marching Band in high school, which in southern culture is a really big deal. My particular high school was a pipeline to FAMU (Florida Agricultural and Mechanical University), and FAMU was home of the "Marching 100." I was a dance girl. The point is that I come from that culture and that was a huge accomplishment; because I was going to be part of the band at my local high school, I ended up deciding to go to this performing arts school (New World School of the Arts) and that radically changed my life. I don't know if I would be here today if I didn't go through that high school. I don't know what would have become of my life. I fell in love with acting. I had auditioned for the Theatre Department and it was a multi-disciplined performing arts school, and I was going to school with people who had extraordinary artistic ability, one of those people being Tarell Alvin McCraney.

Kate Arrington:
I grew up in Raleigh, North Carolina. My parents were both English professors. When I was an infant, my dad was an adjunct at Duke, teaching film, because he's really interested in Hitchcock. He went to a lot of different conferences and gave papers on Hitchcock. When I grew up, I saw every Hitchcock movie—at far too young an age!

Gary Sinise:
Many of my teachers at Highland Park High School started grading me on what I was doing in the plays. We had to take a test on the constitution to graduate. I had been rehearsing or something and hadn't studied, and my teacher, Rose Bogeson, she helped me, because I just grabbed the test and I walked out in the hall and said, "Listen, I haven't studied, I've been doing theatre. I don't know anything on this test. I wish I did. I'll accept whatever hand you deal me. You're justified to fail me. I can't take the test. It's a waste of my time." She gave me a D. She passed me without taking the test. I was one of the lucky ones that found my life's work at a very early age. When I was sixteen, I did my first play, and I've haven't stopped doing plays or acting since.

Francis Guinan:
My family was sort of a black Irish family on both sides. I guess you might call it a strict Catholic upbringing. My high school was one of those separate but equal things, where there was a girls' wing and a boys' wing, and we sort of mixed at lunch, but not really. There were only a couple of classes that actually had both girls and boys. Our principal was Father Daniel J. Delahan—what a reactionary fascist he was. This was the late sixties and early seventies when I was going to school. I remember he gave a sermon once denouncing the Stones' *Let's Spend the Night Together* and the tune *Sock it to Me, Baby*.

John Mahoney:
I was born and raised in England. I did a lot of theatre while I was growing up—a lot of citywide competitions in Manchester. I was halfway though my senior year in high school when I auditioned for the

Birmingham Rep. My parents had a fit and I finished the play that I was contracted to do with them, and then came back and finished school. One thing led to another and I decided to emigrate to the United States.

Rondi Reed:
I think the fact that we had such bedrock training at Illinois State and were told from our earliest days that if you want to do theatre you can do it yourself. You don't have to go to New York. You don't have to go to LA. You can do good theatre where you are. That was deeply imprinted on us from our faculty. They would occasionally bring in some big named stars among them, Karl Malden and Leonard Nimoy, and they would say, "Do it where you can do it."

Mariann Mayberry:
I grew up in Branson, Missouri. When I was seven, my big dream was to either be in the Saloon Show at Silver Dollar City, a folk arts/crafts theme park in Branson, or get cast, and ride a horse, in the local outdoor drama, *Shepherd of the Hills*. My father worked at Silver Dollar City, so there was hope for a foot in the saloon door, but the dream died when he moved us to Illinois to work for Marriott's Great America in Gurnee, Illinois. At fifteen I started working at Great America during the summers and eventually I found my way into *Neptune and Nemo's Dolphin Show* and *Bugs Bunny's Magic Show*. In the Dolphin Show I was the cute little thing with a whistle that did all the tricks with the dolphins, including putting fish in my mouth for the dolphins to leap out and grab. In the magic show, half the time I was Porky Pig, and half the time I was the girl getting cut in half or disappearing.

I eventually found my way into plays in high school, and then, against my parents' hopes, decided to go to college for theatre. I went to Illinois Wesleyan University, but by my junior year I needed something more. I decided I needed an internship, so I went up to Chicago and wandered the streets in a skirt and heels looking for some theatre to take me on. This was back when the Dunkin' Donuts at the corner of Clark and Belmont was one scary place. I actually went in there for a cup of coffee and an officer saw me and insisted on driving me back to my friend's apartment. The following night I found myself in front of Steppenwolf. I went across the street to the Gaslight Bar, went through the phone book, got my quarter out and called over. Kate Richey (who is now married to Francis Guinan) answered and said, "Sure, when can you come in?" I said, "How about now?"

I'd stumbled upon the Holy Grail and my life was completely altered thereafter.

William Petersen:
My mother and I saw *The Sound of Music* at the Shubert with Florence Henderson. We sat in the first row of the balcony and it was a school night and it was late and it was great and it was downtown and it was snowing and it was just too cool. I couldn't believe these kids in the show were out there singing in the middle of the night and performing. My mother had talked to Florence Henderson because she was head of the Evanston Women's Club, so we got to go backstage and I saw all the kids go out the stage door and get into a limousine to be taken to their hotel or whatever, because it was the road show. Every time I saw *The Brady Bunch* after that, I kept going, "God, she was Maria." I just thought, "What a cool life that would be to be my age and be on stage and then be going in a limo someplace." That was literally the introduction I had to the theatre. I didn't think about it that much at the time, but I know it was very momentous for me.

It was just an accident that I ended up in the theatre. A number of years later, I went to Idaho State University, because my girlfriend at the time went there. I was going to try and play football and I ended up in the theatre department because my grade point average was so bad that I had to get my grades up to qualify—and I fell in love with the theatre. I just fell in love with the people that were working on plays and the energy in the department.

Bob Breuler:
I went to Quinnipiac College, which had just three buildings when I went there. I was studying to be an accountant and I failed miserably. So, I transferred to Southern Connecticut where I was in liberal arts and writing poetry. I had been published in the New Haven Festival of Arts. They put my poem on the wall. This was kind of cool. My friend Holly and I were walking down the hall and we decided to audition for *Love's Labour's Lost*. There were a lot of good-looking girls. This was when most guys got into the theatre that way.

Amy Morton:
I went to hippie school. Oak Park River Forest was a big high school, it was like 5,000 kids, but this was the seventies, so there was one blocked-off little section of the high school called the experimental program. You could write your own curriculum. You could get English credit for

keeping a journal. There were wacked-out ways to get credit, so if you were really self-motivated it was great, but if you're a beat-off, you're in trouble if you ever want to go to college. I was not that self-motivated, but I loved it and we created our own little theatre company within that little chunk of the school.

Austin Pendleton:
I was born in Warren, Ohio, in 1940. I'm the oldest of three children. My mother had been a professional actress and even directed professionally. My father saw her, I think, first on the stage when she was a journeyman actress at the Cleveland Playhouse, but playing a leading role. They had an on-and-off courtship for a few years and she just decided to marry him and settle in Warren. This was before World War II. All three children—my brother was born not long before Pearl Harbor and our sister was born two months after VE Day and a week before Hiroshima, so we were all born in and around the War. My brother, not at all incidentally, is now the president of the board of the Cleveland Playhouse, which is where our father first saw our mother.

Ian Barford:
I come from a small town—Charleston, Illinois. A lot of the people, John and Laurie and Terry and Joan and Rondi and Randy, come from small little towns like that. My parents were musicians and theatre was not a big thing growing up, but they did take me to theatre occasionally. They were professors, but their first love was music.

I went to ISU from '84 to '88. I was not intending to go into theatre. I was a tennis player. I was on the tennis team and not a very good student and really had no particular direction. I fell into theatre through a series of strange circumstances.

Anna D. Shapiro:
My mom was an actress for a little while. She married my father, who was a conceptual black and white photographer. Every kind of cliché about being an artist my dad was. I think he wasn't as much of a theatre person as my mom, but the way that he lived his life gave her permission to totally be an actress. My parents weren't rich and it was 1966 and there weren't a whole lot of moms who were out being actors, while they had young kids, so she stopped.

In terms of Steppenwolf, I remember seeing *Balm in Gilead* at the Apollo. I remember seeing *True West* at the Apollo. I remember seeing *Orphans*. I remember seeing *Cloud 9*. I remember everything. I don't remember anything about being a kid, but I can remember those plays totally with almost total recall. My mom took us to everything here at Steppenwolf and I just really remember the feeling of coming here. I remember the feeling of opening the program and being so excited to see who was going to be in it, because I had so much affection for all of them. I fell madly in love with John Mahoney. I wanted to marry him. Still hasn't happened. When I saw *You Can't Take It With You*, I really thought this is what happens when they use their powers for good instead of evil.

I didn't want to be an artist at all. I just wanted to be normal. I thought if I had a trade then my life wouldn't feel so volatile. My dad was an astonishingly wonderful human being but he had a lot of challenges being an artist. It's hard when you're a kid not to relate to the work that they do.

I went to Columbia College to study film. I've said this a million times, but when your parents are artists it's not that different than growing up in a family of cops or lawyers. It's not whether or not you're going to be a cop or lawyer, but rather, it's what kind of cop or lawyer you're going to be. I took this film-directing class and I hated it. I don't remember why, I just thought I'm going to take a directing class in the theatre department from Sheldon Patinkin. My mom and dad knew Sheldon before they were married to each other, so that was just a coincidence. They'd known each other since high school, since college, because my mom was involved with The Compass. I took a directing class and directed a little play. That was that. I was done. I loved it. I haven't stopped since.

Laurie Metcalf:
I grew up in southern Illinois in Edwardsville and other than having a relative, a great aunt who was a playwright named Zoë Akins, who actually won the Pulitzer Prize one year for play called *The Old Maid*. I never knew her or anything about her back then. Other than that, I had no connection to theatre, but we'd weirdly put on little shows in the backyard and charge people to sit in lounge chairs and watch me swing on the swing set.

Frank Galati:
I grew up in Northbrook, but I was born in Highland Park Hospital in 1943. I went to Glenbrook High School and Ralph Lane was my high-school teacher. Ralph had his MA and a couple years after my crowd graduated, he went back to Northwestern; finished his PhD,

and he got the job at Illinois State, where he mentored many of the Steppenwolf ensemble members.

Yasen Peyankov:
The funny thing is I always wanted to be an actor ever since I was a little kid. I don't know what it was or why, maybe it was the play element that was always very attractive to me. In Bulgaria and Eastern Europe in general, the government subsidized theatre and art, because it was a socialist country. My parents took me to my first play when I was maybe six or seven at the local theatre in Varna where I grew up. It was a Bulgarian play, like an old melodrama with a love triangle and some big passions. I remember sitting in the dark in the balcony of this gorgeous old theatre watching those actors and just being mesmerized by the whole experience and I knew this is what I wanted to do. For a child, a play like that would probably be boring, but I just sat there and ate the whole thing up.

James Vincent Meredith:
I was born in Chicago and raised in Evanston. While I was in Evanston, I did a lot of work with the Piven Theatre Workshop. So I was lucky enough to take classes and study under Byrne and Joyce Piven and their daughter Shira. I learned about improv and being comfortable within my own body as an actor. We're talking junior high going into high school, which is the period of time that you're kind of concerned a lot about your body image. It was really useful for me working there and learning under all those guys. It gave me confidence to trust myself on stage and in real life.

I got this Steppenwolf shirt that was tie-dyed. I don't know where it came from, but I wore that thing religiously for years. Like end of high school going into the college and I was like, "Yeah, I'll be in it one day," but I never took it seriously. They are kind of pie in the sky; it's Steppenwolf for goodness sake. At the time, I hadn't even seen a show there. That was like late eighties, early nineties. That was my first time that I gave any thought to Steppenwolf—it wasn't even a dream though because they were just too far beyond my reach.

Martha Lavey:
I was born in Lawrence, Kansas—one of seven kids. My dad's career was with the CIA, so we always lived in the United States, but we moved around a fair amount. In sixth grade we moved to Detroit and I went to a place called Immaculata High School, which was an all-girls Catholic

High School. By the time I graduated it had a majority of African-American students. Our nuns were feminists and liberation theologists and against the war; Jane Fonda came to our high school and spoke. It was just a really progressive cool place and there was a woman named Anne Knoll who was my drama teacher and she had grown up in the Chicago area and it had always been her ambition to go to Northwestern but I think her family didn't really have the resources. She ended up going to Quincy College but when I was a junior in high school, she took me to Chicago and showed me Northwestern and suggested I apply. I got in and that's how I got to the Chicago area and I've stayed here ever since.

Jim True-Frost:
I grew up in the Chicago suburb of Winnetka, Illinois, where I did a lot of children's theatre—and then all school plays, musicals, and dance and chorus concerts for four years at New Trier High School completely immersed in performing. Like Jeff, Gary, and your experience, I had an inspiring drama teacher named Suzanne Adams. She was one of those artist educators who really taught the craft of acting like it was a conservatory program. She knew her stuff about technique, craft, and the literature of the theatre. She also had this fire about truth and integrity in art. She was a real light for me.

Jon Michael Hill:
I wrote a short story when I was in first grade at the magnet elementary school and turned it into a play. It was about my brother getting lost at the zoo. Sitting in the auditorium watching the thing I wrote should have made me want to become a writer right off the bat, but instead I looked at the lead actor playing my brother and said, "Oh, man, I want to do that." I was watching *Mad Max* and *Star Wars*. I always longed to be in those types of films, but it was more just a dream. I didn't really understand the path to do it. I wanted to go to school for engineering and I realized I wasn't that good at math. My buddy said, "Hey, Ang Lee went to the University of Illinois. They have a theatre program. You should audition." I did and got in. It was the only place I auditioned.

Molly Regan:
I grew up in Mankato, Minnesota, a town my family had lived in for a hundred years. We'd go to traveling musicals like *Hello Dolly* and stuff like that in Minneapolis. One of the moments that I knew theatre was special was when my mom and a group of ladies took me to a production

at the Guthrie of *The Cherry Orchard* with Hume Cronyn and Jessica Tandy. I was much too young to understand the play. I could get the basic plot, but I was just totally taken in. It was this overwhelming experience of "I get that. That touches me. That reaches me. Whatever they're doing up there, I understand on some emotional level." I was brought up very strict Irish Catholic and the only way to really express myself was in the theatre. The theatre was a chance for me to really get out what I was not allowed to get out in real life, because of Minnesota stoicism and what I would call Irish Catholic repression. I could do anything on stage because it wasn't me. I think that was a real key for me to wanting to be an actor.

K. Todd Freeman:
I originally got started in theatre in seventh grade and then went to the High School for the Performing and the Visual Arts in Houston. Then I went to North Carolina School of the Arts, the Conservatory in Winston-Salem, so that was ten years of pretty much back-to-back school training. I moved from college to New York and then got a role in a play. It was a pretty straight path.

Tim Hopper:
In elementary school in Chattanooga, we had a few programs that we put on in the school auditorium/lunchroom. I remember playing Woodrow Wilson at some little President's Day event. At the masses every morning at my catholic school I would read the announcements and the epistle. As a junior in high school a friend literally dragged me into the room to audition for a Catholic High School production of *Canterbury Tales*. I think the bug kind of bit there. The next year was *You Can't Take it With You* and I played Mr. Kirby. It was after that I said to my dad one day that I wanted to be an actor. He was great about it. He said, "Listen, it's a flighty profession, but if that's what you want to do then you have to do it." My parents really supported me.

Tina Landau:
My parents were film producers and did a series called *The American Film Theatre*, so I was surrounded by the arts and entertainment. It's interesting though because in my family I was always considered slightly the black sheep because I wanted to do theatre instead of film. I grew up going to Broadway musicals, which was my first love. To this day, I maintain that that art form is most fundamental to my work and most in my DNA.

Kate Erbe:
My dad is a doctor. My mom was an actuary. They didn't want me to be in such a difficult profession with very little stability with a life in the theatre. I saw that as not supporting me and therefore I had to prove them wrong. I actually dropped out of high school and left home when I was sixteen. I ended up at a progressive high school in western Massachusetts—a boarding school. I finished there and applied to NYU to the undergraduate drama program. It was the only school I applied to and I luckily got in, because I didn't have a Plan B.

Ora Jones:
I grew up in the military and we traveled. I woke up one day as a child and thought for some reason the idea of acting was what I was supposed to be doing. My mother was very accommodating and somehow in the jungles of Panama found someone who was doing a production of *Oliver*. I was seven years old and to this day I don't know how she did it, but she got me in.

I consider myself to be very fortunate to have parents who helped us learn about the things we were curious about. They had tough childhoods and worked very hard to get to where they were and they wanted to make sure that their kids worked for it too. The theatre just never left me. I was very serious about what I wanted to do. I just didn't know how to do it. I was again fortunate because I had teachers who wanted to encourage an active interest in their students.

Being from Ohio and Columbus, our family is very sports-minded, so I went to Notre Dame, because I wanted to see the Fighting Irish up close, but the other more important reason I chose Notre Dame was to get a more rounded and complete education. I had been saying since I was a kid that I was going to be an actor, but when it came time to go to college, I was afraid if I went to an actors' training program or conservatory, and then discovered that acting really was not what I wanted to do, I would have been stuck. Going to a university that had other requirements—math, science, history, etc—gave me the opportunity to compare acting with other subjects, so I could get a better perspective.

Coming to Chicago was really a "happy accident." During our senior week, we got on the train and came to Chicago and I met a friend's brother who was an actor and he said, "Do you want to come to Chicago and hang out for a couple of days. You can follow me around and I can show you what I do in a day as a professional actor and maybe that'll help you decide whether this is a place you will want to be." I came to

Chicago on vacation and thought, "I'll be there about a week," and just never left.

Tracy Letts:
My folks were both English teachers and taught in a small state college in a small town in Oklahoma where I grew up. My dad had gone to school on the GI Bill and wound up with a PhD and my mom had a master's degree. These are Depression-era people coming out of Oklahoma—a remarkable generational leap. I kind of defied some of that by not going to college. I did a semester in college and then dropped out. They were actually fairly accepting about it, "You know, he's not going on that path."

At seventeen, I was in Dallas, Texas with my headshot and résumé trying to get work as an actor because it was about a hundred miles north of my hometown and they were making more films like *Places in the Heart* and *Tender Mercies* there, but Dallas is not a great place for any actor to be. I was there for two years before coming up here to Chicago for a summer and this seemed like a much better fit. I wasn't a playwright. I had written my whole life and had grown up in this literate household, so I came here to act in the theatre—and I had a hard time.

My first job here was at Steppenwolf in *The Glass Menagerie*. Jeff Perry's aunt Barbara, "Boots," played Amanda, so I knew Jeff's family briefly growing up. His father passed away very young and both of his parents were educators too. Jeff is one of the best pure human beings I have ever encountered in my entire life—period. I think it was the first thing Fran (Guinan) had directed for the company. I didn't have an audition scheduled and I wasn't going to go, but a friend of mine convinced me, so I walked in at the end. I was the last person who waited in line for an audition. I read for them and the casting director said, "Where are you from?" I said, "I'm from Oklahoma." She said, "Where the hell were you when we were casting *The Grapes of Wrath*, when we needed all the Okies we could get?" Fran said, "Well, thank God he wasn't available for that so he can do my show." It was a nice introduction to the company.

Chapter 2

BALM IN GILEAD: THE DEVELOPING ENSEMBLE PHILOSOPHY AND MOVING FORWARD

Balm in Gilead was just one of those incredibly magical things where the exact right cast finds the exact right play and the exact right director and it's performed in the exact right place at the exact right moment in history.

—John Mahoney

The work of Steppenwolf over the last forty years has included so many meaningful moments in so many productions that there is no possible way to capture them all. I believe the productions I have chosen and their individual production-based stories will illuminate for you, the reader, a strong representation of how many of Steppenwolf's productions came into being, which is a blend of immense talent, a dynamic collaborative approach, unwavering perseverance, and many "happy accidents." There is no specific "Steppenwolf methodology" that was magically revealed along my journey writing this book, but what I found was an ensemble committed to the work of mining as much as possible from each of the scripts they encounter; a group of people, from playwright to director to actor to staff, that is never satisfied unless they have each done all they could possibly do to fully realize the work at hand. At Steppenwolf, it was, is, and always will be about "the work." As Gary, Jeff, and I heard from our mentor Barbara Patterson on many an occasion, "Trust. If you focus on the work and the process, the product will take care of itself." Sheldon Patinkin summed it up like this:

Steppenwolf is totally into doing whatever they are doing. They're doing it because they're doing it, not because they want someone to like it.

In the summer of 1980, following *Quiet Jeannie Green* and just prior to the opening of *Balm in Gilead*, the reputation of the Steppenwolf

Theatre Company in Chicago was at a high point. Ensemble members were among the most sought-after actors in town, and when the ensemble members were not involved with a Steppenwolf production, they eagerly accepted outside offers, despite the fact that, in most cases, even that did not mean financial security. Sadly, it has always been a challenge for the Chicago theatre to be able to pay actors a living wage, and the myriad of companies in town, both large and small, still piece their existence together "paycheck to paycheck." As a result, many members in the ensemble supplemented their income by teaching classes, either at the theatre or as adjuncts of the theatre department at Columbia College, a program that had been revitalized with the arrival of Steppenwolf mentor Sheldon Patinkin as its chair. Many in the company now had theatrical agents in the city, which meant they began to do commercial and voiceover work to augment their incomes. Finally, some were able to make a sustainable living almost exclusively in the theatre or in performance-related activities.

The large cast for *Balm in Gilead*, securing the proper location, and the sizable budget it would take to produce, had kept production of the play on the back burner. Now, the successes and increased visibility of Steppenwolf and their new Hull House home encouraged them to take the risk. The decision to produce *Balm in Gilead* was supported by the new board of Steppenwolf, which had been reorganized under Russ Smith's leadership during the move into the city. The addition of influential, high-profile board members with connections to corporations and funding agencies made the plans for continued expansion more attainable; everybody recognized the importance of the first Chicago season's penultimate production, *Balm in Gilead*, in achieving the goal of becoming a permanent presence in the city's theatrical landscape.

The original production of *Balm in Gilead*, written by Lanford Wilson, produced by Ellen Stewart at New York's Café La Mama and directed by Marshall Mason[14] created a minor sensation when it premiered in 1965. In the intervening period since the initial run of *Balm in Gilead*, only five other professional productions of Wilson's play had been attempted. With its huge cast of 28, difficult overlapping dialogue, and an environmentally-based story with a limited plotline, *Balm in Gilead* appeared to be a questionable choice. But with the commitment and foresight of director Malkovich and a hungry group of actors, Steppenwolf pulled it off with

---

14. Mason would later direct Steppenwolf's production of Wilson's *Burn This* with John Malkovich and Joan Allen.

electrifying results. Still, as Francis Guinan amplifies, there remained uncertainty:

> I remember opening night of *Balm in Gilead*. I was standing alone onstage and Malkovich came out. He and I were the only ones in the theatre standing on the stage before the show and I asked him, "How do you feel, John, do you think this is going to work?" He said, "Gosh buddy, I don't know if this is going to work or not." He was really in doubt, he didn't know. Of course, the reviews came out and it was practically a civic holiday. But we didn't know.

An extended sold-out run attested to the way the audience reacted to the production, and Richard Christiansen's *Chicago Tribune* review eloquently captured the immense enthusiasm of the critics:

> Lanford Wilson's *Balm in Gilead* is not so much a drama, but it is a play filled with marvelous theater, and in the miraculous ensemble production that Steppenwolf Theatre opened Thursday night, it already has given the young Chicago theater season one of those brilliant electric evenings for which the living theatre was made … It is a night to remember, a production to cherish.

Glenna Syse was equally effusive for the *Chicago Sun-Times*:

> If good theater is that which makes you care and hurt and laugh and sorrow, then the Steppenwolf Theatre Company production of *Balm in Gilead* is not merely good. It is simply great.

The opening of *Balm in Gilead* on September 18, 1980 was a red-letter day in Steppenwolf history. The locale for the play is a seedy, all-night, New York City diner, inhabited by hookers, junkies, hustlers, dealers, and drunks. The play's story moves these characters helplessly forward in a metaphoric dance of death. Newcomers to the diner, Joe and Darlene, played by Francis Guinan and Laurie Metcalf, the lovers at the play's heart, are victims trapped in this world beyond their control. In Malkovich's production, the play began with the passionate strains of Springsteen's "Thunder Road" ("We got one last chance to make it real!") as Dopey, played by Gary Sinise, lit a match that let loose the cacophony of the inhabitants of the all-night diner; it ended with the final ear-ripping, cranked-up guttural screams of Springsteen's "Jungleland" ("They reach for their moment and try to make an honest stand"), which framed the show's finale. Along with Springsteen, songs from Tom Waits and Rickie Lee Jones provided an evocative and memorable soundtrack for the show. *Balm in Gilead* remains etched in the collective consciousness of not only the Steppenwolf Company, but also the Chicago theatre, as a symbolic flashpoint that propelled the beginning of a period of historic growth and attention, and became arguably the most important piece of theatre in the history of both.

The play had been under consideration for a long time by the ensemble, as Sinise explains:

> Terry was the Lanford Wilson guy. Malkovich was the Pinter guy. I ended up being the Shepard guy. *Balm in Gilead* had been in Terry's view for a long time, even before we started the company. Obviously, it had thirty characters or whatever, so it wasn't easily producible and certainly in the basement it would have been a real challenge. Once we got to the Hull House we began to consider it for production. I think I showed up opening night of *Bonjour, là, Bonjour*, the first show at the Hull House. I had come back from LA, so I was part of that season and I was picking up little parts and parking cars and doing that kind of thing. We got into the fall and began to work on *Balm in Gilead*. We were finally doing it. Nobody knew what it was going to be like, because we were kind of flying by the seat of our pants.

Terry Kinney adds:

> I really wanted to the direct it, but I think I was telling myself the wrong thing because I mostly was in love with this peripheral character named Fick, because I related to Fick's plight and his vulnerability. When it came time to do the play everyone said, "So, who's going to direct it?" I was sort of the logical choice, but John really threw his hat into it. He said, "Oh, I love this play. I would like to do it." So I just said, "Fuck it, you do it, but only if I can play Fick." It's providence that we did it that way because John had a very clear notion of what he wanted to do with it with the music and everything else.
>
> Fick was such a meaty role, too. I mean it's someone that's drawn so precisely, and the aria you get at the end of the first act makes everything worth it, because then people keep their eye on you for the rest of the play. You don't do much more after that, but you can act silently, which is my favorite thing to do.

In putting the show together, there were a number of elements that came together to make *Balm in Gilead* a landmark production: the creation of an environmental piece of theatre with lots of simultaneous action, designing a set in a small space that could accommodate the large cast, a twenty-five-minute monologue by Metcalf's character Darlene in the midst of the chaos, and, most importantly, the development of Dopey as a sort of onstage stage manager. As Malkovich recalls:

Based on my experiences working with Ralph Lane, one of our professors at ISU, the idea of kind of a master of ceremonies occurred to us. I think in no small part due to the fact that although I've never directed it, *Our Town* was one of my favorite plays. Somehow we hit upon the idea of Gary's character being the kind of master of ceremonies, narrator, observer, participant, or all of the above, so that he gave the sound and light cues and moved the action forward and backward or had moments where he controlled repeat action. He became kind of director on the floor.

Sinise gives further insight:

John had a good take on certain things and the sort of ringmaster circus aspect of it that we discovered along the way just happened. We started playing with things during the run. It wasn't like we went into it saying, "We're going to have Dopey be the ringmaster and have him cue the lights on and off and start the sound cues." We just started futzing around with different things and then at the end, we did it once and then we did it again for another moment and then again for another moment and then it took on a world of its own. I became this guy controlling all the action—the junkie king.

Laurie Metcalf also talks about the "happy accident" that brought that to light:

At the Hull House, the booth was up and in the corner and whoever was calling the show couldn't see, so Gary, who was like slumped in character on the side, said "I'll cue it myself," and he would do that. Then it just morphed into, "Well, just let him call the show," because it's wonderful. It was just an accident. Every once in a while, people would freeze and a spotlight would come down and just hit something. It was theatrical, but also gritty and super theatrical.

This was one of the most difficult productions in the company's history from a technical standpoint; however, the minimalist scene and lighting design, born out of economic necessity, were firmly based in a collaborative storytelling process in which the designer worked hand-in-hand with the director and actors—all of whom had grown up in the rock and roll era of the sixties and seventies. Longtime set and lighting designer Kevin Rigdon remembers the simplicity of the technical storytelling, which led to the intense, raucous styling of this production:

> The first apostle of the church of all white light, you know, which was an interesting thing because it wasn't that. It may have felt like that to the audience, but it wasn't. That was only part of the story. What we did really well as storytellers was to zero in on, and not clutter the story, but to clarify it. What the actors did on stage, I was echoing physically. I guess you could call it minimalist, I think another way of thinking about it is that it was very detailed in its minimalism.

Rigdon chronicles some of the influences and luck that accompanied the set's creation:

> One of the things I've always done is taken long walks or bike rides around the city for inspiration. I remember being near the Chicago Circle Campus when I came across this little hole-in-the-wall diner that had a 24-hour sign, which is what I copied. Malkovich and I went there to see it and he loved it.
>
> There were a couple things that really stood out for me in the design process for *Balm in Gilead*. The Edward Hopper painting *Nighthawks* was hugely influential and having the original sit on the walls downtown at the Art Institute was great. I visited often. It wasn't a sense of copying it, but capturing its essence. I wanted to create a sense that out of this cacophony, audiences could zero in on a very still moment—*Nighthawks* was that moment.
>
> The theatricality of *Balm in Gilead* was so important and all we had were nickels and dimes to rub together from a financial standpoint, so we found a restaurant supplier that was willing to loan us some banquettes and the only ones they had were these God awful orange and yellow ones, so we just embraced it. The actual walls of the theatre were the walls of the set and the tile floor was all painted. There was nothing real. The bedroom was nothing but scaffolding. We had boxed in the scaffolding that we used to focus lights and couldn't get it backstage—because there was no backstage. We ended up just

pushing it off into the wings behind the seating and that became Dopey's hangout. It was just recognizing that you had things that worked and then running with it—the result was absolutely beautiful.

Steppenwolf's Midwest premiere of *Balm in Gilead* at the Hull House Theatre, its subsequent restaging at Chicago's Apollo Theatre, and also 1984's co-production with Circle Rep in New York somewhat miscast the theatre's image with the public. On the one hand, it proved beyond a shadow of a doubt the company's ability to create extraordinary theatre, but it seemed also to pigeonhole the audience's expectations of the work of Steppenwolf in the short term. Beginning with the production of *Balm in Gilead*, people associated the company with a "rock and roll" style, minimizing their more sensitive performances of plays such as John Murrell's *Waiting for the Parade*, John Steinbeck's *Of Mice and Men*, C.P. Taylor's *And a Nightingale Sang*, or the comic styling of a play such as Alan Ayckbourn's *Absent Friends*. The performances of these plays all gained acclaim, but were wrongly given second-tier placement in people's accounts of the company, due to the immense success of *Balm in Gilead*.

Chicago's public broadcasting network, WTTW, televised the thirteenth annual Joseph Jefferson Awards ceremony in 1981. The awards, modeled after New York's Tony Awards, honor the best work in Chicago Theatre the previous season, and were held at the Shubert Theatre. *Balm in Gilead*, nominated for nine awards, was the big winner of the evening. The company garnered seven "Jeffs" included Best Production, Best Ensemble (nominated against the Steppenwolf production of *Absent Friends*), Best Director (John Malkovich, also nominated for Steppenwolf's *No Man's Land*), Best Actress (Laurie Metcalf, who beat Glenne Headly, nominated for *Absent Friends*), Best Supporting Actress (Glenne Headly, also nominated for her performance in Brecht's *Mother Courage* at Wisdom Bridge Theatre), Best Cameo Performance (Debra Engle), and Best Lighting Design (Kevin Rigdon). Steppenwolf's unbridled achievement that evening catapulted their name fully into the consciousness of Chicago's theatre-going public. Jeff Perry speaks of the impact of *Balm in Gilead*:

> It was absolutely the most defining, challenging, vibrant, and fun example of what we had set out to do. It had a structure that has exactly the kind of fertile ground that we had been practicing. This extended tribal community of urban people, whom Lanford Wilson called "losers who refuse to lose," fit in with our emotional and political bent toward the underdog. We felt a great affinity with all of

the people represented in the play, and it has this ensemble structure with multiple focuses and overlapping dialogue going on all over the place—different lives going on all at the same time in different little changing and evolving permutations in this 24-hour diner.

It would be like a group of musicians devoted to a passion for changing classical forms coming upon Stravinsky's *Rite of Spring* and going, "Oh my God, this is what we've been waiting for." It required everything we had practiced and more. We hadn't risked our lives, but it required a sort of Cirque du Soleil level of cooperation for it to work. It had some brilliant writing, some good writing, and some mundane writing, but its structure theatrically has the potential of being thrilling, but it has to be in the right hands. It was a gigantic moment of expression.

Perry's comments suggest the nexus of an underlying purpose that Steppenwolf continues to carry on, which is telling meaningful stories that represent the under-represented and disenfranchised.

Francis Guinan's musical analogy about working on *Balm in Gilead* describes the ensemble's collaborative approach:

It is almost like music—like playing jazz. When you get the bunch of us onstage, anybody can do a riff and people make room. There is a great deal of freedom with that in the individual performances, because other people would give the space away—they give other people the scene. When they were finished, there was a sense that you didn't want to be a pig about it, you know, but when the other person was done, there wouldn't be a beat dropped.

Joan Allen added:

Balm in Gilead was exciting when it worked, because it was difficult, because of all of the overlapping dialogue, but I remember a few times when it was perfect, and it was probably the most exciting time I've ever had onstage. When it all worked, it was like being on a rollercoaster—so exhilarating.

And William Petersen:

We ad-libbed stuff and we tricked each other. It was just so free. None of us had any intention of what it became. We just found it really fun to hang out with each other. We just hung out and sometimes the lights would go up and we'd still be hanging out and then the lights would go down and we'd still hang out. The lines were blurred between the stage and reality. We were all in our twenties and we all thought, "Oh, this is such good fun." Mostly, we were just partying. We were just playing.

Malkovich talked further about some of the other elements that stamped this production as uniquely Steppenwolf:

There were nice examples of people who wouldn't necessarily be playing the parts they played in *Balm in Gilead*, like Jeff Perry playing the transvestite, or Joan Allen playing a violent lesbian. All of those choices or caprices, if you will, seemed to work out quite well. Also, when you open up the script, there's a set of dialogue on the left and a set of dialogue on the right and literally everyone in the play could've had one line, so we had to work on those pages quite diligently and specifically about what had focus and when. There was a very delicate balance throughout, and not just the rehearsal period, but also the entire run, including New York. It was just something that was in constant play and unlike any production I've ever directed. It was never a fixed thing—always in movement—always immersed. We had our entire ensemble in it; Fran, Laurie, Jeff, Al, Gary, Glenne, John Mahoney, Rondi, and Joan, and we were very lucky to get people like Billy Petersen from the Remains Theatre and many others from the Chicago theatre community in the Chicago production and later in New York who contributed a great deal.

Clearly, this production was something to be treasured, a special moment in time on so many levels, but what does it say about the ensemble style that so distinctively defines Steppenwolf? John Mahoney passionately shared his view of what makes the company's approach resonate for him:

I think what we do is take a work that we admire and attack it ferociously and it doesn't mean that we do it by punching each other in the face or playing Bruce Springsteen, but by attacking it ferociously. It could be by Noel Coward as well as Sam Shepard. It means attacking it with an intensity and honesty that pushes all personal considerations aside and concentrates on the work itself.

Mahoney's "attack it ferociously" philosophy sums up what had come to be considered the "Steppenwolf style": removing the emphasis on self-attention by each actor and replacing it with a fierce focus on scene partners and letting the play develop organically through that interaction. To quote Second City alumnus Dave Razowsky, "Everything is important and it all comes from your scene partners if you allow it to." Although each individual actor in the Steppenwolf ensemble may bring a different character development process to the work environment, they remain able to work together comfortably by understanding this core collaborative and selfless philosophy. Mahoney continues:

> This sounds corny but one very important thing is that each of us respects the other's method. I would never in a million years question Al Wilder's approach and Al would never ridicule my, what might seem to him, lack of preparation. I've never heard any single actor at Steppenwolf criticize another actor's method of preparation.

Jeff Perry adds:

> Another common thread that we grew up with as actors, along with, "If you're not working together, you're working alone," was, "If you're not in the moment, where the hell are you? You're in some plan and that plan can't be as good as what could happen spontaneously."

By and large, the ensemble members were/are "doers" and not "talkers." Steppenwolf is comprised of a group of actors, directors, and playwrights who are not deeply analytical or philosophical about what they do. They prefer to let their work speak for itself. Of course, they think about choices and break them down, often ad nauseam, but it is more of a physical/emotional approach that happens in the interaction between characters as opposed to an analytical methodology. One feeling that was echoed repeatedly throughout the interviews was summed up by Sinise at the AT&T Onstage Directing Symposium in 1987:

> Going into the theatre, you want to come out with something. You want to have experienced something. Have been enriched. I, as an artist, want to make you feel something inside. I want you to take it home and think about it. If that doesn't happen, if you walk out of the theatre without having been hit head-on with some kind of feeling hitting your senses, then we haven't done our job.

This commitment to the audience with its focus on eliciting a strong gut-level emotional response is at the core of the Steppenwolf style, if there is indeed a "style." The company members universally believe that one way to accomplish that objective was not only to perform a play intensely and play a character vividly, but also to understand the role of the actor as the chief source for audience involvement. If the audience sees a performer fully involved emotionally in a character, then they are more apt to involve themselves to the same degree. When this happens, then Sinise's objective can be met. With that point in mind, the selection of Springsteen's music for *Balm in Gilead* takes on even greater meaning, because Bruce Springsteen, "the Boss," is renowned for his total emotional commitment to his work and music.

This total involvement in "the moment," and the emotional investment that goes along with it, points to the heart of the contention that the Steppenwolf Company could only have been born in the rock and roll era. In the contemporary world, where the threat of a terrorist attack hangs over our heads moment to moment, and where unrelenting media saturation allows us to see life and death on a daily basis, living for the moment takes on a different and more immediate meaning. The Steppenwolf Company addresses both literally and figuratively the deep concerns regarding the temporary nature of our lives, and thrusts those feelings into the work. What has developed over forty years is the no-holds-barred approach to acting that has become synonymous with Steppenwolf. Glenne Headly in discussing *Balm in Gilead* described the darkly playful nature of this approach:

> When I say go for broke, I mean they might try anything even if it hurts physically and mentally. Some might be a little more wild than others, but it was more like, if you're going to fully commit to that, then so am I. If you're going to go that far, then let's go further. It would just sort of escalate. People would also say to one another, "That was good, but it wasn't good enough." That would force you to be better.

Actors in the company have never been easily satisfied, so if an individual member thought others were giving less than what they were capable of, they would not hesitate to let them know. Headly's observation points out a somewhat dark and self-deprecating sense of humor that marked an attribute of the company's demeanor. This sense of humor, which manifested itself often with pranks during performances, helped to keep the notion of play present in all of the company's work. To paraphrase noted theatre director Peter Brook from *The Empty Space*, "A play is called play for a very important reason, because a play is play." Ensemble member Tom Irwin called Steppenwolf's humor "A healthy irreverence for both the business and the profession of acting." Theatre had to be kept fun. This approach, however, in no way negated the need for hard work and serious dedication, which was particularly key to the achievement of creating the environmental nature necessary in *Balm in Gilead*, as co-founder Terry Kinney recalls:

> It was a pretty relaxed rehearsal period and John sat with a boom box during rehearsal, listening to cassette tapes and cueing them up very quietly, but we would hear music coming from the house where John was sitting. He would be smoking and he wasn't watching us, but he was obviously listening. We only had two techs and then we opened. We didn't have previews back then, so it was important for him to do that during the rehearsal process, but we were on our own a great deal of the time. We were out there really focused and just doing it. Our stage manager, Teri McClure would say, "You just jumped a line." I never quite knew how she knew, because of all of the overlapping.

The chain of events that led to *Balm in Gilead*'s most defining moment, a twenty-five-minute monologue delivered by Laurie Metcalf as the innocent Darlene, began with a chance meeting between John Malkovich and playwright Lanford Wilson. This was one of the first encounters by an ensemble member with a true American theatre icon—an experience that would be oft repeated as they themselves became leaders in the American theatre. Malkovich shares a funny recollection of their meeting:

> We happened to meet Lanford Wilson in the late spring or summer before we went into rehearsal for the original production of *Balm in Gilead* in the fall of '80. We met him in Lake Forest because they were doing a production of his play *Serenading Louie*. We very briefly said hello to him and I told him we were doing *Balm in Gilead*, and the only thing he said was, "You're a braver man than I am. Oh, and cut that monologue. It can't be done. It's unnecessary."

Malkovich continues about his first experience seeing Metcalf's rendition of this difficult, "unnecessary" piece:

> The centerpiece of that play is Darlene's lengthy monologue recounting the story of the day she almost got married. Laurie never wanted to rehearse the piece because she's like that and she wanted to

get it right. Eventually a couple of days before it opened, or before the first preview when we would have our first audience, I told her I really needed to go through the entire thing, so I could set the light and sound cues, because I had not seen it. She started the monologue, and at that point in the play it's only John Mahoney's and Deb Engle's characters and Glenne Headly who played Ann, the character that Laurie's character is talking to, on stage. Little by little, all the other actors came in to watch and listen to Laurie's monologue. Even on the very first attempt, it was utterly spellbinding. It was very, very lean. It was very, very funny. I think everyone got, even then, in that moment, that what we were witnessing was something out of the ordinary in Chicago theatre and in Steppenwolf Theatre.

Metcalf shares a look inside her process for this piece:

Even out of an early reading of *Balm* when I just learned that I was going to play Darlene, there was something about her line where she describes finding her marriage license. She and her boyfriend never got married, but she found the license and it had a big bend across it. For some reason, that just broke my heart. I was just aware that it affected me and so I let it. It was crucial that I played the scene with Glenne even though I did all the talking, because she listened to the whole thing every night and kept it active—kept it a scene and not just a monologue.

Original ensemble member Al Wilder, who played the character of Rake in *Balm in Gilead*, relates his impressions of Metcalf's work:

We were almost in the audience's lap in the small Hull House space, and there's Laurie doing a monologue that to someone in theatre would be considered way too long to hold anybody's attention. And Glenne Headly was being the greatest listener ever on stage. The monologue runs the gamut of really wacky farcical all the way to really sensitive and I never got tired listening to it offstage. I wasn't even in the play at that point. It was a cornucopia—a continuum from terrible and disappointing to marvelous and magical.

Malkovich finishes the story of the monologue, bringing it full circle:

Lanford had never seen us and had certainly never seen Laurie, but he eventually saw Laurie's work in *Balm in Gilead* at an event where I was trying to raise money for the New York production at the house of a wealthy benefactor and theatre investor. Lanford came to see it, and seeing Laurie doing the monologue, he couldn't watch. He found it too upsetting and had to walk out of the room and wait until it was over. When he finally did see it in New York, he loved being around the jazziness of it and the collaboration between Circle Rep and Steppenwolf. That and Gary's production of *True West* inspired Lanford to write *Burn This*, which I was in with Joan Allen.

The monologue ended with beautifully placed underscoring of Tom Waits' classic ballad "Waltzing Matilda," which was meticulously planned to end with the last lines of Metcalf's emotional speech.

The company members worked in every aspect of the theatre both on stage and off developing the tightly knit bonds that held the key to the strength of their ensemble. Joan Allen compares working with Steppenwolf to working with other companies:

> Steppenwolf is like a family, because there is such profound history. There's a lot of trust and deep feeling that is just sort of given. You're in for life, pretty much, and it's a shared experience. That's not always the experience when you go outside of the company. There are people who you act with that want the attention on them and they think their character is more important than yours, and they don't care about the story and how it's told. It's about getting personal attention. I think that is really sad.

John Mahoney echoes Allen's family metaphor:

> We are virtually selfless with each other when it comes to making sure that the other person has what he or she needs at any particular time to get where he or she needs to go, and I just don't think we find that anywhere else.

These traits developed over years in which the company worked together, in many cases lived together in a variety of iterations, socialized together, and were with one another almost all the time. The type of ensemble connection at Steppenwolf's core can only manifest itself over a long period of time and, above all, cannot be manufactured just because people believe ensemble is the desired result.

Along with the company's dark sense of humor came an accompanying trait that can only be described as arrogance; or, in John

Malkovich's words, "confidence." Growing from a belief that the work that they were doing was really special, this arrogance gave them the strong commitment needed to extend to new heights. They never ceased to believe that they could be better than anybody else. Terry Kinney expressed these feelings in an article by Christine Dolen in the *Miami Herald* entitled "Born to be Wild":

> We had a little chip on our shoulders. We went to see a lot of Chicago theatre, but didn't see anything we liked. We wanted the kind of intensity that we saw in the films of Cassavetes; he was our hero.

Kate Erbe relates a story about working with Randy Arney on the Steppenwolf production of Sam Shepard's *Curse of the Starving Class* that takes the intensity question one step further:

> We would have a huddle before going on stage. Randy was around during previews and opening night and he would gather us all into a circle. We'd put our hands in and he would say, "Find the asshole. Tear it open. And stick your head in it." Those were his fighting words for us before we went on stage. That really is the goal. "Find the asshole. Tear it open. And stick your head in it." That's it in a nutshell. It's that visceral. It just makes sense.

Kate Arrington simply summed up this freedom of letting it all go:

> The moment of "Who gives a fuck?" is the most amazing moment. That's the most meaningful thing you're ever going to learn as an actor.

This brashness on the part of many of the Steppenwolf actors added another layer of self-imposed pressure to succeed that forced them to push that much harder to accomplish their ambitious goals and to always work to "tear it open." When discussing their approach, ensemble members often used music and sports analogies; through these metaphors, each individual member expressed the need for understanding one's role not only in terms of a specific production, but also in terms of the individual responsibility to supplant one's own ego for the greater good of the whole and, in a broader sense, to the future of the company.

Jane Alderman, longtime Chicago casting director, said you could always tell a Chicago actor compared to one from LA or New York, because they were just regular-looking people ready to do whatever was necessary to achieve the objective at hand. The character of Rake played by Al Wilder in *Balm in Gilead* captures this indomitable Chicago spirit in the best possible theatrical way:

> The main difference between people in Chicago and New York is that in New York everyone carries an umbrella ... but see in Chicago, there it's this symbol or something. See in Chicago, you're never going to see a construction worker carrying one of those narrow little rapier kind of umbrellas. Or any other kind. It's unmasculine, see. They won't have it. In New York, sure; but in Chicago, not on your life. Fairies and old women, some, not many, carry umbrellas when it's really cloudy. But everyone else stays clear of that sort of thing. Consequently they get rained on a lot in Chicago.

Finding actors of color to participate in the production presented a difficult challenge, as John Malkovich explains:

> At the time it was quite a struggle to find actors of color. I don't even know if there were any Latino actors. It's a long time ago. If there were, we never found one. It wasn't easy to get black actors up to our theatre at the Hull House. We found a few. Our great friend, who passed away a number of years ago, actress Billie Williams, and a girl named Michelle Banks; as well as Bill Williams who would do more shows with us. We found some people.

Juxtapose this dilemma with the myriad of proactive and positive choices Steppenwolf has made to address the issues of diversity and access under the leadership of artistic director Martha Lavey, and one can clearly see the evolution of a theatre focused on telling stories representing a wider span of cultures.

There is no question that *Balm in Gilead* was a watershed moment for Steppenwolf Theatre Company. The ripple effects of that production continue to reverberate; the success both in Chicago and in the subsequent collaboration with Circle Rep in New York in 1984 significantly impacted the growth of the "storefront" theatre movement in Chicago and also positioned Chicago at the vanguard of the American theatre.

The season that followed *Balm in Gilead* at the Hull House location was indicative of pathways for the future with productions of an American classic, *Of Mice and Men*; plays directed by two vital collaborators: Sheldon Patinkin (*Arms and the Man*) and Austin Pendleton (*Loose Ends*); and of course the notorious, aforementioned

Savages, which director Malkovich jokingly called "the worst play in the history of Steppenwolf."

One of the first major upheavals in artistic leadership took place during *Absent Friends*, the play that immediately followed *Balm in Gilead* in the 1980/81 season. H.E. Baccus, artistic director of Steppenwolf since 1976, decided to move on, and Gary Sinise would ultimately take his place. Francis Guinan reflects on the first moments that this change began to be put in motion:

> We were doing *Absent Friends*. H.E. was directing and about a week or two into rehearsals, during a note session one afternoon, he literally stopped in the middle of a sentence and put his hands over his face and then stared at the center of the stage, stood up and said "excuse me" and he went into the back. About 45 minutes later, someone went back to see him, I can't remember, but it was pretty clear that we weren't to go back there, because he needed to be alone for a minute. Malkovich walked by and went into the back office and came back out and said, "H.E. doesn't really feel that he can continue with this, and if nobody has any objections, I'm going to direct it." We all asked, "Is everything OK?" John responded, "He's fine. He just needs to stop for a while." While we were talking, H.E. walked from the back office and out the front of the theatre and I didn't see him again for two years.

Malkovich remembers the importance of the loss of Baccus in philosophical terms larger than the play at hand:

> In a way it was a weird kind of turning point for people. They sort of pulled together. We went ahead and started rehearsing again in a few minutes after H.E. left, with a different director who really didn't know the play. In two days it was fantastic and it didn't open for two weeks. Some of the actors weren't too happy about me taking it over, nor do I blame them, but the point being, that we just went on. We just went on.

Malkovich clearly saw this event as evidence of the company's ability to focus on the immediate achievement of goals as opposed to staying mired in a difficult situation. The cast for the Midwest premiere of *Absent Friends* included Francis Guinan, Laurie Metcalf, John Mahoney, Rondi Reed, Glenne Headly, and Al Wilder; the play demonstrated the company's growth; the youthful vibrancy, which had marked much of their early work, was now being supplemented with style and grace that had been foreshadowed in plays like *The Glass Menagerie*. The company was maturing and beginning to make more informed decisions in terms of their script selection. *Absent Friends* had another symbolic importance, because it provided an opportunity to showcase the strength of new members of the ensemble who had joined during *Waiting for Lefty*. The entire cast with the exception of Metcalf and Wilder had been part of the second wave of actors to join the company. The assimilation of the new members was now beginning to take hold, a little over a year after their initial arrival, and became a model for the ongoing additions to the company that would take place in subsequent years. Although this process took some time, Tom Irwin, one of this new guard, saw the process as an inherent strength of the company:

> The whole success of the theatre has been about adaptability and being able to change. Sometimes that adaptability and change has been smoother than at other times but we've done it. You know, similar theatres to this organization have failed because they haven't been able to do that. They weren't able to adapt and change.

The transition from the artistic directorship of Baccus to that of Sinise was a particularly meaningful moment in Steppenwolf history. Perry remembers the meeting in which Sinise was given the position of artistic director:

> I think at the time people very much hoped H.E. would be back—I'm sure we did. I remember us voting to see who would take his place. Gary said, "I'd be willing to do it. I think I could do it." It was a very bizarre kind of thing. People discussed his merits and voted on him while he was there in the room. I remember years later him saying, "That was not easy to deal with." He assumed that everybody would just go along and say, "Hey great, let's go," but people were split about it. People weren't sure what the next move should be.

The change in leadership, which came on the heels of the enormously successful *Balm in Gilead*, altered the course of Steppenwolf forever and was truly the beginning of the end of an era for the company. Jeff Perry summed up the transition from Baccus to Sinise:

> I've always assumed that H.E. kind of saw the writing on the wall of going from a mom and pop "Garden of Eden" to what he thought

could be a divisive—just because of the amount of change—exploration of fame and fortune by the members, and that these feelings all led to him taking off. It was a big change, going from the personality of H.E. to the personality of Gary as artistic director. Both fiercely talented, multifaceted artists, it was like going from a philosopher king to an unstoppable commander.

Whereas the mild-mannered and introspective Baccus focused on the company's artistic purposes and in many ways allowed members of the business staff to make their own decisions, Sinise entered into the role of artistic director with a serious agenda for growth, from both an artistic and a business prospective. Sinise's ambitious plans included a calculated effort to establish a national reputation for Steppenwolf, as he reflects:

> That was a tumultuous time when H.E. left. What we were going to do and the kind of course we were going to take was up in the air. It was not even two years after I became artistic director that we did our first play in New York.

Terry Kinney describes the impact on the company:

> That was such a big blow when we lost H.E., because he was the one person that we could all agree on was a genuine genius. We knew he was denouncing the moniker of artistic director and that he had been uncomfortable in the role because he had a hard enough time making decisions about his everyday life—making decisions on behalf of the whole company didn't come naturally to him. His version of *The Glass Menagerie* was a complete epiphany production. If anyone could have seen it outside of that church basement—it was our masterpiece as far as I was concerned.

This change in leadership demonstrates how Steppenwolf, in each step in its growth, has flourished where many others have failed, by meeting obstacles head-on and positively building on the changes that occurred.

In his first six months as artistic director, Sinise took a break from acting and directing to focus on his goals for the company. His plans to increase the company's stature quickly began to pay dividends on the business side. Together with his office staff, Sinise developed systems to improve the theatre's process for making business and artistic decisions. The staff, although small in numbers, began to keep a more traditional daily work schedule, which created a more disciplined approach to day-to-day operations. Sinise's assertive style defined his reign as artistic director as one far more autocratic than that of Baccus. Steppenwolf's days of being a young group that "went with the flow" were now beginning to be displaced by a clearly defined plan of action with a strong policymaker at the top. Sinise explains:

> These were the days of the quest for strength and for that power position that would enable us to get $300,000 grants from a bunch of different corporations and to be able to get loans. You can't do that if you've got a bunch of people flopping in the pond and nobody leading the way.

With Sinise solidly in control, the company explored a variety of possibilities for increasing revenue and visibility. Sinise took on three projects, including his first directing stint with Steppenwolf, Sam Shepard's *Action* in the Almost Midnight series. Shepard's darkly sarcastic play painted with broad-stroked caricatures of a family demonstrated the aggressive style that would become Sinise's trademark, and the production developed a cult-like following. Executive director Russ Smith recalls the significance of the Almost Midnight series.

> It was unbelievably important in the archaeology of the theatre. Once we got a subscription season going at the Hull House, we realized that we didn't have enough money to put all these actors on the stage at any given time, so we decided to do plays for friends at midnight. Not only did this give the ensemble members more opportunities to work as actors, but it also gave them chances to direct. In fact, it was where Gary, in many ways, learned how to direct.

Sinise also directed *Morning Call*, a play by Chicagoan Alan Gross that featured the acting of Perry and Metcalf as the story's young lovers, which was presented on WMAQ, the Chicago NBC affiliate, on June 4, 1981. That same summer, Sinise repeated his role as Dopey in the Apollo Theatre restaging of *Balm in Gilead*, which had an extremely popular two-month run. A well-respected Chicago public relations firm, John Iltis Associates, was hired to handle all print and visual media for the theatre. The fiery Russ Smith led the business operations of the theatre in concert with the tenacious Sinise, furthering Steppenwolf's broad vision for the future. The addition of this professionalized promotional approach reaped almost immediate benefits, and the subscription base of the theatre grew dramatically.

Terry Kinney, a Steppenwolf founder, who had not directed for the theatre since the second season in Highland Park, returned to the directorial reins for Steinbeck's classic *Of Mice and Men* in September of 1981 and it became another highly praised production. The performances of Malkovich as Lennie, the strong man with the mind of a child, and Sinise as his partner and protector George, were acknowledged for their sincerity and compassion.[15] The critics in Chicago were beginning to get a sense of the level of success that was soon to come for members of the Steppenwolf ensemble as Glenna Syse prophesized:

> The Steppenwolf Company has done it again. Its production of John Steinbeck's *Of Mice and Men*, which opened the fall season at 3212 N. Broadway Wednesday night is the kind of theater that brings distinction to the Chicago dramatic scene … Lennie is a natural for John Malkovich and his portrayal is yet another chapter in a career that should be attracting attention around the nation.

Syse's comments are supported by John Kennedy's concluding remarks in his *Chicago Reader* review:

> What this production will do is reconfirm, if it needed doing, that Steppenwolf is the most exciting ensemble in town. God help us if some of these folks become stars and fly away.

Their words, although complimentary, suggest a tinge of dread about the consequences of success. Little did anyone realize how quickly Kennedy's foresight would become a reality—the focus of the theatre-going public on the work at Steppenwolf was growing exponentially. Success also brought problems, as evidenced by what happened during the last week of the run of Patinkin's *Arms and the Man*. Laurie Metcalf, who played the role of Raina, had to be replaced by Glenne Headly so she could join the cast of *Saturday Night Live*.[16] Of course, Metcalf's

15. The two would repeat these roles in a 1992 film version directed and produced by Sinise. The work of Malkovich and Sinise in *Of Mice and Men* anticipated their accomplishments in the New York run of *True West* in 1982.

16. Metcalf's work on *SNL* would involve nothing more than a short stint as a reporter in the "Weekend Update" segment, because the show was temporarily cancelled during the 1981 writers' strike. When *Saturday Night Live* started up again, the entire cast was replaced (largely by members of Chicago's Practical Theatre Company, including Julia Louis-Dreyfus among others).

brief presence in the cast of the renowned late night show only added to the special mystique that surrounded members of the company both in and outside the confines of Chicago.

With their production of *Of Mice and Men* in late 1981, the company aggressively solicited group sales and began what would become an ongoing venture—afternoon performances of selected plays for high-school audiences. Post-show discussions among audience, cast members, and directors initiated during the last season would also continue. With the success of Steppenwolf's schedule of public classes, the post-show discussions, increased targeted promotion, and the addition of afternoon performances, the company was following a textbook plan for audience development.

Following *Of Mice and Men* in Steppenwolf's sixth season was Michael Weller's *Loose Ends* directed by Austin Pendleton. Glenna Syse's review of the show sounded a familiar refrain:

> It is interesting once again to examine the chemistry and craft that make up the Steppenwolf skill. In the simplest terms, they are a company in the true family sense of the word. I suspect they are all really related to each other, probably had to share their toys when they were growing up. At any rate, they are always tuned to the same station. They listen to each other, they look at each other and what I like about them is that they take their time about it and they take nothing for granted.

The themes in Weller's play of love, marriage, insecurity, and the death of idealism, also addressed real concerns of a large portion of Steppenwolf's audience. This symbiosis of cast and audience, which had similarly occurred with Pendleton's *Say Goodnight, Gracie*, made *Loose Ends* a commercial success. Scott Fosdick spoke of this bond in his *Daily Herald* review, saying of both cast and audience, "They take to *Loose Ends* like a freak takes to opium-laced hash." His drug reference metaphorically captured the high that Steppenwolf was on at the time. The years of working, playing, and living together forged offstage bonds that tightened their onstage focus, as Sheldon Patinkin captures:

> What makes all of them particularly good actors is their absolute openness to whatever emotion or whatever effect is happening next and they don't fudge on that at all. They are so serious about getting the work done as well as is humanly possible.

Sinise's reign as artistic director surrounded the company with the heady atmosphere of increased recognition, but it also fueled doubts about whether they could stick together in the face of their growing success. The price of the newfound fame, and its impact on the Steppenwolf group dynamic, was a question that continued to trouble the company as they moved forward. Sinise's 1982 production of *True West* would bring those concerns to the forefront with the play's proposed move to New York, a first for Steppenwolf, and a defining moment in the history of the theatre.

The run of good fortune that began with 1980's *Balm in Gilead* and continued through 1982's *Loose Ends* provided Steppenwolf with more creative independence and power than ever. Countless original scripts were offered for perusal and potential production, and the company was now solidly in a position to negotiate for hot New York properties for Midwest premiere. Funding solicitation by the board of directors was meeting with unprecedented success as corporations and contributors eagerly offered to support the burgeoning company's ongoing growth. The list of subscribers continued to grow, and plans that had been in the works for a permanent move to a larger performance space were nearing conclusion. Their focus was on the transformed dairy space formerly occupied by St. Nicholas Theatre at 2851 N. Halsted.

Jeff Perry summed up the time the company had spent in the Hull House space:

> The juices flowed. The Hull House years were arguably the greatest period for the company. We had the greatest amount of years of experience on the court. The ideas were at their greatest density, and the energy was at its highest, and the challenge was the greatest.

Artistic director Sinise had been looking for a play that the company could take to New York ever since he took over as artistic director of Steppenwolf in late 1980. New York producer Wayne Adams had expressed interest in producing the company in New York after becoming familiar with Steppenwolf's work during the Travel Light production of *Say Goodnight, Gracie*. Finding a play that would best exhibit the talents of Steppenwolf while at the same time prove to be economically feasible had become a priority. Discussions involving a New York move for *Balm in Gilead* had been temporarily shelved because of the large size of the cast and accompanying costs, but Sam Shepard's newest play, *True West*, with a cast of four, seemed to offer the company a vehicle that could help them finally stage their work in New

York. Sinise secured the rights to the play and, even though it had recently debuted and failed in New York, plans for a Chicago production as part of Steppenwolf's 1982 subscription season were put in motion.

Director Sinise's affinity with Shepard's work drew him to *True West*, a black comedy about the relationship between two brothers with very different demeanors. Lee, a petty thief and desert rat, moves into his mother's home with brother, Austin, a mildly successful screenwriter, busy at work on a script he hopes to sell. Lee is watching the house while their mother is away on vacation, and the brothers come into conflict when Lee disrupts the stability of Austin's serene work environment. Over the course of the play, the two men begin to reverse personalities as each takes on characteristics of the other. Lee offers a seemingly unintelligible script to the Hollywood producer Austin had been targeting, and the producer is surprisingly interested, which sets the wheels for conflict in motion through an outrageous series of events.

True West had originally premiered at the Public Theatre in December of 1980 with Tommy Lee Jones as Austin and Peter Boyle as Lee, but critical response to the production was generally unenthusiastic. Frank Rich's *New York Times* review commented on the strength of the script but suggested that the actors and director had not interpreted the play very well. His opinion was apparently confirmed when Shepard disclaimed this New York production. Despite the failure of the original New York version, Shepard's play remained a hot property and Steppenwolf's acquisition and subsequent production were greatly anticipated by the Chicago theatrical community.

Steppenwolf's *True West* realized the full power of the play and salvaged it from becoming what might very well have been an under-appreciated piece of Shepard's legacy. Steppenwolf's Chicago production drew strongly favorable response from the critics. Writing for the *Chicago Sun-Times*, Glenna Syse gushed:

> Simply the best dramatic production I've seen in Chicago all season. No sense tiptoeing through the tulips, no ifs, ands, and howevers are necessary. The Steppenwolf production of Sam Shepard's *True West* is a beaut ... a magnificent menace, the kind that keeps you from swallowing, the kind that permits only breathing in, no breathing out. You leave the theater thinking perhaps you will turn back and see blood on the threshold, headlines in tomorrow's papers, crime in your heart ... What is so wonderful about this production is that the horror and the humor are so married to each

other ... This is a script with perfect pitch, a rare sense of diminuendo and crescendo, meticulously punctuated and paced for maximum theatrics.

Her comments suggest that Sinise's direction and Malkovich's acting had achieved a style that reflected a blending of the aggressive intensity of *Balm in Gilead* with the fine-tuned comic tones of *Absent Friends*. Sinise's ability to realize the variety of dramatic possibilities in Shepard's script helped to revitalize opinion about the play's potential and brought Steppenwolf's production solidly to life. The success of *True West* facilitated an extension of the run and a move to the Apollo Theatre. Sinise spoke about the power of Shepard's plays on the *Charlie Rose* show on May 13, 1996:

He doesn't write things that are all logical and linear—just like life, he leaves many questions unanswered ... I think one of the great things about Shepard's writing is that it is like a great piece of music. It shifts emotionally. It shifts dynamically. Like a great piece of music, it can take you through to an emotional, visceral reaction. You're not sure why you are having that reaction inside, but you know that something is speaking to you ... its beauty or its power, or its range that it operates in. Any great play does that, and his plays do that.

The triumph of this production of *True West* renewed Sinise's hopes for a chance to take a play to New York. Producer Adams and partner Harold Thau began to put the pieces in place for an Off-Broadway opening, but the Steppenwolf company members remained surprisingly apprehensive, and in some cases downright opposed to the move. The rise of the company from their humble beginnings to the high profile that they now enjoyed had happened at such a rapid pace that many ensemble members feared a move to New York would begin to unravel the delicate dynamic that the company had worked so hard to achieve. In the back of the minds of some in the company was the experience of the Group Theatre and its demise after many of its members, most notably Clifford Odets, defected to Hollywood, and they feared a similar fate for Steppenwolf.

Debate over the proposed move featured heated exchanges among company members during a number of meetings designed to resolve the growing impasse. Sinise remained resolute in his desire to take the show to New York. He said, "It became necessary for our own growth to leave Chicago," and he felt that the move would ultimately bring national recognition and greater opportunities for the artistic growth of its members. Malkovich, a pivotal player in the debate, wavered between the two sides of the question, but eventually opted for the New York plans that Sinise had championed. Malkovich harkens back with great detail:

> New York was never a goal of mine. I'm not a big fan of New York. I personally didn't really see the point. Because in 1982 when *True West* opened, *Balm in Gilead* was already in our rear view mirror. We had some blows. Principally, when H.E. our artistic director had left us after *Balm in Gilead*. That was a very sad day for a lot of us. Some of us, at least I did, thought it would be a fatal blow.
>
> It wasn't easy in the early years. We all loved each other and simultaneously drove each other nuts, but we had a lot of respect for the work of the people in the company. We had lost Nancy Evans a couple years before, which I was not very happy about because I thought she was super-talented, and then H.E. left and I think people started to think that everybody would drop like flies. We didn't know anything about the business of theatre or getting funding or any of the things that one should probably have some idea about before they start a theatre. But, by 1982 we had had a good deal of success and *True West* was just another production to us. I don't think many people at Steppenwolf would have thought much more highly of *True West* than they thought of *Absent Friends* or Gary's incredibly hilarious production of *Action*. But, people came from New York, Wayne Adams and Hal Thau. *True West* was a very good production, but it wasn't something that we viewed as overly special.
>
> Gary always felt that our work merited attention and needed the national exposure to give us the oxygen to survive in Chicago. But, nothing had ever really been a success that went from Chicago to New York, so when the whole subject came up and we had an offer to take our production there, I didn't particularly want to go. I also felt that there were others who didn't want to go, either. My feelings kind of went through a change because people responded to Gary's entertaining of that option so negatively that it kind of changed my mind in the opposite way from, if everybody thinks it's such a bad idea then it must be good. Of course, in the end, Gary was right. But everybody else was right, too, in that it profoundly changed the nature of the day-to-day experience of being in the Steppenwolf Theatre Company.

Malkovich's decision to go tipped the scales and the move was put in motion.

John Malkovich played Lee and Jeff Perry played Austin in the original Chicago run of *True West*; however, Perry decided to remain in Chicago as artistic director of the company and did not make the move with the show to New York. As a result, Tom Irwin, who had replaced Perry during the Chicago run for a couple of months in the remount at the Apollo, was slated to play Austin for the New York run. The harsh reality of the New York theatre was demonstrated when the New York producers unceremoniously replaced Irwin with Sinise after a single rehearsal during what was Irwin's first ever trip to New York. Suffice to say, the emotional events and decisions surrounding *True West*'s move to New York, even thirty years later, still generate deep feelings among many of the early ensemble members.

True West opened at the Cherry Lane Theatre in New York on October 17, 1982, and critical response exceeded all expectations. Mel Gussow's *New York Times* review began with these words:

> The production of Sam Shepard's *True West* that opened last night at the Cherry Lane Theater is an act of theatrical restitution and restoration ... Seeing the play in revival, one realizes that it was the production not the play that was originally at fault. The new version—using the same script—is an exhilarating confluence of writing, acting, and staging. As performed by John Malkovich and Gary Sinise, two members of Chicago's Steppenwolf Theater Company making their New York debuts, and as directed by Mr. Sinise, this is the true *True West*. The compass needle is unwavering.

Stanley Crouch echoed Gussow's comments in the *Village Voice*:

> In *True West*, John Malkovich invents a masterpiece of vernacular American acting ... The performance is endlessly musical, a tawdry recitative that flares with withdrawals, maintaining its invention and spontaneity every moment ... Malkovich if he is capable of the same invention in a variety of roles could become a very important actor.

The positive critical reaction to *True West* was further substantiated when Malkovich and Sinise won Obie Awards for their work as, respectively, actor and director. Malkovich was also awarded a prestigious Clarence Derwent Award as the "Most promising male actor on the metropolitan scene." Randy Arney commented on the New York reception of the play and foreshadowed some of the challenges that lay ahead for the company:

True West was over the top. I mean Jackie O and Kurt Vonnegut and others were lining up to see it. It was such a phenomenon, so Steppenwolf started to get a real vibe at that time. There was a centrifugal force going on that was pulling members away in many ways.

The showing of *True West* on PBS's *American Playhouse* in 1983 was the first time Shepard's work had been presented on television and further added to the company's mushrooming national exposure. Ian Barford remembers *True West*'s impact on him, when he was an ISU student:

I saw a PBS tape of *True West* very early on when I was taking basic acting courses—that was electrifying. That performance of John's spoke to something very primal in me that made me think, "If there's a way you can get paid to do that, that's what I want to do."

Shepard's words from *True West* again figuratively capture the mixed emotions that the ensemble felt in the place they now found themselves:

So they take off after each other straight into an endless black prairie. The sun is just comin' down and they can feel the night on their backs. What they don't know is that each one of 'em is afraid, see. Each one separately thinks that he's the only one that's afraid. And they keep ridin' like that straight into the night. Not knowing. And the one who's chasin' doesn't know where the other one is taking him. And the one who's being chased doesn't know where he's going.

The overwhelming acclaim Steppenwolf received from *True West* signaled the beginning of what would become an ongoing relationship between the company and the New York and international theatre communities; and ultimately began to allay some of the initial concerns within the company about the show's move to New York. Steppenwolf was now poised for even greater things for both its individual members and for the group as a whole.

Figure 20. Laurie Metcalf, Gary Sinise, William Petersen, *Balm in Gilead*, 1980 © Lisa Ebright-Howe.

Figure 21. Jeff Perry, *Balm in Gilead*, 1980 © Lisa Ebright-Howe.

Figure 22. Glenne Headly, Joan Allen, Kathi O'Donnell, and John Mahoney, *Balm in Gilead*, 1980 © Lisa Ebright-Howe.

Figure 23. Laurie Metcalf, *Balm in Gilead*, 1980 © Lisa Ebright-Howe.

Figure 24. Gary Sinise and John Malkovich, *True West*, 1982 © Lisa Ebright-Howe.

Figure 25. Laurie Metcalf, *Coyote Ugly*, 1985 © Lisa Ebright-Howe.

Figure 26. Rondi Reed, Joan Allen, Moira Harris, and Laurie Metcalf, *Waiting for the Parade*, 1981 © Lisa Ebright-Howe.

Figure 27. *Absent Friends*, 1980 © Lisa Ebright-Howe.

Front: Rondi Reed, Francis Guinan, Glenne Headly

Back: Alan Wilder, Laurie Metcalf, John Mahoney

Figure 28. Ensemble photo 1981 © Lisa Ebright-Howe.

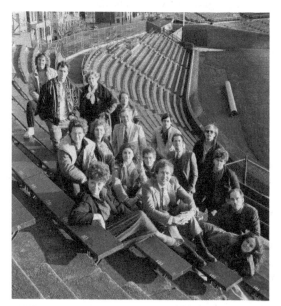

Figure 29. Ensemble photo 1982 © Lisa Ebright-Howe.

IN THEIR OWN WORDS: ON GETTING INTO THE ENSEMBLE

Sally Murphy:

I was first cast in *The Common Pursuit* at Steppenwolf and expected the Ensemble members to be quite intimidating. They were after all, members of the hottest theatre company in America and I remember being in college when they did *Balm in Gilead* and had heard the line for tickets went around the block.

When we first began rehearsals I was completely floored by their warmth and generosity. There was not an ounce of hubris among them. It was almost alarming. There also was an undeniable confidence and intelligence about them. This group knew how talented they were and were completely comfortable with that fact. Honestly though, during that time I remember laughing really hard and having epic ping-pong games.

Being asked to be an Ensemble member of the company was one of the most meaningful days of my life. It was abundance beyond the imagination and I am grateful every single day.

Kate Arrington:

It was surreal and, to be honest, it was almost not helpful. I was so fucking nervous. We happened to be the show during the Gala, and so there's this Sunday night after the Gala that all the company members come to see whatever play it is. It was just all this pressure because it was our opening. All the people that I could barely be in a room with were sitting in their theatre watching me on the stage. I had a boyfriend at the time that came to my dressing room and I just couldn't stop crying. I said, "I'm not leaving. I'm not going out there. I'm so humiliated. I can't." But, you work here long enough and realize that that's the thing that makes it special. These people do what they do every night and they take it for what it is. There are no products to deliver. They are all true. Like Fran (Guinan)—there's no good or bad—every night he just goes out there and does it. There's nothing to prove.

Mariann Mayberry:

Steppenwolf had only had one or two interns before me. It was a newer concept to them. I did a lot of xeroxing and everything/anything else. I got to know everyone and learned by getting to sit in on auditions. I returned to college for my senior year and Steppenwolf called asking me to come back after I graduated. Under Rondi Reed's tutelage I basically stage-managed the Steppenwolf Summer High School training program and started working in the box office, house managing, running the concessions, and later went upstairs to become the receptionist.

All the time, I was staying with a friend, and sharing her one-inch thick futon. There were days I would xerox for eight hours straight. I'd go home weeping from the monotony of copying on a prehistoric machine that could only do one page at a time—nothing else! It was one of those days that I first ran into Terry Kinney. I thought he was a homeless man who had wandered in. I'd never met him. He was sitting there at the big table with his long crazy hair and I said, "Can I help you?" and I started to usher him out. Thank goodness he laughed.

I just kept sticking around and became a part of the family that way. Then one day I realized I was never going to be "an actor" to them. I needed to quit, but couldn't quite bring myself to do it. Then the day came when I smarted off to Steve Eich, the managing director, and he fired me. A week later his wife, Rondi Reed, suddenly cast me in *A Midsummer Night's Dream*, a Steppenwolf Outreach production. I was the head fairy and I was in heaven. A couple of years ago, during *August: Osage County*, Rondi revealed to me that Steve had actually asked her to cast me in it, because he felt bad that he'd fired me. Twenty-five years after I got fired—I actually found out Rondi and Steve were in on starting my Steppenwolf acting career.

Midsummer was followed by *The Geography of Luck, Wrong Turn at Lungfish*, and then *Ghost in the Machine* directed by Jim True. I cut my long blond hair very short and dyed it mahogany. It was one of those plays where everything came together into a great production. After that people's perception of me was altered. I wasn't an intern anymore and I'm sure that I wouldn't be an ensemble member today if that play hadn't happened.

Randy Arney:
I got my bachelor's at Eastern Illinois and then went to ISU to get my MFA. I would talk to Malkovich on the phone and he'd say, "You don't need an MFA—drop out—come up here and do plays." I would say, "You're crazy. You think this little thing you're doing in the basement of a church is going anywhere?"

I finished my MFA degree. I was trying to decide whether to go to New York or California or Chicago, when John called and said, "I'm directing a play called *Balm in Gilead* and there's a part for you if you'd like to be in it. Nobody's being paid anything, but if you want to come to Chicago you can join this cast." It was really just the offer of work so I followed that lead to Chicago. I got there in the summer of 1980, went into rehearsal for *Balm in Gilead*, and pretty much never left.

Ian Barford:

I was sitting backstage with Martha and she said, "You know, why are you in LA? You know, you're not an LA kind of guy. You're a Chicagoan. Why don't you come back to Chicago?" I said, "I've spent a lot of time in Chicago and now I live in LA." She said, "Well why don't you come back to Chicago?" She said, "Maybe we'll make you a company member." I said, "Well, OK. Let's talk about that." So not too long after that, she called me and she said, "We're going to make you a company member, but we're trying to diversify the ensemble and after we figure out the others we're going to bring in, we'll bring you in as a group." So, I knew that that was going to happen quite a long time before it actually was announced.

A year later in 2006 I was brought back from California to do a show called *Love Song* with Francis Guinan and Molly Regan and Mariann Mayberry directed by Austin Pendleton. It was during that show that Anna (Shapiro), who I'd known for many years, and I began to go out. We were both single and had always been with other people. Suddenly we sort of became aware of each other in a different way. And then being brought into the company and with that relationship starting, it was clear to me that I was going to move back to Chicago.

Frank Galati:

Gary and Terry and Jeff and all the Steppenwolf people came to see the shows that I did in Chicago, because Al Wilder was the butler in *Travesties* and Chasuble, the minister, in *The Importance of Being Earnest*. I knew Al and we got to be really good friends and I had met Jeff and John and Laurie. When Gary was artistic director he called me and said, "You know, man, we've never done like a funny show for the holidays, but we're thinking of doing *You Can't Take It With You*. What do you think? Would you be interested?" I said, "Yeah, I would be. I love that play."

I think it was the second week of rehearsals, Gary said, "Would you stop up at the office? I want to chat with you for a minute." Gary said, "Man, we'd like you to join the ensemble." I was bowled over. The whole idea of joining the ensemble had never occurred to me. I didn't know what the process was by which you became a member of the Steppenwolf ensemble. I guess I found out when he asked me. I said, "Gary, are you kidding? I would love to." At Steppenwolf, when you're in, you're in, so I was deeply honored and thrilled.

Jim True-Frost:

I was doing *Killers*, my second play at Steppenwolf, and in the company offices they'd made a decision they wanted to add some younger, new company members. I had become a member of the Remains Theatre Company after *Road*, which had been a year earlier, and Randy Arney didn't want to invite me to Steppenwolf and just sort of pluck me out of Remains. I went to his office and he was saying it in a way that was sort of like, "If you were available, we'd like to ask you to join the company." He kind of left it in my hands to make myself available, which I did, so I formally told the folks at Remains I was going to leave the company.

To be asked to join Remains after *Road* was a huge signal to me that I was really in my career. I was probably twenty-one or twenty-two at that point. When I was at Northwestern, certainly after I graduated high school, I didn't know I wanted to be an actor. I didn't have the sort of ambition of, "This is what I'm born to do and I want to be an actor." I remember feeling sort of swept up at that moment in time towards the theatre.

Eric Simonson:

I knew when I moved to Chicago that my goal was to get into Steppenwolf, which was very hard to do because it was 1983. The cat was already out of the bag and Steppenwolf was a big thing in town. It was hard even to get an audition. I joined a small upstart storefront theatre called Lifeline, which is still around. I was one of the first six members. Boots, Jeff Perry's aunt Barbara, was head of the outreach program at Steppenwolf and we became friends. It was impossible to even get an audition for the outreach program at Steppenwolf. You had to sit by the phone in the morning, like 9:00 when they opened the lines to get on the list to audition for Steppenwolf. You'd sit by the phone, because cell phones weren't around and you would just dial over and over and over. It was always busy. I could never get an audition. But Boots offered to put me and other people in Lifeline on the list, so, that's how I got an audition. I auditioned for the "Page to the Stage" program and got in a Shakespeare Sampler. There were five of us including John C. Reilly. Anyway, that was my first acting experience.

Jon Michael Hill:
My theatre professor Peter Davis at the University of Illinois during
my junior year was doing some dramaturgy and understudy work
for Steppenwolf's production of *The Unmentionables* by Bruce Norris.
Anna D. Shapiro was directing and they were searching for a kid to play
a sixteen-year-old African kid and hadn't quite found it, so they asked
Peter if he knew of anybody and he mentioned me. I worked on the
accent for a long time before I went in and already had the physicality
and accents put together, because I had a month to prepare and it just
worked out. As the story went, Erica Daniels and Bruce looked at each
other after the audition and were like, "This is the kid."

Prior to this opportunity, I had very little knowledge of Steppenwolf
Theatre. At school, when everybody found out I had this audition, we
started having conversations about what Steppenwolf was, who started
it, and what it means for actors in Chicago when they can break into
that family. There was all that added pressure and I knew there was a
dangerous folklore about the company. It was exciting. I had always
loved Gary Sinise. I just didn't know he started a theatre company.

Getting in the room and collaborating with everybody on *The
Unmentionables* was a really big deal, but I just did my work. After the
show closed, we had started school again, and Martha emailed me and
said, "Hey, do you want to come up and do a reading of this two-hander
with Tracy Letts? And, stop in my office before the reading." My
girlfriend at the time said, "They're going to ask you to join the company."
I just laughed. I said, "That's the stupidest thing I've ever heard. I've done
one show with them." I went to Martha's office and she was there with
Amy Morton. They just said, "Listen, we could tell from the rehearsal
process and what you did in the show that you just kind of fit our
aesthetic. So, if you want to join the company, we're going to bring in
some new people, and you could be in that group." I said, "Of course."
They were looking to bring in new ensemble members and diversify the
ensemble, so I came in with Ian Barford, Kate Arrington, Alana Arenas,
Ora Jones, and James Vincent Meredith. After they asked me to join, I
had to pull myself together, so I could do a reading of a two-hander with
Tracy Letts—the most intense actor I had worked with at that point.

Tracy Letts:
My first Equity job was *Picasso at the Lapin Agile*, the Steve Martin play
that actually inaugurated our upstairs space at the theatre. I was twenty-
eight and newly sober by maybe a month or two. I'm still sober
now twenty-one years later. A lot of changes were happening in my life

at that point. I had just opened my first play at the Next Lab in Evanston, *Killer Joe*, a play I had written and had spent a couple of years trying to get done—trying to find a theatre that would do it. Steppenwolf wouldn't do it, and I was bitter about that because I had tried to write something really in the kind of rock-n-roll mode that I thought they operated in, but they were in the new space and they were a little less rock-n-roll.

Killer Joe was in this forty-seat theatre in Evanston and it was quite a success. It got terrible reviews but it got one important great review from Christiansen in the *Tribune*, so we were selling out up in Evanston. It was going great. At the same time, my phone rang and it was Randy calling me to offer me the job in *Picasso*. No audition—just an offer at Steppenwolf. I had understudied a couple of shows and my introduction to the company was *The Glass Menagerie* for the Educational Outreach Program, now called Steppenwolf for Young Adults, in 1988 when I was twenty-two or twenty-three. That was the first show I did with the company. That was at the same time as they were doing *The Grapes of Wrath* at the Royal George.

After a particularly harrowing experience on the Steppenwolf Mainstage as an understudy where I kind of got thrown to the wolves during a production of *The Road to Nirvana*, they had called again to ask me to understudy and I said, "I want more money." They said, "The pay is the pay." I said, "You know, after the harrowing experience I had and came through with flying colors; I think you guys should pay me more money." They said, "We're not going to pay you more money," so I said, "Then forget it." It was one of those times where you kind of take a risk of "I'm never going to work there again. I've just turned down this job. I'm not playing the understudy game." I also had an intuition that if I kept accepting the understudy job that's how I would be thought of. So, I turned it down and then Randy calls and offers me *Picasso*. I wound up doing 468 performances of *Picasso at the Lapin Agile* both here and in Los Angeles, when we transferred the production.

Martha Lavey:
I saw a production of *Say Goodnight, Gracie* that Austin Pendleton directed and I thought, "Oh, my God, if I could ever act with people like that who were that good that would just be heaven." My first class at Steppenwolf was with John Malkovich in his scene-study class. There were a couple of other people in that class that he also cast in his precious *Savages*. This was when they were at the Hull House—a tremendously exciting time. I think the next show I was in was *Aunt Dan and Lemon* in 1987.

I was living in New York when Randy (Arney) called me up in 1990 and asked me if I wanted to come back and do *Love Letters*. *The Grapes of Wrath* was in New York at the time and I would take these long thirteen-mile runs right there in Midtown and I just happened to run into Terry Kinney who was there working on *Grapes*. In any case, I did *Love Letters*, which kind of facilitated my being able to come back to Chicago, and allowed me to finish the doctoral program at Northwestern, and then Jim True cast me in a production of *Ghost in the Machine*. Randy was in that too and shortly after they asked me to join the ensemble in 1993 Randy asked me to be an associate artistic director. Then came the leadership transition, and Gary, Jeff, and Terry asked me if I would be the interim artistic director. I had that interim title for a year and then they made me artistic director.

K. Todd Freeman:
In college at North Carolina School of the Arts, everybody knew who Steppenwolf was. We all ran to the TV when Steppenwolf came on PBS for *True West*. It was a big deal. I wasn't one of the lucky ones who had gotten to see *Balm in Gilead* in New York, but my classmate Joe Mantello, who is now a big Broadway director, went and shared his experience and brought back some of that energy.

Somewhere around 1992, I auditioned for a play called *The Song of Jacob Zulu* when I was living in LA and Eric Simonson directed it. I think Jeff Perry was there at the audition and Tom Irwin and Gary Cole who was living out there at the time. I got the gig. The next year, we took it to Australia and Broadway. When we were on Broadway they asked me to join the company—pretty much a year from having booked the gig originally. Of course, I said, "Yes." I mean who wouldn't?

Amy Morton:
I started with the Remains Theatre in Chicago and we hung out with everyone from Steppenwolf, who for the most part probably thought they were always better than us because Steppenwolf always thinks they're better than everybody and it's usually true. I mean it's one of the things that got Steppenwolf to where it is, a really startling arrogance.

My first actual job with Steppenwolf was *You Can't Take It With You*. Their company manager at that time, Aubrey, called me and said, "Yeah, do you want to do this play?" They didn't make me audition for it. I can't even tell you how excited I was—such a great first play to do because it's so familial and joyous and Frank is such an amazing director.

They had asked me to be in the company in the eightiess right around *Coyote Ugly*, which I understudied. Gary asked me to be in the company and also Billy (Petersen), and we both said, "No, we got to be true to our school." When Remains finally folded Terry was nice enough to bring in an orphan, so that's how I became a member. It was during *A Streetcar Named Desire*, and Terry said, "Do you want to think about playing Blanche?" I said, "No." I had no desire to play Blanche. If I go crazy it isn't in Blanche's style. It's not something I felt I could pull off well. I said, "No, but I'd love to do Eunice." I'm sure Terry went to Martha first, but he was the one that said to me, "Would you like to be a member of the company?" I was like, "You bet you." It was really a great day. I felt so at home.

Gary Cole:

Malkovich directed Remains Theatre's second show in our little space—a play called *Harry, Noon and Night*. In those days people would just collaborate. Malkovich invited Gary and the rest of the company over to a preview and they gave him notes and he gave us notes. Two years later Steppenwolf decided to remount *Balm in Gilead* at the Apollo. They came to us and ended up putting the four male actors from Remains into that production.

Over time we just kept working at Steppenwolf. We worked at each other's places—more so we worked there as opposed to Steppenwolf working with us. I think at some point for Remains other things started to happen in people's careers, which took people to New York and Los Angeles and into movies, so it became a different situation. Somewhere in the midst of that I decided to join Steppenwolf. It was the mid-eighties and I had gone to New York for the first time ever, because Gary Sinise asked me to come in to *True West* in New York. They hired Jim Belushi and he was working with an actor and that wasn't working out, so Gary asked me.

I don't think I was a member of Steppenwolf until '86. I just decided I wanted some more certainty, if there is such a thing. Steppenwolf had a place. They had a season. At least, you knew what was going to be happening within the next couple of years. At Remains, it was like, "Are we doing a play? Where are we going to do it?" It was so random.

Anna D. Shapiro:

I don't think there's much that Martha Lavey is not capable of. I think if you give her an assignment she really can figure it out. I was just out of graduate school and I needed a job. I was just flying by the seat of my pants in trying to figure out what I could contribute. At that point I just wanted to be able to direct, but I really tried to focus on the New Play Lab and figuring out the best way to move new plays through a building that new plays hadn't moved through. I did that with Martha and Michele Volansky. Of the three of us I was probably the least effective. I was fine, but they were probably more innovative in their thinking. I was a good face for it and I think that I was very good with the plays. I wanted to direct and I was getting jumpy about it. Then Gary said, "Well, we have to give her an opportunity." So they built a little theatre in the garage here for me and I directed a play in there. And then they started to let me work. I basically learned how to direct. I knew something, but I didn't know what I knew. I mean I had my MFA in directing from Yale. Directing was all I did. I've never acted. I never wanted to, but the level that you just get kicked up to here is about ten levels higher working with these people.

Tina Landau:

The way I got hooked up with Steppenwolf was through a musical I wrote and directed, called *Floyd Collins*, which was running in New York. Frank Galati unbeknownst to me came to see it and called Martha Lavey, who had just become the artistic director and said, "We have to produce this show. This belongs at Steppenwolf. It's extraordinary." Martha flew to New York and saw the show. I did not know any of this.

I'll never forget my first conversation with Martha, because she said, "I'm interested in this piece" and she went on to talk about the wonderful verticality in the world I had created and all sorts of very complex metaphoric readings of the work. I thought, "I need to work with this woman." I mean, she used the word "verticality." Steppenwolf had done a Tom Waits musical piece, but had not done much else in the musical genre. It became very clear that it was a little out of the wheelhouse in terms of what I was asking for and needed, so Martha asked me to direct something else. I did Chuck Mee's *Time to Burn*. Martha invited me back the next year to direct a play I was writing called *Space*. The morning after it opened, Martha and Gary took me to Vinci and said, "We'd like you to be in the ensemble." I told them I couldn't see how that would be possible, because I was a director not an actor. Of course, I accepted once I realized they weren't joking.

Alana Arenas:

I was pounding the pavement. I would get auditions for Steppenwolf, but I would never book anything. Everyone's heard the saying, "Don't call us, we'll call you." Finally, I just said, "I'm just going to have to break that rule." I called casting director Erica Daniels and said, "What am I doing that's not getting me the part? I know I'm not supposed to call you, but I don't want something I don't know to hold me back." She said, "You're fine. I keep calling you in because I like you."

Then came *The Bluest Eye* by Toni Morrison. I was invited to be a part of the readings and workshops. I really wanted to be in that show and I ended up doing it. I really wanted to be in that play. It was a Steppenwolf for Young Adults show and we ended up taking it Off-Broadway in New York. When I got back, Martha Lavey sent me an email. I was really slow on the uptake when it came to email. She finally called me and said, "I sent you an email." And it's like, "Oh my God. It's Martha Lavey and I did not respond to her email right away." This is when it was just getting to the point where the expectation was for everybody to have a computer and my agent was constantly saying, "Did you get my email?" I just want to say for people who don't have a lot of money, it was a different thing about having email in your home and being held accountable to checking it all the time. Of course, I immediately thought, "What the heck did I do in New York?"

I finally met with Martha, and she said, "Alana, we would like to invite you to be a part of the company." I said, "What does that mean? What are the requirements? What do I need to do?" Martha said, "It basically means that we prioritize you and in turn we ask that you prioritize us." I said, "OK. What would you have to do to be kicked out?" She said, "You don't get kicked out." I said, "Well, you know I just made up my mind that I'm going to move to New York." I just was so oblivious. Martha then shared a little bit about her life and said, "What I would advise you to do is just take this and see where it goes." I said, "Yeah, OK. That sounds good."

Yasen Peyankov:
It happened right after the run of *The Time of Your Life* in Chicago in November 2002. I had just worked with Jeff Perry for the first time, and it was my sixth show with the ensemble. Martha called me and said, "Can you come to my office? I want to chat with you." I had a feeling. It's the kind of thing that you always wish for, but stays in the realm of dreams.

During the meeting Martha and I were chatting about my plans and where I was at this point of my life. At some point, Martha just said, "How would you like to join the ensemble?" I immediately said, "Yes," and Martha added, "You can think about it if you want." I replied, "No,

I've thought about it for a long time. I'm not going to change my mind!" After it happened I shifted all my energy to Steppenwolf. It is my artistic home and I belong here.

Bob Breuler:
I got a call from Gary. He said, "We need somebody to play Big Daddy in *Cat on a Hot Tin Roof*." They had some guy coming in who had quit. Gary said, "Can you come in to audition?" I said, "Well, I'd love to, but I'm under contract at the Guthrie for a season, and in order to get out of it, I have to pay a month's salary to get out." He said, "Come in anyway." I thought I was just going to come and read something. We're up on the third floor at the old building at 2851 N. Halsted. It's the middle of July and there's no air conditioning. I'm doing the whole Big Daddy scene. Gary's sitting out there and I am acting with none other than Austin Pendleton. He's playing Brick and we have the scripts in our hand and we're doing the whole scene.

They asked me to do it. I went back to talk to the Guthrie and I gave them the whole story that I was cast as Big Daddy, and they said, "Go ahead with our blessing. We're not going to charge you for the four months."

I said to my wife at the time, "I really want to be in this company." That was 1982. It really connected with me, because that's the way I work, physically and so forth. I was really attracted to them right then and I just put it in the back of my head and sent out the vibe. And it came back to me.

Then they cast me in *A Lie of the Mind*, and my wife and I moved here. She's a cabaret singer and had worked in Chicago before. During that run, Gary and Jeff asked me if I wanted to become a member of the ensemble. And I said, "What are my duties?" They said, "Well, there aren't any. If you want to do a play, just let us know and we'll do the same. We just put your name on the wall with your picture." I said, "That sounds like nobody owes anybody anything." So I joined. It was so casual and so crazy.

Chapter 3

TRANSITIONS, *THE GRAPES OF WRATH*, AND A NEW THEATRE

Doing *The Grapes of Wrath* for the first time helped us realize that you can travel a thousand miles by crossing thirty feet of stage floor.
　　　　　　　　　　　　　　　　　　　　　　　　—Frank Galati

The early 1980s were a turbulent period in the Steppenwolf narrative due to the sudden upsurge of fame, and the opportunities and problems that came with it. But in retrospect, according to Sinise, "This was also one of the most important and defining moments in time in Steppenwolf's early history." The discussion about moving *True West* to New York happened at the same time as the move from the Hull House space to the converted dairy and former home of St. Nicholas Theatre at 2851 Halsted Street. These simultaneous occurrences created angst and inflamed strong feelings among the company and board of directors, a board that had continued to gain a more prominent voice in the day-to-day decision making of the theatre. When Gary Sinise and John Malkovich moved to New York with *True West*, the theatre lost their artistic director (Sinise) from its home base, as well as the director (Malkovich) for their next show, *A Prayer for My Daughter*, scheduled to open at the new theatre at 2851 N. Halsted in September of 1982. The short-staffed office and limited ensemble flexibility with fewer available members was proving problematic.

The direction of the company's future at this pivotal moment was discussed and debated among the ensemble members, the board, and the Chicago theatre community at large. Co-founder Terry Kinney spoke of the concerns Steppenwolf faced in the wake of the success of *True West* in an article in the *New York Times* on November 27, 1983:

One by one, people are getting snatched up because they're becoming more successful ... It's become a problem morale-wise. We're thinking of expanding the ensemble so that people can work once a year or once every two years. We've got to expand, because Steppenwolf may never again be this group of fifteen people who make that space in Chicago their first priority. We want to keep our ensemble real strong in Chicago, but at the same time we're all opening our arms to new challenges.

In the five years that followed the opening of *True West*, Steppenwolf took one show per year to New York, including *And a Nightingale Sang* (1983), *Balm in Gilead* (1984), *Orphans* (1985), *The Caretaker* (1986), and *Educating Rita* (1987). These shows helped to raise the profile of several ensemble members, opening doors for them in New York and Los Angeles.[17] However, this also added fuel to the apprehensions that had divided the company regarding the decision to take *True West* to New York in the first place. Over time, in large part due to the rousing reception for these shows by the New York audiences, some of the fears gradually began to subside. But, immediately following the move to the theatre at 2851 N. Halsted, and even into 1984, Chicago audiences, press, and particularly the funding community had trepidations about what the future held for Steppenwolf in Chicago.

The story of the immensely successful and commercially innovative St. Nicholas Theatre and its rapid fall from grace had intensified the pragmatic sensibilities of prominent arts supporters in Chicago, who had generously backed the growth of St. Nicholas, only to see founders David Mamet, William H. Macy, and Steven Schacter move eastward to pursue a broader landscape of opportunities. Sadly, St. Nicholas Theatre's relocation had contributed to the financial over-reach that led to its economic failure and forced the company to shut its doors. This situation was fresh in the funding community's minds as they continued to see the rapid success of Steppenwolf ensemble members outside of the city of Chicago. Would a mass exodus of ensemble members follow, put Steppenwolf's future in Chicago in question, and lead to the same kind of dissolution that happened to St. Nicholas? This question was intensified not only by the successes, but also by the fact that Steppenwolf had been in the midst of a financially leveraged move to a new space at the same time that *True West* had moved to New York. To alleviate the growing concerns and to answer this question, the company held an important press conference in July of 1984 on the stage of their new

---

17. Examples include Joan Allen in *And a Nightingale Sang*, Laurie Metcalf in *Balm in Gilead*, and Kevin Anderson and John Mahoney in *Orphans*.

theatre at 2851 N. Halsted to demonstrate their continuing commitment to the future of their ensemble in Chicago. Jeff Perry, who had stepped out of the cast of *True West* and into the role of artistic director, said at the time:

> The rare trust and knowledge between ourselves and our audience, coupled with the fact that we can be left relatively free to create in Chicago without the overwhelming economic and media pressure, make it imperative that Chicago remain the base of our operations.

Sinise further attempted to calm the waters by affirming that Chicago was their artistic home:

> It's like when we moved from Highland Park to Chicago to get a larger audience. We didn't go to New York to split up; we went there to make us stronger.

Perry reflected back on this vital period over thirty years later:

> Gary and John's instincts to roll the "for-profit" dice in NY amounted to a gigantically important self-recognition for our ensemble. The artists we had gathered were too curious, too talented and too ambitious to limit their work opportunities. It was a profoundly important moment where *True West* carved out our ongoing ability to "have our cake and eat it too," in terms of the variety, compensation, and visibility of our work.
>
> Pretty much every ensemble of note in American theatre history had crashed and burned on the rocks of "fame and fortune vs. art." *True West* was the first glimpse of Steppenwolf's now established ability to surmount that obstacle. Of course, what was required was that our artists returned with regularity from "fame and fortune" gigs; no example more striking than Laurie Metcalf returning to Steppenwolf almost every *Roseanne* hiatus over a ten-year period to, as she put it, "Make sure I could still act."

Co-founder Kinney speaks of the anxiety that surrounded this decision:

> Jeff sort of took over the reins and didn't go to New York so Tom Irwin went instead. The producer decided that he didn't like Tom's version of it and forced Gary to go into the role himself. The revelatory reviews were the kind that suggested that we might never see John and Gary

again. Some of us got resentful. We were left with a brand new theatre that we couldn't afford. We were left without our artistic director and without, I think, one of our most creative and popular actors. We did feel a little bit abandoned, but as it turned out it was just that we didn't understand what it meant for the destiny of the company over the long haul for that to do so well. I think Gary had that vision and we just couldn't align with it at that moment—eventually we did.

The question of whether or not the move of *True West* to New York was a detriment or a gain for the company would continue to be a debated for a long time; however, the subsequent successes and the longevity of the company make moot this question. Sinise remembers an important element that affected all future out-of-Chicago productions:

Jeff and Fran did not want to move with *True West* to New York, so I was going to have to recast the roles of Austin, the younger brother, which Tom Irwin would initially go into; the role of the producer, Saul Kimmer; and, even though Laurie was absolutely hilarious in her role as the mother, there was the thought that her part needed to be recast with an older actress. With only two out of the four actors coming from Steppenwolf, the company members voted that we could not bill it as a Steppenwolf play. This was not something John or I wanted, but the company voted and as John and I were swimming against the tide, we could not argue. That is why the poster for Steppenwolf's first show in New York does not have billing as a Steppenwolf Theatre Company Production.

To me, it was always a Steppenwolf show. It was only because the bios for John and I that were in the program reflected mostly credits at Steppenwolf Theatre in Chicago for both of us that the critics all picked up on that and mentioned Steppenwolf in every review. After that, we billed all the shows moved to New York or anywhere as a Steppenwolf Theatre Company Production. This was an important lesson we learned when the next show, *And a Nightingale Sang*, had to be recast with a few New York folks as well.

The company eventually embraced its New York and international achievements and continued to thrive in Chicago—Steppenwolf's one true home. Laurie Metcalf speaks to the significance in a broader sense:

Without people like John and Gary to move us into action, some of us might still be in Highland Park in the basement doing plays.

To which Glenne Headly adds:

> A theatre that is really good does not rely on one or two or three or even six people, it really has a life of its own. The theatre should be more important than the individual. It should live beyond its members.

In the intervening years between the premiere of *True West* in New York in 1982 and the opening of *The Grapes of Wrath* at Chicago's Royal George Theatre in 1988, Steppenwolf's growing reputation was clearly reaching new heights in terms of national and international recognition. When the theatre received the 1985 Tony Award for Regional Theatre Excellence, the company was placed squarely on the map as a leader in the American theatre. From their earliest roots in a basement in Highland Park, barely ten years had passed for the company to attain this level of accolade; and, ironically, the theatre had become an established theatrical institution, which had been the very antithesis of what the Steppenwolf founders' earliest visions had been. Sinise, Perry, and Kinney had a strong aversion to the entire concept of "institution," and now they had become that very thing. Nonetheless, the stars were aligning, as Randy Arney remembers:

> I remember a press conference on 8/8/88 where we announced the plans for the new theatre at 1650 N. Halsted. At that press conference, we also announced our plans for *The Grapes of Wrath*, and that night, I was at Wrigley Field when they put the lights on for the first time—8/8/88.

There were big plans ahead, but the challenge for the company became how to simultaneously maintain its fierce independence and unique dynamic; move forward with plans for a major expansion; sustain the company in Chicago; and continue to build upon its impressive national/international stature.

Steppenwolf had opened its first show at the 2851 N. Halsted Street location in 1982, only two years after their move into Chicago and the Hull House space; and now, only two years later, they were already looking for yet another move to a larger theatre. The massive growth and increased notoriety of the company had created unforeseen challenges. Shifting artistic leadership was the norm during this period, with Gary Sinise returning as artistic director in 1985 until 1987. Sinise:

Jeff had the reins for just over two years from fall '82 until early '85 when I returned to Chicago from *Balm in Gilead* in New York. I left that show just before Christmas '84 and it closed in January '85 after a ten-month run in NY. It was shortly after I got back that I took over for Jeff—a simple hand-off as I recall. I was ready to do it again. Jeff was ready, and unlike the previous transition from me to Jeff when there was a lot of tension; it was just smooth sailing without a lot of discussion.

In the fall of 1986, Sinise appointed Arney and Jeff Perry as associate artistic directors. Upon his resignation in early 1987, the two would become co-artistic directors for one year, with Arney finally assuming leadership responsibilities as the sole artistic director in 1988. Amazingly, at Sinise's behest, Arney had directed his first professional show, *Bang*, only eighteen months earlier as part of Steppenwolf's 1986 subscription season. Arney, a relative newcomer, faced an immediate onslaught of noteworthy events for the theatre when he began his tenure as artistic director as he shares:

> The glory, excitement, and buzz around Steppenwolf Theatre Company was tied to about ten or twelve people. It's easy to forget now, because the theatre has become this wonderful strong institution in Chicago, but there was a point where it was literally a handful of individuals; and many of those people were leaving Chicago at the time and finding other opportunities. They wanted the theatre to continue. They wanted it to be something. They would have hated to see it go away, but nobody had solved the question, "How does this place exist beyond these ten or twelve personalities?" Our first reviews when I was artistic director would lead with how many ensemble members were or weren't in the play. So, before it was judged as a success as a play, the theatre was sort of judged on its success of having ensemble members in it.
>
> There was much consternation in town whenever shows would be done that didn't have ensemble members in them. The company itself was looking at the question, "What are we?" Gary was living in Los Angeles and John was living wherever and these were the people that everyone couldn't wait to see no matter what the play was. One of the first things I did was institute a new wave of people who were asked to join the ensemble—more at one time then had ever been added since the original ensemble.

As part of this new wave in the mid-eighties, some familiar and some new names became official ensemble members during the leadership of

Sinise, Perry, and ultimately Arney. The new members included former ISU students Rick Snyder, Gary Cole, and Arney, as well as Frank Galati, Austin Pendleton, Molly Regan, Kevin Anderson, Bob Breuler (who had initially come from the Twin Cities to play Big Daddy in *Cat on a Hot Tin Roof* directed by Austin Pendleton), Jim True-Frost, and Tim Hopper. The company also made strides nationally and internationally with multiple excursions to New York; and trips to the Kennedy Center with productions of *Coyote Ugly* directed by John Malkovich and *Streamers* directed by Terry Kinney; Sydney and Perth, Australia festival performances of *Lydie Breeze* directed by Rondi Reed; and a restaging in London of *Orphans*, directed by Gary Sinise. In its Chicago incarnation *Orphans* had introduced the dynamic work of Anderson, working alongside Mahoney and Kinney; and in London the show featured Albert Finney and Jeff Fahey, stepping in for Mahoney and Kinney. The addition of a major international star such as Finney shed even greater light on the company's work.[18]

The rapid growth and multiplicity of opportunity forced Steppenwolf to go through a maturation process at hyper-speed on both the artistic and business fronts. Randy Arney talked about the role of artistic director at Steppenwolf:

> Artistic direction at Steppenwolf is very different from artistic directing anywhere else because it's about the care and feeding of a group of people as opposed to going into an office, closing the door and picking plays solely.

There were two primary pieces to the puzzle at hand for Arney as he took over as artistic director of the theatre. The first was to keep the momentum moving forward in the search for a new performance space. The second was the ongoing artistic mission of the theatre in terms of season planning, and particularly the continuing development of *The Grapes of Wrath*, which had been commissioned by the theatre in 1985 when Sinise was still at the helm. The pairing of these two tasks paralleled what had occurred in 1982, when the company balanced moving *True West* to New York with the opening of the theatre at 2851 N. Halsted, but on a much grander scale from an economic perspective.

18. The company would come back to Finney again in Ronald Harwood's *Another Time*, which was the premiere performance in the new theatre at 1650 N. Halsted in 1991.

The journey of bringing the theatrical production *The Grapes of Wrath* to the stage in many ways mirrored the Joads' struggles at the heart of the original story. When the Steppenwolf ensemble set out to realize this conquest, they could not possibly have surmised the enormity of the task that they had laid out for themselves, or the shared devotion that it would take to move this play through a lengthy development process from the original run in Chicago to the eventual triumph on Broadway. The play had been commissioned in 1985, but did not open in Chicago until September of 1988, so the path was not only filled with a myriad of bumps and grinds, but also required a perseverance that was truly remarkable. Frank Galati shares his memories of the first discussions about the possibility of doing *The Grapes of Wrath*:

> I was still rehearsing *You Can't Take It With You* at Steppenwolf, when Gary said, "You know, you ought to think of something that you would really like to do that you think would be good for a big ensemble." I said, "Gary, what about *The Grapes of Wrath*?" I can still see his face. His eyes lit up. He instantly knew that it was a good idea. By that time the company had a New York reputation, so when the publisher went to Mrs. Steinbeck and said Steppenwolf Theatre Company in Chicago wants to do an adaptation of *The Grapes of Wrath*—she had seen *Balm in Gilead* or *True West* and was very impressed, so she gave us rights to do it. We sent her the script and she approved it and became one of our most passionate advocates and supporters.

Galati continues on about the difficulty he faced in the process of adapting the script and what finally opened him up as a writer:

> Once we got permission from Elaine Steinbeck, Gary said he wanted to direct it and I thought, fantastic. I started to work on the adaptation. I didn't get very far. I never got a full draft. I didn't let myself think about what the physical production was going to be, because Gary was directing it. I was only thinking about the storytelling and the text and for some reason that kind of gave me a block. Then Gary resigned from his artistic directorship and moved to California and began his career in Hollywood. Jeff Perry took over as interim artistic director, and he said, "Gary is gone. You're going to have to direct it. You have to keep writing it and you're going to have to direct as well."
> It completely freed me, because I immediately thought of how to do it, which I didn't let myself think about. I thought, I know how to

do this. I need a bare stage. I have to have a truck. I have to have fundamental elements of earth, air, fire, and water. That's all I need. Then came the whole idea of music to drive the story—to be the engine that moves the truck to California. I got turned on to composer and performer Michael Smith, who just sort of blew me away with his beautiful sultry voice. I thought, "What the fuck? I'll call him." He didn't know me, but I called him up and said, "Michael, have you ever thought about composing for the theatre?" He said, "No, but I'd love to."

We never had a workshop. We never even had a reading. Who would do an epic play that is God knows how long based on the number of pages without actually reading it out loud? The first reading of the text was the first day of rehearsal.

The first steps in moving forward were the continuing work on script development and the all-important casting process, which was complicated by the fact that the show had far more cast members than there were ensemble members. This would be the largest cast in a Steppenwolf show up to this point in its history. Adding to the challenge was the fact that the artistic staff was virtually non-existent, as Arney captures in describing his relationship with his then assistant to the artistic director Phyllis Schuringa:

The two of us were the artistic office. It was just Phyllis and me. We read the plays. We sent them to the ensemble. I chose the plays. She cast the plays. There were only two of us there for all of those years, 1987 to 1995.

This is an astounding fact when one considers the aforementioned Tony Award and the company's stature at the time. Only two people running the artistic side of the dreaded "institution," while Stephen B. Eich ran the business side. Schuringa became, out of necessity, a kind of ad hoc casting director at Steppenwolf, which would become a more formalized position when Martha Lavey took over as artistic director in 1995. Schuringa remembers the daunting task of finding additional actors for *The Grapes of Wrath* who could meld easily with the ensemble members.

The first cast of *The Grapes of Wrath* had forty people that were young, old, children, adults, and really old people—it ranged far beyond the demographics of our company. We had cast parts outside of the company before, but this was way beyond that.

My constant challenge was that I needed to find people who could stand toe to toe with our ensemble members—and, I couldn't let them down. When we needed to find somebody to add to the cast to fill a role that wasn't apparent for an ensemble member—we were relentless in our search.

Arney adds:

This relentlessness in the office and in the casting process was equal to what was on stage with our actors. It was never "Let's get a local actress because that's cheaper." We just didn't think like that. It was without compromise.

Schuringa talks about the casting of the pivotal role of Ma Joad:

We needed somebody to play Ma Joad in *The Grapes of Wrath* and we didn't know anybody in Chicago. I started calling casting directors in New York, and they would say, "You know I get paid for this, don't you?" And I said, "Yeah, but in your dreamy dream casting of *The Grapes of Wrath*, who would be your Ma Joad?" We were trying to get them excited by the project. Eventually, Lois Smith started coming up over and over again. We decided to fly Lois to Chicago to have her meet with Frank. Flying someone in for an audition was quite an ambitious move for us at that time. Lois couldn't have been more gracious. Frank met with her, she auditioned, and the choice was perfect.

Galati shares:

Lois was well known to many connoisseurs of theatre and film. After all, she was in the film of *East of Eden*. She played a couple of scenes with James Dean as the barmaid in the brothel. Laurie Metcalf had done a live TV gig with Lois and was just blown away by her and said to Randy, "You have to check out this Lois Smith. She might be perfect for *The Grapes of Wrath*." Lois agreed to fly to Chicago from New York for an audition. She was not automatically offered the role.

Vividly etched in my memory was entering the office, turning the corner and there was this woman sitting on this sofa. It was Lois Smith. I had no memory of what she looked like and I wouldn't have recognized her, but she was so magical in her presence sitting there in the office that she kind of knocked me over. Lois read some scenes or some speeches and we cast her instantly. She was shocking. She was so real. Lois was so much in the aesthetic of Steppenwolf. She had that unspoken commitment to truth and to honesty in acting, the relentless interrogation of one another's inner truth.

The equally significant role of Tom Joad was yet to be cast either, as Galati explains:

> We're auditioning and putting the cast together and Randy says, "Who are we going to get for Tom Joad?" I said, "I think we should ask Gary [Sinise], because he was the father of the project. He was the one who said yes to it and who launched it and he's perfect for Tom Joad." Of course, in those days, '86, '87 or whenever it was, he wasn't a big television star yet. He had lots of irons in the fire, but it wasn't as difficult for him to say, "OK, I'm going to do a gig at my home theatre and I'm going to play a role." There was no idea or ambition that it was going to go beyond playing here in Chicago. We didn't have a clue.

Sinise adds:

> I was directing my first film *Miles from Home.*[19] Somewhere in early 1988, they said, "Frank's working on *The Grapes of Wrath*." They started talking about the production and who could be in it. I was probably editing the movie at the point when they called and said, "Frank is directing it, do you want to be in it?" I said, "Of course."

One last addition to the Chicago cast of *The Grapes of Wrath* was John C. Reilly in one of his first professional theatre roles as the mentally challenged Joad brother Noah. Schuringa had found Reilly when she observed the final class projects of the students at the DePaul School of Drama in Chicago. Subsequently, Reilly had done some work with "Page to the Stage," which was an early forerunner to Steppenwolf's Theatre for Young Adults program that was set up to introduce area schoolchildren of all ages to the theatre. Schuringa:

> I saw in John C. Reilly a real sense of the Steppenwolf dynamic. I knew he would mesh well with the ensemble members in terms of style. He was so easy and natural and fit the role of Noah so well.

19. *Miles From Home* starred Richard Gere and included ensemble members Laurie Metcalf, Terry Kinney, John Malkovich, Kevin Anderson, Bob Breuler, Randy Arney, and Francis Guinan.

With casting in place, the focus shifted back to the ongoing development of the set design and script. Kevin Rigdon was once again tapped to be the scenic and lighting designer for the production, as well as co-designer for the costumes. Rigdon fondly remembers:

> Out of all the new plays I've ever done, *The Grapes of Wrath* was the most unusual way of working. The design of the show came before the script. Frank and I met in my office in the scene shop and looked at pictures and talked about things. I went out into the scene shop and beveled some pieces of plywood and came back in and stuck them in the box in response to the Dorothea Lange photographs entitled *The Cultivated Fields*. By the time we were done that day, we had a schematic design for the show that Frank took with him as he wrote the script.
>
> That set pretty much carried through. There were a lot of ideas that we scuttled along the way that never ever made it to the Chicago production. Between the novel and the John Ford film, we knew the elements were so important; the sense of the earth, where we see the burying of the grandfather, the fires were so elemental, the water, and the sky. One of the early questions we had was the whole thing about the truck. We felt that the real truck with all those people in it was really an important image.
>
> We don't invent in a vacuum. There are so many things that we see and like that inspire us. For me, photography has been a huge part— there's always some kind of a visual influence that sparks an interest in me. For *The Grapes of Wrath* it was pretty easy. You go to Dorothea Lange. Her work was a huge influence on the set and lighting.

Malcolm Ewen, a longtime Steppenwolf stage manager and frequent collaborator with director Galati recounts the next steps on the arduous road to opening night in Chicago:

> When we opened at the Royal George Theatre, the play was still in major development. We had a run of eight to ten weeks with only four or five weeks of rehearsal. The first preview was 3½ hours long and it was on a Thursday and we had a rehearsal day on Friday and a preview that night. And, on Saturday back in that era, Steppenwolf had 5:30 and 9:30 shows. Frank knew that 3½ hours was too long, so he went home that Thursday and wrote notes and proposed cuts. He went to Kinko's at probably 5:00 in the morning on Friday and xeroxed new script pages for everybody with his cuts on them. He

came in during that five-hour day on Friday with about a suitcase full of paper and passed out the cuts. Terry and Gary said, "Look, this is an awful lot of stuff. There are cuts in the first scene between Jim Casy and Tom Joad. We'll work on it ourselves and save you the rehearsal time." The rest of the cast worked through these big piles of cuts and later in the day, Gary and Terry came back to Frank and they said, "These cuts don't make any sense because we can't go from this to that." Frank said, "Oh, no. I only xeroxed the pages on which there are changes. The rest of the scenes stay in play." So they were trying to cut it down from a ten-page scene to a three-page scene when Frank only meant to cut a minute or two of dialogue out of it.

I think our first preview was our first run-through, which is one of the reasons why it took so long. It was epic. It's one of the great American stories. We had a lot of talented people working on it, but they were still a little too close to the woods to see the trees. We were just trying to cope with "How do you even fit forty-five people in the dressing rooms that probably could accommodate twenty people at the Royal George?"

At that time, we hadn't developed a lot of sophistication from a technical element standpoint. The truck just slid across the stage in a straight line and when it got to a point where it stopped, the cast would get out and then push it to either face downstage or upstage. It didn't stop automatically. It hardly ever hit its spike, so the lighting specials that lit the front of the truck were a little wider to accommodate for the inaccuracy of stopping. Of course, it broke every now and then and at least one guy threw his back out trying to move it. It was definitely a team effort.

The interesting thing about the original production in the fall of '88 was that we kept working on it after we opened. We kept making huge changes all the way along. After the first week or two of performances, Gary said, "We're all here, we should just keep working on it. Let's not sit on our hands. Let's make it better." Frank is really good at looking at things to see them with an audience and then saying, "Oh, they're not following, or they're bored, or it's a sidetrack from what we're trying to achieve, which is telling the story of Joads and their suffering." We kept cutting and changing all the way through the Chicago run.

Arney provides his perspective:

The Grapes of Wrath, the collaborative nature of how a project of that magnitude came together artistically is amazing. The show took the biggest leap artistically on Friday night of our first week of previews. We had two shows on Saturday, four hours apart. We'd already sold the tickets. The audience was coming. Frank cut—it was "the night of the long knives." He came in the next day and he'd cut fifty total pages and another fifty other pages had cuts on them. By having him go through it and deciding what was truly important—it was like polishing a diamond. Frank literally did this in one night. The next day the whole cast sat in the auditorium at the Royal George and Frank talked everybody through the cuts. Rick Snyder raised his hand and said, "Do I still need to come? I'm happy to." We realized at that point he had been cut from the show entirely. We reworked it so that Rick was playing some other parts. It was about serving that thing. It was an incredible process and such a journey.

Galati also describes the fortitude of the company to work on *The Grapes of Wrath* and bring it to a place that the company truly believed it was destined to go:

There's no point in playing a four-hour play when you know it's got to be cut. So, why play what we're going to lose. I handed out cuts before the first show and everybody is looking and they're reading; Al (Wilder) was berserk, because the Muley scene at the beginning of the show had been cut so much. That was sad, because it is a truly gorgeous scene in the novel.

I realized instinctively the purity and the simplicity of the opening of the simple Steinbeck narration from the text. I did not choose the very first words of the novel, but rather three or four paragraphs into the narration at the beginning, and the line is "The dawn came but no day," and then it goes on.

We got very mixed reviews. Christiansen, as he always was in his long tenure as a critic, was supportive. What I've always loved about him, and he has often been very critical of me, but it was always for the good. I've always learned from his criticism.

We were open. We were alive. It was happening. The company was willing to continue to rehearse even though they weren't really being paid to rehearse. The project was bigger than all of us and needed all of us to be accomplished. Even the thinking inside of the story, "We're the people—we go on—we survive—we can only do this together." Ma says, "You know, there's twelve of us going now and we can't fit on the truck, we might as well take another one." And then getting to the so-called Promised Land and finding out that there's no promise for them.

Ma's words did not fit the journey of the Steppenwolf Company completely, because there would indeed be a Promised Land for this production of *The Grapes of Wrath*, but the journey was just beginning. Jim True-Frost adds his thoughts:

> *The Grapes of Wrath* was a marriage of some incredible things that just fit together in the right way. It was Frank and his gifts as an adaptor and director. It was Gary and Terry and Jeff and all the other company members that were in it bringing just the right sensibility to their characters and the Steinbeck material. And, it was the company mounting what was not fated to be just another production on our stage, but was also destined to move to other venues. We all knew that we needed and wanted to show this to more people in other places.

Despite all the passionate hard work leading up to the opening in Chicago, critic Richard Christiansen, who had been instrumental in giving the company much-needed attention in their earliest days in the basement in Highland Park and had generally been one of their biggest champions, pulled no punches in the opening lines of his September 19, 1988 *Chicago Tribune* review of *The Grapes of Wrath*:

> It takes a very long time for Steppenwolf Theatre's *The Grapes of Wrath* to finish, and when it is all over, in director Frank Galati's reverent and ambitious adaptation of John Steinbeck's novel, admiration for its effort must give way to disappointment for its results ... For a production graced with some of Steppenwolf's best actors, *Grapes of Wrath* has amazingly little to offer in strong performances.

Hedy Weiss's passionately worded *Chicago Sun-Times* rave was in sharp contrast:

> Fire, water, earth and the ferociously resilient human spirit. These are the elemental and combustible ingredients with which John Steinbeck built his great novel of social protest, *The Grapes of Wrath*. They are also the building blocks of the Steppenwolf Theatre Company's breathtaking and emotionally wrenching stage version of the 1939 classic, which received its world premiere this weekend at the Royal George Theatre. Any analysis of the individual components of this triumphant production will fail to suggest its overall grandeur and nobility ...

A cry for social justice and compassion, and a hymn to the endurance of the common man, Steppenwolf's production of *The Grapes of Wrath* is also a celebration of theater as a place where great stories must be re-enacted. The play is here for only a limited run. But it would be an unpardonable sin if it did not receive an extended life, both in this country and abroad.

Weiss's words bolstered the Steppenwolf leadership's confidence. Arney explains his thoughts and those of director Galati and managing director Stephen B. Eich:

We knew we wanted to get it to New York, so Steve and Frank and I met the morning after the opening in Chicago to make a plan. We knew we needed two things—we needed somebody to pay for a full rehearsal rework of the thing, and we needed a better set of reviews.

The impact of the press's critical response on Steppenwolf's endeavors provides a fascinating glimpse into the role of the critic as a positive influence on the artistic process. That seems to be particularly true in the case of *The Grapes of Wrath*, where Weiss's review provided hope and belief, and Christiansen's written assessment gave the company an honest view of issues that needed to be addressed if the show were to move forward.[20]

Steppenwolf moved ahead with plans for *The Grapes of Wrath*, finding an ally in artistic director Des McAnuff at the La Jolla Playhouse, who provided a home for the continued development of the play.[21] In a rare collaboration between regional theatres, La Jolla Playhouse included the show in its 1989 subscription season. This was followed by a run in London at the Royal National Theatre of Great Britain's Lyttelton Theatre which included another complete rehearsal process

20. Richard Christiansen's unfettered coverage of the Steppenwolf, spanning a couple of decades, put him in a unique role as both critic and supporter. The respect of the Chicago theatre community for Christiansen's work is clearly evidenced by the fact that a theatre is named after him in the Victory Gardens Theatre complex in Chicago.

21. Jeff Perry took over from John C. Reilly as Noah in La Jolla, because Reilly had his first meaningful opportunities as a film actor, which drew him away. Reilly's departure provided an example of the depth of the Steppenwolf "bench," and was a forerunner to more changes that would take place along the journey of bringing this play to Broadway.

and ongoing cultivation of the script. Sinise shares the unwavering commitment of the company to move the show forward:

> We stayed with it. The productions in La Jolla, California and London were critical, because it was after those versions that we were able to make the Broadway production happen. It was only because we put the Chicago production up and were able to experience what we had that allowed us to know that we must go back to it. After that run we knew we needed to rework the script and figure out what worked and what didn't. Frank did tremendous work in between Chicago and La Jolla.
>
> During the La Jolla production, we cut more things, molded it, moved stuff around, and restaged things. We dramatically reconceived it and then it had the shape of more of a play rather than a big sprawling theatre piece. Michael Smith and his music became kind of this outside voice looking in and commenting on things as we went along. That became part of the new concept of the play.

Jim True-Frost describes his feelings about the process:

> The memories day to day of this amazing experience of *The Grapes of Wrath* and sharing it everywhere was just so humbling. I say humbling because knowing that it was something sort of historic just made you feel like, "I have to be on my game and really work hard and continue to grow." Even in the beginning doing it onstage in Chicago, there was a sense of momentum to it. The work was so intense and the material so demanding and beautiful that it was just rattling and resounding constantly.
>
> We rehearsed it and came away from it, and got back and rehearsed it again, and again. How many shows do you do that with, where you read, rehearse and continue to craft this piece of art? To continue to hone it and detail it; the specificity of the work by the time you're finished with that type of process is incredible. I'm sure everyone had similar experiences. It just taught us how demanding it is to create something truly extraordinary.

The two-year process of bringing *The Grapes of Wrath* to the Broadway stage, as much as any production in the history of Steppenwolf Theatre, exemplifies the ensemble members' ability to stay with a project and mine as much detail as possible out of the script to create the most honest and truthful story possible.

Terry Kinney talks about the La Jolla Playhouse run:

> There was a confluence of styles that didn't merge with each other when we were finished with the run in Chicago. They were interested in taking it to La Jolla and that's when Gary said, "We have to ask Frank to take us back to the novel and get rid of everything and go back to the actable parts of it and make it realistic." Frank happened to be thinking the same thing, so we started working together on the page, rehearsed it here, but by the time we opened in La Jolla, it was a whole different animal. Frank stayed for the run and kept adapting. Then on to London where we had a short rehearsal period and kept growing the piece into the more pared-down essentials of the mythology coming out of the realism of it. By the time we were in London it was I think at its peak and then coming to New York was the gravy.

Lois Smith speaks about the Steppenwolf ethos and how ideas from unexpected sources resolved an unsettled moment at the end of the play:

> There is a true sense of working together and a kind of freedom and openness with each other at Steppenwolf and *The Grapes of Wrath* exemplified that for me. Frank Galati with his largeness of spirit and understanding was at the center, able to take in the strong, opinionated, and sometimes rowdy input from, first of all, the founders of the theatre who were a part of it, and a large company all working intensively together to make this thing happen.
>
> We had taken *The Grapes of Wrath* to La Jolla and continued to work on it. One night somebody's friend came to the show. There had been a section that was extremely hard to figure out where the family moved from the boxcars at the end. It was a desperate time after Rose of Sharon had lost the baby. There's a horrible storm and so they leave the boxcars in this terrible weather and end up in a barn. There had always been this problem about how to make that transition work. We tried so many things. I remember days of rehearsal in Chicago just trying something else to find the key.
>
> This friend said something like, "I wondered why they left the boxcars—the boxcars were so comfortable." Sally Murphy, Gary and I talked about it at a restaurant in La Jolla and took it in. Of course, the boxcars are flooded and somehow it hit us all, "Oh my God." That somebody could have that response: "The boxcars were so comfortable." I think Gary got up and called Frank. We immediately the next day altered a few things.

There were two little children's swimming pools set up on the two sides of the wings, and during the narration Sally and I rushed off stage, immersed ourselves in the water and were drenched. We came back for the exodus from the boxcars, all comforts were removed from the boxcars, and we couldn't have been more miserable. The end moment was always wonderful, but the trip from the boxcars to the barn had always been problematic and now we finally knew how exactly to make it work—how to make us miserable enough, and it came from that little comment.

Frank Rich's *New York Times* review captured the last image in the play that Smith's story set up:

> The evening concludes with the coda the movie omitted, in which the Joad daughter, Rose of Sharon (Sally Murphy), her husband gone and her baby just born dead, offers to breast feed a starving black man (Lex Monson) in a deserted barn. As acted and staged, in a near-hush and visually adrift on the full, lonely expanse of the wooden stage, the tableau is religious theater in the simplest sense. There is no pious sermon—just a humble, selfless act of charity crystallized into a biblical image, executed by living-and-breathing actors, streaked with nocturnal shadows and scented by the gentle weeping of a fiddle string.
>
> Some of the audience seemed to be weeping, too, and not out of sadness, I think. The Steppenwolf *Grapes of Wrath* is true to Steinbeck because it leaves one feeling that the generosity of spirit that he saw in a brutal country is not so much lost as waiting once more to be found.

Smith adds:

> The end moment had always been brilliant—that's what's Steinbeck started with and that's what wasn't in the movie, so that was an extraordinary thing in every way—always had been.

The time at the La Jolla Playhouse provided the creative team with an opportunity to step outside of the project, by virtue of a new location, and gain much-needed perspective as they crafted the show into a more fluid piece of theatre for their ongoing pursuit of a New York run. Arney speaks of the importance of the London run of *The Grapes of Wrath*:

> A friend of managing director Steve Eich named Thelma Holt was running an international theatre festival at the National Theatre of

London. We could get only ten performances, so we built two sets, one in La Jolla and one in London. We took thirty people and did the play at La Jolla, and then flew the cast to London. La Jolla got us the rework we needed, and the London reviews got us into New York.

With financial backing from AT&T and some ardent Steppenwolf supporters, *The Grapes of Wrath* opened to glowing reviews in London; and Steppenwolf was the first American theatre company to ever play at the National Theatre. Longtime London theatre critic Jack Tinker's review in the London *Daily Mail* in early June of 1989 unhesitatingly validates that Steppenwolf's hard work had paid off exceedingly well:

> *The Grapes of Wrath* … is as shatteringly a perfect piece of American Theatre as you are likely to experience in a lifetime of trans-Atlantic travel.

John Peter writing for the *Sunday Times* added:

> It is the best kind of American acting, gritty and gnarled with a simple rhetoric, which knows that it has no need of bombast or hysteria. The actors are sharply individualized and yet self-effacing.

By the time of the London run, even Richard Christiansen had come full circle in his assessment:

> Gary Sinise, as the embittered Tom Joad, stands as the powerful focus of Steinbeck's anger against social injustice. Jeff Perry delivers a heartbreaking portrayal of the Joads' retarded son Noah, and Tom Irwin, in a smashing bit of virtuoso acting, searingly portrays a farmer driven mad by the despair of poverty. The smoothness of the performance was all the more remarkable considering that the cast had had only a technical rehearsal and one run-through before its London debut.

Tom Irwin's detailed account of opening night sheds a little light on the personal chaos he faced on the big stage of the National Theatre of London on opening night:

> Taking *The Grapes of Wrath* to the Royal National Theatre with its rich theatre history was thrilling. Vanessa Redgrave threw a party for the cast and meeting her left me speechless, but to be standing on a stage that I remember reading about in my theatre history class was

mind-blowing. Steppenwolf was performing on the stage where the legendary Richardson, Olivier, Gielgud and others had played; it was profound because we became part of this history. That's a long way from my hometown of Peoria, Illinois.

I vividly remember the feeling in the pit of my stomach opening night of *Grapes*. Our dressing rooms were in the center of a complex of three theatres built around a courtyard. You could look in the windows across from you and see the actors in different costumes preparing for three different shows. "Okies" from Depression-era Steinbeck walked the halls with soldiers from *Hamlet*. In each dressing room there was a monitor with a dial that switched between the different theatres plus a speaker for your "places" calls. *Grapes* opens with a spotlight coming up on a man playing a saw followed thirty seconds later by a spotlight on the opposite side of the stage that came up on the character I played giving the opening narration to the play. I was switching back and forth on the monitor between listening to *Hamlet* starring Daniel Day-Lewis on the Olivier stage and the audience filing in to our show in the Lyttelton. I was happy and excited and also slightly concerned because I wasn't getting any additional calls from our show; I didn't have a way of contacting the stage manager and there was no assistant director to be found.

Sitting in my room, I switched the speaker back to our stage and could hear the music of the saw and I knew that I was fucked. I had thirty seconds to get in place. I tore out of my dressing room, down a hallway, threw open a set of doors and it was a rehearsal room. I was completely lost and the building is a maze. We had only been in the space two days before we opened and no one knew the layout. I kept throwing open doors until I finally found one that led to the front of the stage, but my path was blocked by the Joads' truck. I ran around to the backstage entrance and ran up a small flight of stairs, but in the dark I didn't see one of the actors sitting on the stairs. As I fell over him, I saw my spotlight start to come up on an empty stage. I had to gather myself and slowly, purposefully, and as dramatically as I could, make an entrance into that spotlight. I hit the stage, opened my mouth, and couldn't speak. What came out was a long, high-pitched wheeze. I was sweating profusely. It took what seemed like an eternity to form the first word. The speech must have seemed long, very odd, and weirdly melodramatic.

Later, at the opening night party, Frank Galati came up to me, tears in his eyes, grabbed me by my shoulders and said in a way only Frank Galati can, "Tom, I don't know what you decided to do with that opening narration, but my god, it was brilliant." That was my introduction to the National Theatre of London.

And finally, Kinney shares a moving recollection of the closing night of the London run that symbolizes the level of respect and admiration that Steppenwolf had garnered:

> The most glorious moment I ever had in my life as an actor was the closing night in London. We didn't know that everybody in the building was so fond of us. Thelma Holt the producer, who eventually was part of our New York experience too, was this lovely old-school British producer who arranged on closing night as we were taking our curtain call for roses. I can't tell you how many roses were dumped out of the grid onto us, but we were up to our knees. The entire stage just rained down with roses on us.

All that remained in this lengthy journey was bringing the show to Broadway. In the minds of most ensemble members, "making it on Broadway," although a fantastic achievement, represented, more than anything, an opportunity to share their work with an even greater audience for a play that they felt warranted a special level of recognition. Even today, most ensemble members continue to call Chicago home, even if the myriad of opportunities that have accompanied their successes have taken them beyond the city's potential to fill their creative needs. Sinise:

> I'm so proud of the work we did on *The Grapes of Wrath*, because it was a two-year journey from fall of 1988 to fall of 1990 when we closed on Broadway. Two years in the life of a play and two years in all our lives.

Frank Rich's March 23, 1990 review in the *New York Times* for *The Grapes of Wrath* provided the icing on the cake, but further indicated the values at the core of the Steppenwolf Company; values that still drive them twenty-five years later:

> As Steppenwolf demonstrated in *True West, Orphans* and *Balm in Gilead*—all titles that could serve for *The Grapes of Wrath*—it is an ensemble that believes in what Steinbeck does: the power of brawny, visceral art, the importance of community, the existence of an indigenous American spirit that resides in inarticulate ordinary people, the spiritual resonance of American music and the heroism of the righteous outlaw. As played by Gary Sinise and Terry Kinney,

Tom Joad and the lapsed preacher, Jim Casy—the Steinbeck characters who leave civilization to battle against injustice—are the forefathers of the rock and roll rebels in Steppenwolf productions by Sam Shepard and Lanford Wilson just as they are heirs to Huck and Jim. They get their hands dirty in the fight for right …

Like the superb Miss Smith, Mr. Sinise and Mr. Kinney, the other good actors in this large cast never raise their voices. Such performers as Jeff Perry (Noah Joad) and Robert Breuler (Pa Joad) slip seamlessly into folkloric roles that are permanent fixtures in our landscape. **They become what Steinbeck believed his people to be—part of a communal soul that will save America from cruelty and selfishness when other gods, secular and religious, have failed.**

The New York run of *The Grapes of Wrath* and the acclaim that came with it further cemented the company's place as a leader in the Chicago theatre community and helped to provide a symbolic foundation for the final phases for the construction of their own theatre building. The intrinsic problems of the great success that accompanied their meteoric growth through the 1980s made the move to a new space absolutely essential to the theatre's ongoing survival. The theatre, for all intents and purposes, was bursting at the seams, as Arney explains:

> We had a five-show season at 2851 N. Halsted where the demand for tickets had gotten so high that we were either going to have to quit and cap subscription sales, which the board said we couldn't do, or for a while we had to run a fifty-six-week year. We'd start the season September 1 of one year, and then we had to start the next season on October 1 of the following year, so that we could literally get all of our subscribers through the door.

This scenario, to be so popular, might seem like a very good thing for a theatre, but at that moment it was problematic for Steppenwolf; the theatre was in such high demand that they could not keep pace with the desire of an adoring public to see their work. This was a conundrum, much like a business that has a product that hits the marketplace to immense success, but cannot keep up on the manufacturing end.

Fortunately, Steppenwolf's board of directors, and specifically board president Bruce Sagan, were visionary in their pursuit of the development of a new theatre complex. Complicating matters was the fact that all of the planning for the new theatre was going on simultaneous to the enormous success of *The Grapes of Wrath* in La Jolla, London, and

New York; and further there was the residual pressure of simply keeping up with the day-to-day operations of the theatre. There were in-depth discussions among board members and the theatre's leadership about how to proceed forward in the quest for a new theatre space. The question as to whether the theatre would be able to sustain itself economically by generating enough revenue through corporate and private sponsorships as well as ticket sales, while at the same time paying down the debt burden that they would inevitably incur in a move, was at the forefront of the board's planning process. Arney:

> I remember a board meeting where they said, "We're going to build this multi-million-dollar theatre. Is the ensemble going to come and be in it? Will the audiences follow?" Former Chicago Bear Gary Fencik, one of our board members, quoted the famous movie at the time, *Field of Dreams*: "If you build it they will come." We knew that John Malkovich and Gary Sinise couldn't continue to come back to Chicago to a 200-seat converted dairy and do a play—a play that had to run four months, because we had so many subscribers. My time as artistic director was a combination of finding a way to stabilize what was going on in Chicago and create excitement at the home base to do two things; one, grow that home base; and two, make the center hold so that all of those people that were leaving would have something that they would want to continue to return to.

There is a reason that there is a single tribute plaque in the lobby of Steppenwolf Theatre dedicated to former board chairman Bruce Sagan: without his incredible vision for the theatre's future, the company might not have made it through this delicate time of managing a huge production with *The Grapes of Wrath*, while planning for and opening a new and expensive theatre. Sagan:

> We were taking two huge risks all at the same moment, but you know Steppenwolf has always been an entrepreneurial place, so when I became chairman in 1987, I said to everybody, either we make a new theatre space that suits their artistic capacity or we will never see them again.

Sagan, along with artistic director Arney, managing director Stephen B. Eich, and the rest of the board set out to make this dream a reality. Michael Gennaro, former Steppenwolf executive director from 1995 to 2003, said of Sagan:

Bruce Sagan is one of the greatest visionaries I've ever worked with for what he saw for the future of Steppenwolf. I came to realize that even though I didn't understand necessarily where he was going at the time, I knew it would happen. He just foresaw things. Fortunately, we had a board that was made up of a lot of entrepreneurs that were very smart about business. Steppenwolf has without question the best board I have ever worked with.

Designer Kevin Rigdon, a key player in the development of the new theatre, adds to Gennaro's comments:

Bruce is an inspirational leader. He was not afraid of what he didn't know. The whole process of building the theatre was Bruce saying, "We can do this. Let's ask questions, look at it, and not come at it from a preconceived notion." This had been exactly what we did as a theatre company of actors from the start, so his approach modeled the art we had been creating. It was a very pragmatic, practical approach to building and construction management. Many times the questions that we asked of the engineers and the architects were the ones that solved the problems, because we weren't going to be satisfied with a conventional answer. Usually what happens in a building is you hear from architects, "Don't worry about that, we'll take care of it." Bruce and I would go through that building every single day and we'd walk from the top down and observe what was being done. We worried about every detail and as a result, we got a building that was pretty phenomenal.

Randy Arney sets the scene for the building project:

When we started the plan to be at the place at 1650 N. Halsted, we were just going to rent a third floor of a building there that developer Royal Faubion was opening. Royal owned the Royal George Theatre and the land that sat across the street. He was a sort of mad dreamer who wanted to create a theatre district down at North and Halsted. Steve Eich and I would drive around the city on our lunch hours looking for possible spaces, and then come back to the theatre and call the board and talk about this warehouse, or that place etc. Royal came with a plan that he wanted a building where we are now. The place would be retail space on the first floor and we were going to get the third floor as a rental from Royal. It was going to be like what Second City had when they created their new space. Movie theaters and something on the first floor and then up an escalator to a theatre where we could do our plays.

Things changed a bit, and by the time Sagan had finished negotiating a lease with Faubion the Steppenwolf space was a real theatre, with entry on the first floor and three floors of theatrical space. Arney continues:

> When we started, it was really a shady neighborhood. A board member asked at a board meeting, "Where the hell is Cabrini–Green [a notoriously bad housing project—now gone] in relationship to the theatre?" We went out to see if we could raise money. We didn't know if we could, and Royal was only going to provide us with empty space. He wasn't going to outfit it as a theatre. We were going to have to do the seats in it. We were going to have to do the decorations and the complete outfitting of the theatre.
>
> Royal went about making his plans and building and he was going to sink the foundation very deep because, in Chicago, you have to go down hundreds of feet to bedrock. He started to do all that while we went out to raise our money to outfit the theatre and I started to plan the very first show. That's when I talked to Albert Finney about being in our first show. We had dates on the calendar for a year and a half. Then we started to notice Royal slowing down. All of a sudden the cranes weren't moving. We couldn't figure it out. Our clock was ticking. We were going to open this season at a certain time and Royal seemed to be slowing. Subsequently, we learned he had run into some cash flow problems and ran out of money at some of his other developments and that's why work had stopped.
>
> We had our season planned, but it was then that Bruce Sagan remained cool, and said, "You know what, Royal needs cash now. He is in deep trouble as a developer; I bet if we went to him with a cash offer, we could get this for a steal." And through that, we learned that Steppenwolf actually seemed to have the wherewithal to raise the kind of dough we needed.

Bruce Sagan filled in the details in an interview with Martha Lavey:

> We had this crazy scheme in which we were going to have to raise about $3 million to do the inside of the theatre. We had architect John Morris and we had Steppenwolf's lighting designer Kevin Rigdon. Those two guys had such an instinct about what Steppenwolf wanted that the new theatre got designed out of that understanding.
>
> We had this terrific thing going on when Mr. Faubion went bankrupt. He had made the mistake of trying to produce himself in his theatre at the Royal George and the effect of that was that we were

able to convince the board that we should go try to do the theatre ourselves; that we needed to figure out how we could do it and how we could make it happen. We had a lucky break. There was a wonderful governmental program, which provided the ability to get a mortgage for a cultural facility by selling bonds on the facility in the open market. It's a little complicated.

First, we got some help from one of our subscribers, Melvin Gray of Graycor Construction who had taken over Inland Construction. They did an analysis of the plan and said, "If we were very careful and they help us as construction management this is going to cost $9 million." Fundraisers had told us that if we were lucky we could raise $2 million. So, the question was how is it possible for us to get to $9 million? It turned out that there was state legislation, which made it possible for the State of Illinois to issue bonds. The state does that to build schools, to build lights, to build roads; they do it for all kinds of things. They could do it for a private not-for-profit institution, if the institution could find somebody to buy the bonds, because the state wouldn't guarantee them.

This process had started many, many years ago with college dormitories. It was a post-Second World War gimmick that allowed colleges to do something about the vast field of returning veterans. We had to find somebody who would buy the bonds. By the time I got to look at this, the state was doing cultural institutions. For instance, the whale tanks and the auditorium down at the Shedd Aquarium were done with a bond issue. We thought, "How did they do that? Well, the law says cultural institutions, do we fit?"

We actually created a circumstance in which the State of Illinois floated a bond issue for Steppenwolf Theatre for $5 million and what we did was we went out to raise $4 million, which was just under half of the cost of the building, but the bonds were not guaranteed by the State of Illinois. We had to find someone who would buy the bonds. Who would do this crazy thing? It turned out that we got William Blair & Company, which is an old Chicago investment banking company with a long history of helping Chicago arts and educational organizations. They went looking for what can only be described as a high-risk bond fund, which means that the bonds in the fund are paying a higher interest rate than normal because they're risky. The idea was that this fund would put together a whole passel of these bonds. These were mortgage-backed securities. Blair brilliantly found this fund in Boston and came back and said, "You're going to have to pay a terrible interest rate, but you can have it." We paid 9 percent tax-free to the buyers of those bonds and that was at a moment in time when a bond for the city of Chicago would have gone for 5 percent. We were almost paying double, but it was tax-free to the buyer because it was this crazy state-issue circumstance that had started with dormitories and wound up with whales and came and did us.

Needless to say, the bond fund comes to investigate and what do we tell them? We're only asking for half the value of the building. If we go bust, you own the building because it's a mortgage. We even showed them how they could turn it into a store. It was at the time when Terry Kinney was on the TV series *Thirtysomething* and this guy comes to investigate and we have this long conversation. He wants to know all about this one actor, Terry, who he had been seeing on television. That helped flip it, and he said, "We'll take you. We'll buy your bonds." And so we suddenly had $5 million and we had to go and raise the rest. I hired a young development director, Judith Simons, as a fundraiser and we went after finding the money with the team in place: Rigdon and Morris to see to the creation of a "Steppenwolf" theatre space; artistic director Arney building the ensemble and the international reputation of the Theatre; managing director Eich who was running a not-for-profit theatre that was economically breaking even and whose subscription base was exceeding 100 percent of the seats; and a development director not afraid of the fact that we had never raised a penny of capital.

The opening of the theatre was the inception of the Steppenwolf Gala. That was the first gala where we sort of invented the idea that you have a theatre experience and then you go have dinner and talk and have a good time and drink. Everybody's now doing it. We've really been imitated since, but this was 1991.

We got it built at that unbelievable price and we met the $9 million goal. Albert Finney wanted to see this theatre first, before he committed, and he came while we were building the theatre. He got up on the stage and saw this lovely house, which was only ten rows deep, a curving balcony and a total of 500 seats. He turned around and looked at the stage and the scenery fly system, which is essentially a Broadway stage, and said, "How did they let you get away with this?"

Sagan's story typifies the blend of entrepreneurial spirit, financial acumen, thorough planning, and plain luck that has been a hallmark of the business side of Steppenwolf. When Michael Gennaro joined the theatre as executive director in 1995 for what would be a seven-year reign, he said, "I want to make sure that the business side of the theatre is as successful as the artistic side." When one considers the humble roots of Steppenwolf in Highland Park, started by a group of young actors with no business experience, and the perch they now inhabit, it is clear that the lessons of business have been well learned and Gennaro's goal has been met. Arney summed up the massive company growth of the 1980s:

> We won the 1990 Tony Award for Best Play for *The Grapes of Wrath*. The following year we opened our new theatre space at 1650 N. Halsted. Starting in 1985 when there was nobody around to 1991 and having the new building and the Tony Award ended for the first time the lingering existential question about our staying power, "Is this company going to be here a decade and then stop?" We weren't asking ourselves that question anymore.

In the aftermath of *The Grapes of Wrath* and the establishment of a permanent theatre space, Steppenwolf was now poised to embark on further building the strength and reach of their institution as they moved forward towards a new millennium.

Figure 30. Gary Sinise, Terry Kinney, *The Grapes of Wrath*, 1988 © Michael Brosilow.

Figure 31. Sally Murphy, Lois Smith, *The Grapes of Wrath*, 1988 © Michael Brosilow.

Figure 32. Sally Murphy, Gary Sinise, Jim True-Frost, *The Grapes of Wrath*, 1988 © Michael Brosilow.

Figure 33. Lois Smith, Gary Sinise, *The Grapes of Wrath*, 1988 © Michael Brosilow.

Figure 34. Gary Sinise, Jeff Perry, *The Grapes of Wrath*, 1988 © Michael Brosilow.

Figure 35. Rondi Reed, William Petersen, *Fool for Love*, 1984 © Michael Brosilow.

Figure 36. Kevin Anderson, John Mahoney, Terry Kinney, *Orphans*, 1985 © Michael Brosilow.

Figure 37. John Malkovich, *The Libertine*, 1996 © Michael Brosilow.

Figure 38. Martha Plimpton, *Hedda Gabler*, 2001 © Michael Brosilow.

Figure 39. John Malkovich, Joan Allen, *Burn This*, 1987 © Michael Brosilow.

Figure 40. John Mahoney, K. Todd Freeman, *The Song of Jacob Zulu*, 1992 © Michael Brosilow.

Figure 41. Ensemble 1985 © Michael Brosilow.

Front: John Malkovich, Glenne Headly, Laurie Metcalf, Moira Harris, Kevin Anderson, Terry Kinney

Middle: Gary Sinise, John Mahoney, Gary Cole, Alan Wilder, Rondi Reed

Back: Francis Guinan, Austin Pendleton, Rick Snyder, Frank Galati, Robert Breuler, Jeff Perry, Randall Arney

Figure 42. Medal of Honor 1998 © Michael Brosilow.

Front: Rondi Reed, Austin Pendleton, Tim Hopper, Moira Harris, Sally Murphy, Martha Plimpton, K. Todd Freeman, Alan Wilder, Molly Regan, Tina Landau.

Second: Glenne Headly, Kevin Anderson, Francis Guinan, Kathryn Erbe, Mariann Mayberry, Eric Simonson, Robert Breuler, John Malkovich, Tom Irwin.

Third: Amy Morton, Frank Galati, Terry Kinney, Gary Cole, Jim True-Frost, Martha Lavey, Laurie Metcalf, Gary Sinise.

Back: Lois Smith, Joan Allen, Randall Arney, Jeff Perry, Rick Snyder

Figure 43. Rick Snyder, Martha Lavey, Randall Arney, Mariann Mayberry, *Ghost in the Machine*, 1993 © Michael Brosilow.

Figure 44. Amy Morton, Martha Lavey, Rick Snyder, *The Memory of Water*, 1998 © Michael Brosilow.

Figure 45. Gary Sinise, *One Flew Over the Cuckoo's Nest*, 2000 © Michael Brosilow.

IN THEIR OWN WORDS: MY FAVORITE STORIES

Tom Irwin:
We weren't thinking, "Oh my God we're creating history here." We were entertaining ourselves and wanted to take audiences on the best ride we could. Some really talented people, through a lot of luck, came together at the same time, with a common sensibility, a commitment to truth and a very high level of irreverence. There was a Chicago-like work ethic; we didn't sit around stroking each other's egos, or patting ourselves on the back; you did your job and you wanted to bring it because you felt a real responsibility to the character and to everyone on stage with you: "If we're going to do this, let's really go for it." We took great comfort in that we couldn't wait to get on stage and play with each other. Big dumb choices—victims with attitudes, trying to make someone crack up, and bringing someone to tears; it was as much for each other as it was for the audience.

If you weren't in a show you were parking cars or working the box office or being an usher. No one had money. After shows we would throw some bucks into a hat and go next door for cases of beer and gyros and sit on the set and party and then come in early the next day and get on the phone and try and sell subscriptions. Then do it all over again. There was so much laughter. We didn't know what tomorrow was going to bring and didn't really care.

Stephen B. Eich (Managing Director)
Once around the time of *And a Nightingale Sang*, Mary Miller, John's sister Mandy Malkovich, and Phyllis (Schuringa) were all in the box office and they came up to me and they said, "We got to tell you something. This is really interesting. We've had a bunch of people call and they want to see the show on Saturday night and we don't have any tickets left." And so we pushed them into the Saturday night and at the end of the conversation, the purchaser, who's on the other end of the phone, says, and, by the way, "What's playing?" People had started to come to the theatre to see Steppenwolf, not necessarily for the shows. That was a real benchmark.

Gary Sinise:
I remember I called Lanford Wilson's agent to inquire about the availability of *Balm in Gilead* for a New York run. I said to her, "We'd

really like to bring the play out there." To which she replied, "My dear man, this is New York. You are 'out there!'"

Kate Erbe:
I saw *Balm in Gilead* in New York and saw in Steppenwolf this fierce commitment to being the best they can be and fiercely American. To sit there in that theatre and hear Bruce Springsteen blasting out of those speakers was amazing. I was a high-school dropout and eventually went to a therapeutic high school in Western Massachusetts. I was a part of the drama program there. They took us to see *Balm in Gilead* at Circle in the Square downtown on 7th Avenue. As a confused teenager struggling to find my place in the world, to be witness to their work, I just felt like, here were people telling a story that I could relate to—specifically for me—for my generation. They were speaking to my artistic and human soul in a way that I had never experienced.

John Mahoney:
One of my favorite theatrical experiences as an actor was *Balm in Gilead*. I mean when "Jungleland" was coming up in the end, every single night of that run, both at Hull House and the Apollo, my hair stood on end.

Francis Guinan:
There's a scene up in the bedroom between Joe and Darlene in *Balm in Gilead*, which was originally written for them to be in their underwear. Laurie and I right at the beginning of rehearsal looked at each other and said that that was stupid; I mean, they've just fucked like rabbits, so of course they're naked. There was a matinee and we had some women in from Skokie, some garden club or something like that, and I was standing there having just gotten out of bed, and I heard somebody in the audience say, "Is he circumcised?"

Tom Irwin:
Before we opened *Balm in Gilead* in Chicago we didn't know what we had—sometimes it felt like barely organized chaos. I had a great entrance to Tom Waits'"Red Shoes" and ensemble members were getting paid $50 a week. My favorite memories were the music, watching Laurie's monologue, and John Mahoney's hairdo. We were big on hairdos, because if you came up with a good "do" you had 90 percent of your character.

In New York, half the cast was from Steppenwolf and half was from Circle Rep, and we performed in their space, a beautiful little theatre in the West Village. It was so small the audience had to walk through the diner's bathroom to get to their seats. We had our opening night party in a grade school gymnasium and a couple of days later most of the cast came down with a really severe case of the measles or chicken pox. We had to shut the show down for a week. It was several weeks before pregnant women were allowed in. Terry (Kinney) and I were sharing a crappy apartment on the Upper East Side. He had the bedroom and I had a pull-out sofa that had a bar in the middle of it, which was killing my back and there was no air conditioning; it was 100 degrees in the middle of summer and we both had the measles. Tough. But once we got over it—we were in NYC in a hit show that people were begging to get in to see. What a time we all had.

Rondi Reed:
In terms of *Balm in Gilead*, I want to say that fully three quarters of us had never been to New York, and it was all about New York street life. It was how we imagined it to be, or how we had seen it in the movies of Cassavetes and Scorsese, or in films like *Midnight Cowboy*, which we saw during our college years. That was our amalgam of what we thought New York was, and it was very gritty and romantic.

Tim Hopper:
I was at Michigan getting my MFA. I was getting ready to go to New York and a friend said, "While you're there, you have to see this production of *Balm in Gilead* with this company called Steppenwolf." I was sitting there before the show began in an aisle seat and there's some guys sitting next to me, but Gary comes up to us bumming change in character, and says, "Hey, you guys a couple?" We're like, "No, we don't know each other." He says, "Well, you should be. You look good together." That was my first time to ever speak to Gary Sinise and to see Steppenwolf's work. I was just blown away. I said, "I didn't know you could do stuff like this."

Malcolm Ewen (Stage Manager):
Gary once told me a story that occurred after we had just finished building our new theatre here at 1650 N. Halsted. He went into the bathroom and found some guy stealing rolls of toilet paper and said something to him, and the guy said, "Oh, I'm from …"—I can't remember the name of the theatre, it was some little theatre company—"and we're so poor we can't afford toilet paper, so I'm stealing these five rolls to get us through the next weekend." Gary actually let him go, because he said he used to do the same thing at the Goodman.

Francis Guinan:
A high school came in to see *Of Mice and Men*. During the bunk scene, some kid kept putting his foot up on the bunk. Malkovich had some blocking over there and sat on the bunk and this kid kept kicking it, so during part of his business Malkovich turned around and looked at the kid, and this kid gave a sort of a defiant kick a little harder. Anyway, the scene was over and the lights went down. Malkovich jumped over the top of the bunk and reached up and grabbed the kid by the ears in the blackout and put his forehead up against the kid's and said, "Get your feet off this stage or I'll tear your goddamn head off," and he ran offstage. The lights came back up and John said that the kid's eyes were like huge silver dollars. He was scared to death. Some monster grabbed him in the dark.

Rondi Reed:
In *Death of a Salesman*, John Malkovich and Terry Kinney played the brothers. During the production, John's father passed away and so we had to close down the show for a couple of days, because we didn't have understudies in those days. Real life goes on as well as the stage life goes on and you sort of navigate around it. We had a spate of people getting married back in the eighties and we cut a run of *Loose Ends* short, because we had weddings. You could do that back then. Now, you have to be covered and you've got subscribers and different responsibilities, so you have to figure out how to navigate. In the earlier days, we just sort of tried to accommodate everything within our life because we had no other choice.

John Mahoney:
Let me define charisma for you. If John Malkovich and I were on stage together and I was one side of the stage standing upside down, naked with a sparkler sticking out of my ass, and John was on the other side of the stage fully clothed and just looking at his finger, everyone would be looking at John.

Randy Arney:
I went on in *True West* as an understudy. I don't think I'd had a rehearsal. It was, "Let's just do this." I'd been watching rehearsals with them all along, so I went on. The first night I was a little hyped and kind of just trying to do my job. Malkovich stood and talked to me for a while onstage as his character Lee and at one point he turned with me, took me by the arm, and walked me upstage. I thought, this isn't in the blocking. We've never done this before. We got upstage and he took a

pee in the sink on the set. He had to down two or three beers during the show, so he had to pee. To have that level of relaxation, "I got to pee so I'm walking up," and dealing in the moment—wow!

Ian Barford:
We were doing *The Libertine*. John (Malkovich) was playing the Earl of Rochester. The play takes place in the Restoration era, 1660s. There's a scene where John's character comes up to a constable who is keeping us from going to a tavern. The tavern is closed and we're trying to convince the constable to let us in, and during the run of the show, John determines that he's going to start talking to the constable through his asshole. So, he rolls over on his back and grabs his butt cheeks and starts talking to the constable out of his asshole. What kind of actor would do that? A Steppenwolf actor.

John Malkovich:
I don't anticipate. I don't know what people are doing or think about anything, and I don't care. That is my curse and my gift. I didn't really know what would happen with *True West*. I never gave it a second thought. I packed clothes for a couple of days. I certainly never anticipated all the things that would ensue from the production. If I had to do it over again, it would still be a judgment call, and I say that completely honestly.

Todd Rosenthal (Scenic Designer):
I saw *The Grapes of Wrath* and found it riveting. It was my first encounter with Steppenwolf. I said, "I would love to work at Steppenwolf Theatre." It stuck in my brain, so when I finally moved to Chicago, I parked myself on the doorstep. I knocked on their door every day. I remember seeing Frank Galati in the hallway up in Northwestern once and I told him my story and he broke into tears.

John Mahoney:
I was doing John Guare's *House of Blue Leaves* with Stockard Channing in the eighties and she came up to me and said, "John, you're amazing! You even act when you're facing upstage."

Ian Barford:
At ISU, they had a weeklong seminar with Uta Hagen. I didn't even know who she was at that time. Chain smoking up there on the stage. I wasn't invited to audition for the faculty to get to work with her during

her week of workshops, but on the third day she said, as she put out her cigarette, "I'm sick of all these scenes. Anybody who wants to do something, you come up here and we'll find something for you." I got up and there was a girl behind me. Uta said, "The two of you—do this, its a story by J.D. Salinger called 'Just Before the War With the Eskimos.'" We went back to her dorm room and we wrote it out in play form. I had no idea it was a comedic scene. We came in the next day with the scene memorized and everybody's cracking up. I didn't even know the thing was supposed to be funny. The scene ends. Uta stubs out her cigarette, walks up to me and kisses me on both cheeks and says, "This is what I've been talking about." From that moment on I was an actor. I didn't even know who this woman was.

Gary Cole:

Gary (Sinise) was very passionate about *Tracers*. He decided to create a four-week mock boot camp to prepare us that had nothing to do with the regular rehearsals. Gary and the entire cast went up to Sawyer, Michigan to this frozen campground. The late, great Dennis Farina, who was the drill sergeant, would abuse us for hours and we wore our uniforms everywhere before we ever started rehearsing. Gary created an environment that was unlike anything I had worked on. By the time we started doing the play we were way ahead of where we would have been had we just started on day one and said, "Here's the play, let's read it." Gary had it all laid out in his head. The guy is a theatrical genius as far as I'm concerned.

Gary Sinise:

During my return as artistic director in the period from '85 to '87, great things were coming our way, while at the same time not everything was always smooth sailing. *Frank's Wild Years* in 1986 was a pretty big deal. As artistic director, I made a decision to put it into the season and along with Terry Kinney helped our business guys secure some additional funding to put it up.

Terry, who was directing, had been developing it with Tom and Kathleen Waits after meeting them during the NY run of *Balm in Gilead* when they came to see it. It was going to be a big show, with eyes on NY, and a bunch of outside investors were brought in. During rehearsals Terry and Tom/Kathleen began to see things very differently. I tried my best to help them all get through it, having meetings in my office and mediating between them to try to help get them back on course. But, it seemed the writing was on the wall and they were not going to be able to get past their creative differences.

The last thing I wanted to do was to step in on a show that my dear friend had been talking about for a few years and had developed from the ground up. A lot was on the line and we had to get something up on stage. About a week or so before our first preview, Terry stepped away and I took over as director. I cut it way back and started with a new concept and brand new staging with a simple objective: get a show up that would be fun and entertaining and allow Tom Waits to do his thing. While the show never moved on from that run, it ended up doing very well that summer.

Tracy Letts:
Picasso at the Lapin Agile wasn't my introduction to Steppenwolf, but it was a solidification of the relationship between the company and me. Steve Martin had written *Picasso* and was in town to work on the play. I had been a huge fan of his as a kid—*Saturday Night Live*, his tours and his albums. I was starstruck by Steve. He was a very nice, very smart, down-to-earth guy. At some point he became aware of this play, *Killer Joe*, that I had written that had opened elsewhere in the city and he was curious about it. I said, "Well, I'd love for you to see it." I warned him that it was pretty down and dirty stuff. He was wowed by the show, really blown away. He said to me, "I have to look at you in a whole new light." I thought, "Why? Why do you have to?"

We were trying to raise money to take *Killer Joe* to the Edinburgh Festival. We had to raise about $16,000, which was an astronomical amount of money for us. We did bake sales, kissing booths, and everything else to raise that $16,000, but Steve gave us a check for $5,000 to take the show. He was largely responsible for us being able to take the show, which was not only successful at Edinburgh, but so successful that from there it went to the Bush Theatre in London.

Yasen Peyankov:
I was not an ensemble member yet, but I was constantly being invited to do shows. I was in *The Odyssey* at the Goodman Theatre with Mariann Mayberry. Mariann and I already knew each other because we have done several Steppenwolf shows together. She was starting rehearsals for *Hysteria* by Terry Johnson, directed by John Malkovich. Two days into rehearsals, she says, "Al Wilder had to drop out and they're looking for somebody." I said, "What about me?"

They were losing their minds because they had to find Freud, the lead role in the play. They were talking to the guy who did it in London. They were talking to Terry Kinney and F. Murray Abraham. Mariann calls Martha and says, "What about Yasen?" I got the sides on a Thursday. We had a matinee of *The Odyssey*. I read the script in between shows. I got home after 10:00, and worked on the scenes until 2:00 in the morning. The next day at 10:00, I go to the audition. John shows up with Martha and he's in a denim jacket, very casual, and shakes my hand. We'd never met. I'm beyond nervous. I'm numb at that point—I mean, coffee and cigarettes all night to study lines. He was reading my résumé, talking about projects and plays that he wanted to do that he saw on my résumé. It felt like we talked for a long time.

I did the first scene and Martha was my reader. John says, "OK, let's do the second one," which was a little more explosive. When we are done with that, there was a long pause. I'm thinking, "He's going to give me direction now." And then, he just looks at me and says, "Can you start tomorrow?" My eyes just fell on the floor. It's the last thing I expected would happen at that point. I was so in shock that Martha looked at me and said, "Aren't you excited?" I said, "I'm super excited, I'm just stunned!" And I continued, "I'm sorry John, but I have admired your work for so many years and meeting you under these circumstances I still can't like really comprehend all of this." He just gave me the biggest hug, and said, "You had the part after the first scene. I made you do the second one because I just enjoyed your acting." He proved to be such a generous artist. His confidence is contagious, it kind of rubs off on you.

Francis Guinan:
There's a new book about Tennessee Williams and this guy has discovered that Tennessee for years had a photograph of Lois Smith right over his typewriter so that as he was working he could look up and her face would inspire him.

Austin Pendleton:
I left the original production of *Fiddler on the Roof* the same night that Zero Mostel did. Bert Convy, who played the part of Perchik, also left that night. It was announced to the cast one night, "Mr. Mostel, Mr. Convey, and Mr. Pendleton are all leaving August 14," like a year into the run; to which Zero then announced to the whole company, "The reason that Bert and Austin are leaving the same night as me is that Bert and Austin are drawn to me sexually." He was an outrageous man.

Erica Daniels (Casting Director):
My first business trip for Steppenwolf was on September 10 and 11, 2001. I went with Martha Lavey and Amy Morton to do auditions for

Glengarry Glen Ross, which was scheduled on the 10th, and a couple hours on the 11th. Amy and I were staying at one hotel and Martha was at a different hotel. Amy and I checked out of our hotel to go get some coffee and a bagel and the events at the World Trade Center occurred, Amy and I were like, "What's happening?" We got to the audition space to find Martha. None of us had cell phones at the time and we were stuck in New York. Tim Evans and Michael Gennaro were in Toronto at a film festival and were stuck there. None of us had a change of clothes. We were able to rent a car and drove back on Friday, September 14.

Michael Gennaro (Managing Director):
Tim and I called each other on September 11 because our wives had called us and said, "You've got to turn on the television." We saw what was happening and I called downstairs and said, "I've got to rent a car immediately." I remember being in touch with those at the theatre. It was tough because of the closeness of everybody. When we all got back, Martha and I immediately called a company meeting. It was definitely a moment that I will not forget; it was as if all of us needed to get in that room and just feel that we were all there together.

Amy Morton:
One of the things that got Steppenwolf to where it is was a really startling arrogance. Case in point. Every other theatre, most not-for-profit theatres are LORT (League of Regional Theatres). We are not, because Gar, Per, and Ter (Sinise, Perry, and Kinney) went, "We're not going to do what everybody does." It was either them or Gennaro that marched into the SDC (Union of Professional Directors) offices and said, "We're not going to do this LORT thing. We're going to come up with our own contract." And they did. When David Hawkanson came in, not knowing any of that history, he said, "Well, I think we should make the company LORT. It's just going to make things a lot easier." All of the directors in the company just went, "Nope. No way. Not going to happen. We're not going to be LORT." It's that complete confidence that allows for those things to happen.

Tracy Letts:
My folks were both born and raised in Oklahoma. My mom was lower middle class and my dad really came from poverty just after the Depression in Oklahoma. They taught at Southeastern Oklahoma State University in Durant, Oklahoma. My dad grew really disenchanted with the college politics and took early retirement and started to follow what

had been a childhood dream of his, which was to act. The first production I ever remember seeing was *To Kill a Mockingbird* with my dad playing Atticus at my college, when I was probably ten years old. The first play I did was a community theatre production of *Solid Gold Cadillac* with my father. The director wanted my dad in the play, but he wasn't going to do it. He wasn't going to drive the hour to Tishomingo, Oklahoma, to go to rehearsals and do this play. She asked me to be in the play at fifteen knowing my dad would have to drive me to rehearsal and as long as he was driving, he would be in the play himself.

My father started to find himself in a lot of demand. He was in his fifties and he had a great weathered look. He probably made forty movies and TV shows in and around Dallas in his second career. There was always a need for a sheriff, a judge, steamboat captain, and he worked with good people including Clint Eastwood, Francis Ford Coppola and Robert Zemeckis—really legitimate stuff. He's in the movie *Castaway* with Tom Hanks and he played Governor Connelly in *A Perfect World*, a Clint Eastwood movie with Kevin Costner.

My mother also took early retirement from teaching. She wrote a short story called "Where the Heart Is" and her agent advised her to try to turn it into a novel. It was selected by Oprah for her Book Club and was made into a film with Natalie Portman and Ashley Judd. All this changed my parents' life. They became wealthy as a result of this. Schoolteachers who had remarkable second acts to their lives.

Erica Daniels (Casting Director):

Penelope (2011) was a piece that Amy and Tracy had seen over when they were doing *August* in London and they loved it, so Amy decided to direct it. Casting it wasn't easy. It was a bunch of men in their bikini bathing suits around an empty pool. John Mahoney's brother passed away and he had to leave the show. We had to figure out what we were going to do and it was Thanksgiving week right before tech. There was an understudy in place, but we couldn't use him, because we had sold the show with Mahoney's image. That's a challenge when you've got someone that people are so excited to see. We were exploring some New York actors, but the one we wanted passed on the offer. It was just crazy.

Martha was nervous. Amy was in rehearsal, which was about to end. I was going to have to tell her that we hadn't found anyone. I was a nervous wreck. My phone rang and it was Tracy and he said, "What's the update? Is he doing it?" I said, "No, he just passed on the offer. I don't know what I'm going to do." He said, "What are you thinking, Erica?" I said, "Tracy, I want you to do it. I need you to do this role." He said, "OK." He was driving to his mom's for Thanksgiving. "I'll turn around and be there tomorrow."

So, Martha walks in and I say, "Tracy is coming back." Now, just do the math—from John Mahoney to Tracy Letts, it's not like he was perfectly cast for the role. He was supposed to be the old one in the play. It was completely bizarre, but we just needed a good actor at that point. Martha is on the floor lying down out of relief. I'm crying. Amy comes up and is immediately like, "Oh shit." I said, "Tracy has turned the car around. He's doing it." Amy bursts into tears and we're all hugging each other. She says, "He's totally wrong for the role." I say, "I know and we don't care." It was one of those great moments. Of course, he was brilliant. Tracy saying, "I'm turning around. Amy is my best friend and I'm not going to not be there for her." That was a very telling thing.

Francis Guinan:
The first professional show I ever directed was *The Glass Menagerie* for the Theatre for Young Audiences program. Anyway the first break of the first day of rehearsal, we'd read the play and the actors start asking all sorts of questions. Everyone goes downstairs and I turn to my assistants, and say, "Fucking actors." I've been acting all these years and my first directing job, "Fucking actors." Funny. People who both direct and act feel much more in possession of their membership and think, "This is my ensemble too." I felt really tied into this place when I was directing.

David Hawkanson:
You could see the pride of the older members of the ensemble that were invited to the opening of *August: Osage County*. It was a very emotional night. The joke was, "We'll get it open, it'll be under our banner, it'll be a Steppenwolf production, but it won't run and we'll get home for Christmas." Tracy had this smirk on his face and said, "Man, there are a lot of people tomorrow morning that are going to be hung over, but that won't be the worst of it. They're going to realize that they are stuck in New York through June." The irony was that it went on to become one of the longest-running straight plays on Broadway in the last decade.

Jeff Perry:
I'm a basketball freak. The San Antonio Spurs inspire me because their style is such an interesting throwback. They're like Bill Russell's Celtics and there is such a rarified communal link in those guys. They all could have made more money as 99.9 percent of their peers have done in a

millionaires' league, but they love the system and love the attitude of "If we put this team first, we can probably beat anyone." They were selfless. That has been true at Steppenwolf as well.

Austin Pendleton:
I'd been away from the New York theatre for a while as my daughter grew up, but when she was older, I decided I wanted to direct again. I called around at all the places in New York where I used to get asked to direct, and it was like, "Once you step out of that river, you are out of that river." I called Martha at Steppenwolf and she said, "Oh, I'm glad to hear this." Shortly after, she called me and said, "Will you come next year and direct Laurie (Metcalf) and Yasen (Peyankov) in *Frankie and Johnny in the Clair De Lune*?" She got me started directing again. She was the only artistic director who gave me that chance. Of all the ones I called in New York, I never heard a word from them and I'd been a little bit in demand as a director before I sort of retreated from it.

I directed *Frankie and Johnny* and had a wonderful time with Laurie and Yasen. And then Martha just began to call me regularly. All of that got me back in the game and then I began to get New York opportunities again, and all of this arising from a remarkable woman, Martha Lavey, but also from Steppenwolf, this theatre company that I had fought so bitterly against the very idea of going out there to work with in the first place.

Kate Arrington:
Fake written and directed by Eric Simonson might not be one of the most historic productions in Steppenwolf's history, but it is historic in my life because I got to work with Eric and Fran (Guinan). Eric is one of the loveliest human beings that I know and Fran and I ended the play with a twenty-minute scene—just the two of us. I will never learn more about acting from anybody else than I did just being alone on the stage with Fran for twenty minutes.

Alana Arenas:
I thought, "I cannot believe these people have invited me to be in their company as their peer. I have to live up to that expectation." It was beautiful being in my first Mainstage show with Fran Guinan in *The Crucible*. I played Mary Warren and he was Judge Danforth. When he was in character, he would scare the living daylights out of me. His command of the script and the character made me feel like I owed it to him to meet him there.

One thing that I've always really admired about this company and the amazing actors in it is that they give fully of themselves. There are bitter people in this profession and if you hang around sometimes with actors that feel like they haven't gotten as many opportunities as they deserve, you hear them talk about who sucks and so on. To be working with these people who are the most humble, artistic heroes I have ever had the pleasure of meeting is an honor.

Francis Guinan:
I have never worked with an actress like Alana. We were doing our scene in *The Crucible* and at one point she looks at me with fear in her eyes and I saw her pupils actually dilate. She actually physically manifested what the character was feeling. I've never seen anything like that.

Eric Simonson:
I had a personal tragedy take place in my life. My wife contracted a very aggressive breast cancer. Five months later she was dead. I had a one-and-a-half-year-old son to take care of. That's when things kind of like changed for me—my life certainly, but also my relationship with Steppenwolf. Martha really rallied the troops. She got a notice out to all the ensemble members because I had to give up my work for a year. I was never in real danger but she put together a fund from the ensemble members to help me get through that time. I never really understood what it meant to be in this company. We'd all go back for an ensemble meeting or the yearly gala and people would say, "This is just like a family. It feels like a reunion." But this time really drove that home.

Jim True-Frost:
There was a great outpouring of support and friendship from my friends in the company when Leo was born with cerebral palsy and we were in a stressful time working out the early stages of what was going on with him. Martha was one of the best and consistently sent me messages that she was thinking about us and wanted to know if there was anything she or the company could do to help.

I guess when Leo was born, six and a half years ago, really started a time where I was just unable, and continue to be simply unable, to commit to doing plays in Chicago. I miss doing plays there, but as the record shows, people have gone away and come back many times. Through forty years of a company, people at all different stages of their life are more or less active. I feel very much like a time will come when I'm sort of able to be more of a participant.

Ora Jones:

The Violet Hour was the first time I had been asked to do some things that would truly elevate my work and how I think about acting and storytelling and about trusting the other actors on the stage. Terry (Kinney) was asking me to try things that meant I was going to have to shred everything that I thought I knew and go out blind and just see what happens. I just couldn't get at the truth of what we wanted to do. I went to my cast mates Tim Hopper and Josh Hamilton and said to them, "Guys, I don't want to be unpredictable, but I just need to break through this, so if I have to somehow emotionally bring myself out, that's what I'm going to do." Every time I came out on that stage, those two men were out there and saying, "Whatever you got, give us whatever you got. We will do it. We will meet you." That broke down everything for me. I could fly anywhere I wanted on that stage. I could reach emotional heights and depths that I had never been able to do before. They put themselves in the position to receive anything that was offered.

Molly Regan:

After the opening night of *The Herd*, we were having drinks with the playwright Rory Kinnear, who is also an actor and had just won the Olivier Award for playing Iago at the National Theatre, and he said, "Tonight was the happiest two hours of my theatrical life." For a highly esteemed actor, someone who has enormous accomplishments in the theatre to say that our production of his play was the happiest two hours of his theatrical life, that is just such a great gift.

Chapter 4

AN "ONGOING EXPERIMENT," A NEW
MILLENNIUM, AND *AUGUST: OSAGE COUNTY*

I took my wife and kids to see *August: Osage County*. I didn't want
my kids to not know what Steppenwolf was. I wanted them to see
August: Osage County, to see what Steppenwolf actually did—to see
the ensemble in full attack mode. My kids couldn't have seen *The
Grapes of Wrath*, because they were too little and they weren't born
during *True West* or *Balm in Gilead*, or any of the plays we did
before. *August: Osage County* captured who we were and what
we did.

—John Malkovich

I'M RUNNING THINGS NOW!

—Barbara, End of Act Two, *August: Osage County*

Tracy Letts calls Steppenwolf "An Ongoing Experiment." The resilience
that the company has demonstrated throughout its history is a testament
to the fact that the experiment is working. The sixteen-and-a-half-
year period bookended by the closing of the Tony Award-winning *The
Grapes of Wrath* on Broadway in September 1990 and the premiere of
August: Osage County at Steppenwolf in Chicago in June 2007 was a
time in which Steppenwolf had matured considerably. The company
had moved from a fierce force of youth to a thriving entity at the peak
of its powers, where unbridled energy and innovation blended with
well-earned wisdom and experience to position the theatre for the
monumental things that were to follow. The status of the theatre as a
major international institution solidified during this time as a result
of the continued commitment of a growing ensemble, a much larger
and more resolute artistic and business staff, and a group of persistent
and visionary leaders focused on the changing face of the Chicago and
American theatre marketplaces. These tireless trailblazers remained
determined, with the support of the entire company and staff, to create

new and dynamic storytelling through theatre. The efforts of Steppenwolf gradually influenced changes throughout the American theatre and fueled the ongoing paradigm shift that had begun to ease New York's stranglehold on the industry, and helped to shift attention out to the many regional theatres across the country, for which the Steppenwolf story was an inspiration and a guide.

The new theatre complex at 1650 N. Halsted had a grand opening gala on April 13, 1991. The event was sponsored by Citibank, whose corporate clout figuratively captured the growing expanse of the power position that the company had achieved in only fifteen years since their 1976 official beginning in Highland Park. The theatre had survived the tumultuous growth spurt of the 1980s and could now move forward with the security of a permanent artistic home and relative economic stability. However, that stability was being challenged with greater competition for audiences, stemming from a variety of other entertainment and media options including more movies on release annually, cable television's growth, online outlets providing a myriad of choices, and an ever-expanding Chicago theatre market. The National Endowment for the Arts in their 2008 study entitled *All America's a Stage: Growth and Challenges in Non-Profit Theater* paints a dour picture of running a non-profit theatre of any size:

> Since 1992, the percentage of the U.S. adult population attending non-musical theater has declined from 13.5 percent to 9.4 percent. As these trends worsened in the last six years, even the absolute size of the audience has declined by 16 percent.

Despite challenges in the market, the new theatre opened triumphantly with *Another Time* by Ronald Harwood featuring Albert Finney. Richard Christiansen's review gave kudos to the acting:

> Finney gives the role a real ride. Hair slicked back, voice roughened, figure stunted and eyes shifting about in his "Scrooge" mode, he comes up with some spectacular physical stunts for the first act; and in the second act, playing close to his own age of 54, he's a handsome, vigorous celebrity, still haunted by family demons.
>
> The Steppenwolf players portraying members of his family— Rondi Reed, excellent as the mother; ... and Terry Kinney, shrewdly milking his laughs as a sly philosopher uncle.

With these strong notices, the new theatre was up and running, and plans were in place for an active season, including Sam Shepard's

classic *Curse of the Starving Class*; an original adaptation of Anne
Tyler's *Earthly Possessions*, adapted and directed by Frank Galati;
a timeless American comedy *Harvey*; and ensemble member Eric
Simonson's mainstage directing debut with David Hare's *The Secret
Rapture*. This fifteenth season would set the tone in terms of planning
for the next few years, in which originality would mix with tradition. In
the years immediately following the opening of the theatre, several new
ensemble members would officially be added including Kathryn (Kate)
Erbe, Martha Lavey, Eric Simonson, Sally Murphy, Mariann Mayberry,
Lois Smith, and K. Todd Freeman, some of whom already had long
histories with the company. Steppenwolf was beginning a slow move
towards greater balance and diversification in terms of gender and race
with the addition of five strong women and the first person of color to
be a member of the ensemble, K. Todd Freeman. He shares his early
experience:

> In the Chicago North Side theatre community for many years I was
> the only person of any color. The black theatre community in Chicago
> was really weird about it. I don't live in Chicago, so I didn't even know
> that there were feelings, but apparently there was stuff brewing that I
> just didn't even consider. At that time, I didn't consider myself a
> Chicago actor. I was just a guy who got this gig at this major theatre
> that I wanted to be a part of.

As Freeman's account suggests there still existed a geographically
defined racial separation in the Chicago theatre community, which was
matched in many marketplaces nationwide, where available scripts had
not featured many meaningful opportunities for people of color.[22]

Steppenwolf had utilized the services of actors of color in productions
such as *Balm in Gilead*, 1984's *Tracers*, Steppenwolf for Young Adults
productions, and others, but Steppenwolf's 1992 production of *The Song
of Jacob Zulu* directed by Simonson and featuring Freeman working
alongside the famed South African a cappella singing group Ladysmith
Black Mambazo was a strong step by the company and demonstrated
their commitment to the mission of increasing diversity. Importantly,

22. New trends and an emerging number of young writers of color, including
Steppenwolf's internationally recognized Tarell Alvin McCraney, are moving the
diversity needle in a better direction, but this is still an ongoing challenge for the
American theatre community. Major regional theatres, Steppenwolf among
them, have continued to take notice and are aggressively pursuing a path to begin
to break this long-held pattern.

The Song of Jacob Zulu also represented one of Steppenwolf's first attempts to systemize the development and commissioning of original scripts from up-and-coming playwrights, as Simonson shares:

> We had just moved into the brand new space, which, of course, was a challenge. At the same time, the ensemble gave Randy (Arney) a directive to produce new plays. The ensemble came up with this crazy playwriting contest where they asked a writer to submit ten pages from the start of a play; then a full-blown outline of that play and a letter of intent. We got a mixed bag of submissions from Jon Robin Baitz (successful playwright of many plays including 1999's Steppenwolf production of *Mizlansky/Zilinsky or Schmucks*) all the way to a high-school student. The project was one of my first jobs when I became artistic associate. I sold Randy on the idea and said, "I can initiate a new play program if that's what you guys want. I've worked on new plays. I know how to do this." So, it was kind of dumped on me. There were sixty finalists that we had to sort through. We were supposed to whittle it down to ten and we would offer those people a commission of $2,000 to write the full-blown play and guarantee them that we would have a reading of that play in front of an audience.

Arney puts the scope of this project into perspective:

> We advertised in *American Theatre* magazine and other different places. Our ads said that "Steppenwolf is interested in a few good ideas for plays." We were going to take as many ideas as we could get. I think we got an insane number of ideas, like 500 or 1,000 or 1,500— who knows?

Simonson narrows it down:

> One was a submission by Tug Yourgrau who lived in Boston. He was a white South African expatriate US citizen who had court documents of this case that happened in South Africa in the 1980s regarding a young black terrorist. Tug imagined a sort of courtroom drama based on the real transcripts of the trial and he wanted Ladysmith Black Mambazo acting as a Greek chorus. Everyone on the committee reading these submissions loved Tug's idea. It was the top vote getter.
>   So, I'm thinking, "How are we going to get Ladysmith Black Mambazo to do this?" It was not far after Paul Simon's *Graceland* and

they were pretty hot. The other thing was the play was sort of a mess. It was just transcripts and Tug had never written a play before.

Arney:

I'd only known of Ladysmith Black Mambazo from Paul Simon's "Diamonds on the Soles of Her Shoes." But they sang with Paul and so we thought, "Fuck, let's ask them." Joseph Shabalala, the leader of the group, said, "My God, that boy was my cousin. He was the son of a preacher and I've been in that church. I've sung in that church." Joseph himself was a minister and said, "We're in." It was that easy. Tug had told him about this and Joseph felt that it was something that was ordained and that he should be involved, because it was literally his family.

Simonson:

We engaged in dialogue with Mambazo and committed to a weeklong workshop. At that point, Randy didn't have a director. I was knocking on his door and saying, "We've got to have a director. We have a South African singing group coming here and twelve other actors and they're expecting a director." One day Randy just came in and said, "You direct it." I was young and cocky at the time, so, I said, "Yes." We did a workshop and we staged the first ten minutes and people just loved it! So, we commissioned Tug to write the entire play and got a commitment from Ladysmith Black Mambazo.

The play was not a good play at that time. It needed a strong draft. Tug was green; he was not used to the collaboration that was required in making a new play. We enlisted Zakes Mokae, a successful South African-born actor, and John Mahoney and Al Wilder and a bunch of other really good Chicago actors to be in the cast. From one rehearsal to the next, there'd be blowups. It was not an ideal process. We had a lot on the line, and there was some bad behavior. We'd isolate Tug. We'd kick him out of the rehearsal room and tell him he wasn't allowed back in until a certain point. It was a trial by fire.

We did the workshop. Mambazo went back to South Africa, but they were committed to the production. While they were back in South Africa, Joseph's brother, Headman Shabalala, was shot by a white off-duty security officer because he thought Headman was driving drunk. He wasn't. Mambazo doesn't drink because they are Christian and sober.

Arney:

> We were afraid this might be off because Headman was killed. Joseph
> said, "All the more reason I want to do it. It's important we do it."
> When we gathered again it was without one of the two leaders of the
> group. I think it was Steve Eich that came up with the idea that we
> should do a benefit for Headman's family. Paul Simon came to
> Chicago and did a benefit in our theatre. He sat with his acoustic
> guitar and played and sang for 500 people and we raised money for
> Headman's family back in South Africa. This was all happening while
> we were moving forward with the show.

All of the pitfalls imaginable that could happen with new play
development, many obviously unexpected, were part of the process to
bring *The Song of Jacob Zulu* to the stage. But the play met with great
acclaim, as Richard Christiansen's assessment substantiates:

> *The Song of Jacob Zulu*, a play from South Africa that he (Simonson)
> picked, shaped and staged in a triumphant production, was his
> miracle. It became an instant hit last season in its sold-out engagement
> at Steppenwolf, developing such a momentum in its emotional
> mixture of drama and music that its eventual move to a larger
> audience was inevitable.

The play would go on to become the first show after *The Grapes of Wrath*
to make the move to Broadway, which Simonson describes:

> Steppenwolf had a very strong relationship with the Shuberts. We
> had produced *The Grapes of Wrath* with them and when General
> Manager Albert Poland saw *The Song of Jacob Zulu* and recommended
> it, the Shuberts committed to it on the spot.
>   We went to the Perth Arts Festival first with plans to go directly to
> Broadway. While we were in Perth, the first World Trade Center
> attack happened in the parking garage. Of course we were all very
> concerned. It put things in a different light because *The Song of Jacob
> Zulu* is a tragedy about a terrorist, Jacob Zulu, and you were supposed
> to be empathetic to this guy. The thing that strengthened the play
> is that you totally expect the theatre audience at the end of the play
> to understand this young black South African man, because he was
> given the shaft. The white establishment was really out to get him and
> did something devious to prove an innocent man guilty. But, that was

not the story. The story was that he actually did commit this act. The conclusion of the play was that he understood his own actions and atoned for his sins.

What we were trying to do was take a distanced approach to a tragedy like that and understand it in an artistic, emotional, and intellectual way. When you're dealing with a real-life incident like the World Trade Center, you're dealing with harsh, cold reality. Subsequently, we didn't have a long run in New York. At that time, Frank Rich's reviews in many ways dictated what went on Broadway, and what didn't go on Broadway.

The economics and longevity of runs of plays in the New York theatre at that time were directly affected by the power of Frank Rich's reviews, particularly non-musical work. Straight plays had only a limited audience to begin with due to the public demand for primarily musical entertainment on Broadway, so *The Song of Jacob Zulu* was already swimming upstream. Rich's *New York Times* review on March 25, 1993 included the following:

> The music of Ladysmith Black Mambazo rises to greet the audience as if sound were a tidal wave. These nine male a cappella singers from South Africa, who are at the heart of the new Broadway play *The Song of Jacob Zulu*, make music so insidiously penetrating that you seem to absorb it with your whole being rather than just the ears ...
>
> Because their unaccompanied music rises out of nowhere, the group's first entrance in *Jacob Zulu*, from a deep well far upstage at the Plymouth Theater, has a theatricality so stunning the rest of the evening is hard pressed to match it (and never does) ...
>
> The acting ensemble and pungently atmospheric production surrounding Mr. Freeman are of the same consistently high quality that Steppenwolf last brought to Broadway in *The Grapes of Wrath* ... Eric Simonson, a superb director making his New York debut, brings a choreographer's finesse to the stylized storytelling that is the most adventurous aspect of Mr. Yourgrau's script.

Simonson provides compelling insight into the New York theatre at the time and the Shuberts' philanthropic spirit:

> Today in 2015, everyone is fighting for the real estate on Broadway. That wasn't the case back then. When we went there, there were only about six or seven straight plays being produced that year. You had to

be given a rave review, not just a good review, but a rave review from Frank Rich to succeed on Broadway.

I think the Shuberts did a certain amount of producing that was, I won't say charity work, but it was really life-affirming work. *The Grapes of Wrath*, my first show with Steppenwolf, certainly fell under that category. I think the Shuberts knew they weren't going to make money with a cast of thirty people and scenery and everything. It sold at like 95 percent capacity a week and they still couldn't make enough money to make it run.

The story of *The Song of Jacob Zulu* in terms of the history of Steppenwolf is significant because it was the first attempt of the company to produce a new play developed in collaboration with a playwright solicited directly by the theatre. The fact that the play received national and international exposure furthered the theatre's mission through a story that again focused on the plight of the disenfranchised; in this case a South African black man. In many ways, *The Song of Jacob Zulu* set the course for pathways that the company would follow in their future with regards to a move towards greater diversity, continuing play development, and ongoing outreach to a broader audience.[23]

In the years that immediately followed, Steppenwolf kept a very busy schedule with many memorable productions and continued trips to Broadway and beyond. In May 1993, Steve Martin's first play in its world premiere, *Picasso at the Lapin Agile*, was the inaugural production in the Steppenwolf Studio Theatre and had an extended run. Later in the season, *The Rise and Fall of Little Voice* opened in Chicago and then moved to Broadway. These shows illustrated the company's growing status both in Hollywood and New York. Steppenwolf's nineteenth season included *A Clockwork Orange* in its American premiere with a visually stunning staging and adaptation by director Terry Kinney; *Nomathemba (Hope)*, another collaboration with Ladysmith Black

---

23. Another play developed through the process initiated by Simonson, *My Thing of Love*, by Alexandra Gersten and directed by Terry Kinney, immediately followed *The Song of Jacob Zulu* and also found its way to Broadway, although it was not billed as a Steppenwolf production. Kinney recalls:

> I was asked to direct it, but since the producers wanted to replace company members in the cast, I said no. As it turns out, they used two company members anyway (Laurie Metcalf and Tom Irwin), so that was a funny turn of events. They used our barely disguised set and our music with my blessing. There were no hard feelings.

Mambazo, directed by Eric Simonson; and William Faulkner's *As I Lay Dying*, adapted and directed by Frank Galati.

Without a doubt though, the most important event that occurred in 1995 was the establishment of an executive artistic board made up of the founding members of the company: Sinise, Perry, and Kinney, who in turn appointed Martha Lavey as the interim artistic director and successor to the immensely influential Randy Arney. Sinise:

> We had a discussion with Randy after opening the new theatre about the fact that it was a good time to re-energize the company by bringing in some new members. Martha was one of those that came in and she started as an actress. Martha was always very intelligent, knowledgeable, and practical.
>
> This was a very tricky time. We had built a big sprawling building and we weren't used to having that much size and space, and we needed to kind of get the building going, set the building on fire and get it rocking. There was a little bit of a difficult transition and we had to select a new artistic director at that point.

Randy Arney recalls this moment in time:

> I had brought Martha Lavey and Eric Simonson into the artistic office to be my artistic associates and we all worked closely together. In 1994 or 1995, Jeff, Gary, and Terry went to the board and asked that a committee of the three of them as founders be installed in the hierarchy of the structure of the theatre. For me, having done the job already from '87 to '95 without that entity, I thought it was a good opportunity and time for me to transition. I didn't know how I was going to be able to work as artistic director for this group of three, none of whom lived in Chicago anymore. At the time we used fax machines, and I said, "It would be like trying to run the theatre by fax."
>
> I felt really good about delivering the building at 1650 N. Halsted and the creation of *The Grapes of Wrath* and kind of having brought that to fruition. The company had stabilized a lot, and literally when I took the job there were not a lot of people home. By the time we built the new building, all of the sudden both people from out of town and in town felt like we were reinvested in the company, so it felt like a good transition time. Steve Eich and I had been talking informally to Jeff, Gary, and Terry frequently as founders of the theatre, but the idea of actually formalizing that in the structure where the artistic director would answer to the founders seemed kind of untenable to me. So it was time for me to move on.

Sinise continues on about the search for a new artistic director:

All of our artistic directors prior to that: H.E., Randy, Jeff, and me had been people that directed plays. We thought we were looking for another director from within the company. Martha hadn't done that. She wasn't a director, but we thought that she had great administrative skills and intelligence and could be nurtured and supported with regards to possibly taking over the company and moving us forward.

Terry and Jeff and I were a big part of that transition process and had ongoing discussions with our board members. We were always looking for folks from inside the company. That's all we ever knew and that's all we ever thought we needed. Martha and I discussed the possibility of whether or not she would be interested in considering being a candidate for the job. She was a little surprised, but also interested, because she hadn't really thought much about it and had never done anything like that before.

The thing that our artistic directors have now that we didn't have back in the early days was the overall experience of the theatre behind them. Everything we did in the 1970s and 1980s, and then building the theatre was all brand new. We do many things now that we've done frequently in the past, but we've learned from our mistakes and a lot along the way about what works and what doesn't work. We were able to provide a blueprint when Martha came in to work, some guidelines, so things could be achieved early on in her tenure. For the first ten years or so she relied more on some of the folks that had been there before, and in the last ten years she's relied on her immediate allies— her confidants that had been cultivated around her artistic directorship; just like I had mine, and Randy had his. You develop a circle of folks that are helping you to achieve what needs to be achieved.

Martha Lavey also shares her perspective:

Randy built the theatre into a place that he had never really originally signed on for. Whether it was taking *The Grapes of Wrath* to Broadway or the advent of the building of our theatre complex in 1991. It completely changed what the job of the artistic director was. That coincided with this diaspora of the ensemble. They had had big success in New York with *True West* and *Balm in Gilead*. The individual actors, the original members of the company, started to seek their careers in places like New York and Los Angeles. Randy and his artistic brain trust now faced new demands, primary of which was to fill a 500-seat theatre, and there was no infrastructure in the theatre to support him. He didn't have an artistic staff in the same way that we do now. That's what's developed over time and so I think Randy concluded his desire to do that job.

Gary, Jeff, and Terry stepped in because they felt the theatre was not in a place artistically that they felt it should be. They decided it was up to them to choose the next artistic director because that had always come from within the ensemble. I always say that the learning curve on the culture of Steppenwolf was deeper than the learning curve on being the artistic director.

They knew that I knew the culture, which was very important to them. I think Frank (Galati) was probably an important voice as they were making that decision. I think he endorsed me. So, I was put in the chair and then ever after. I felt like they gave me a kind of charter. They wanted to engage the ensemble and make the theatre more outward facing. It had become too insular. Gary said, "Look, if you build a project around an actor that's a little shakier proposition than to build it around a director, so we have to start working with a bigger pool of directors. And, we need to create a play development program. We should have that strength." That was what led to Anna D. Shapiro being hired to be the director of the New Plays Lab.

The shift in leadership was indeed a bit rocky, but history shows that it has worked out well for all involved. Randy Arney went on to become the artistic director of the Geffen Playhouse in 1999 and has continued to be a frequent contributor at Steppenwolf.[24]

On July 22, 1996, Steppenwolf celebrated its twentieth anniversary. This moment in time was attached to so many of the events from the earlier history of the company. *Molly Sweeney* by Brian Friel was playing on the Mainstage, which harkened back to Sinise and Perry's first directing project at Highland Park High School of Friel's *Philadelphia, Here I Come!*; another Sinise-directed production of a Sam Shepard play, *Buried Child*, had closed an enthusiastically received Broadway run just a few weeks earlier, which surprisingly was the first run of a Shepard play on Broadway. The twentieth season closed with John

24. Arney's Steppenwolf productions include *The Beauty Queen of Leenane* by Martin McDonagh (1999), *I Just Stopped by to See the Man* by Stephen Jeffreys (2002), *The Seafarer* by Conor McPherson (2008), and *Slowgirl* by Greg Pierce and featuring William Petersen (2013), some of which have had follow-up runs at the Geffen.

Malkovich's return to the Steppenwolf stage after a four-year absence as the sexually ravenous main character in *The Libertine* by Stephen Jeffreys and directed by Terry Johnson. In his *Dramatic Publishing* introduction to the play, Jeffreys had this to say about working with Malkovich, and by extension the Steppenwolf collaborative process:

> My play *The Libertine* is about John Wilmot, second Earl of Rochester, who was the leading figure at the court of Charles II. Rochester is now recognized as one of the major poets of the 17th century, but in his own lifetime his career as a womanizer, drinker, atheist, pornographer and rebel gained him more attention than his serious writing ...
>
> The American premiere of *The Libertine* was given in 1996 by Steppenwolf with John Malkovich in the lead role. Malkovich, with his immense stage presence and his flair for making dangerous choices, was an ideal Rochester, but from a playwright's point of view the most interesting feature of working with him was his ability to help refine the text in the rehearsal room ... I was unhappy with the second half of the play and eager to make changes ... it involved a difficult gear change for the lead actor in the middle ... I rewrote the scene twice during rehearsals (and discovered Malkovich's underexploited gift for zany comedy) ... After the second preview, John told me he had given it his best shot but it wasn't going to work and could I rewrite the middle of the second act by tomorrow? This I did and was deeply impressed to see Malkovich and the Steppenwolf Company take the new material in front of an audience after a single rehearsal.

Sadly, this tour-de-force performance would be the last that Malkovich would grace the Steppenwolf stage with for another eleven years, when he would return in another collaboration with playwright Jeffreys and director Johnson on *Lost Land*. *The Libertine* also represented ensemble member Martha Plimpton's first work with the company.[25]

Steppenwolf needed to develop stronger business systems throughout the 1990s in response to the company's growing financial obligations. Sadly, subscription numbers had begun to fall, impacted by overall industry dynamics and in part by a fateful production in February of 1993 of Arthur Kopit's *Road to Nirvana*, a dark scatological comedy

25. Plimpton had already had a much-celebrated film career.

about the business of Hollywood. The play's harsh tone proved upsetting to many of the longtime Steppenwolf faithful, leading to residual damage to the theatre's short-term reputation.[26]

Fortunately, the artistic shift in leadership that was in process was being matched step-for-step on the business side. The hiring of former managing director Tim Evans was one of the first changes and helped to right the ship. Evans provides the details:

> In late '91, Randy and Steve Eich called me and said, "Well, we've got a little problem. We've opened the theatre with about 19,000 or so subscribers, because everybody wanted to come to the new building. And, in less than 18 months, we're down to 12,000 subscribers. Everybody's freaking out. Do you want to come and take on marketing?" I said, "Of course, that would be fantastic." I went back in spring of '92 and became director of marketing, audience development, and communications.

Processes for rebranding the theatre's image and growing the staff, which numbered only sixteen, were initiated to help revitalize the theatre and to poise it for growth that could match the demands of the physical space, as well as the expectations of a national and international audience. Shortly after Evans's hiring and Martha Lavey being instituted as the new artistic director, Stephen B. Eich moved on to manage subsequent productions of *Picasso at the Lapin Agile*, so a national search was commenced for a new managing director, which would become Michael Gennaro. *Variety* wrote on October 23, 1995:

> Son of Broadway choreographer Peter Gennaro, he won out over 59 other candidates for the chief business position at one of the nation's leading theaters. Steppenwolf is operating in the black, so Gennaro won't immediately face a financial crisis ...
>
> Gennaro talks about "re-energizing the company and re-engaging" with the rest of the theater community. As Steppenwolf's star has risen on the national and international scene over the last 20 years, the

26. Tracy Letts, an understudy for *Road to Nirvana*, working in what was his first Mainstage Steppenwolf experience recalls that "People were going to the ushers after the play, ripping up their programs and throwing them in the ushers' faces. They lost thousands of subscribers because of that show is what I was told."

company severed most contact with other Chicago theater companies
… But that attitude is changing, Gennaro says. Following the opening
night of its current production of *Buried Child* Steppenwolf threw a
party for the entire Chicago theater community …

Jeff Perry, one of the company's founders echoed the greater meaning of
this inclusiveness:

> These years were marked by the theatre committing itself to trying to
> create repeatable relationships with playwrights and with mentorship
> of fellow Chicago theatres. It was really a "pay-it-forward" thing that
> we had felt from Sheldon Patinkin and Bernie and Jane Sahlins, and
> Joyce Sloane at Second City.

Gennaro and Evans, with input from Lavey, the board, and staff, moved
forward with an aggressive outreach plan building on initiatives Evans
had already begun. Gennaro:

> I believe I was the first managing director from outside of the
> company. They wanted someone who had experience and who could
> help mentor Martha in becoming an artistic director. Right around
> the time I was getting there, they had just done a five-year strategic
> plan that John Fox, who subsequently became board chair, had
> created. Within two years Martha and I had blown past everything
> that was in the strategic plan, so we said, "Well, we'll just keep going."

Evans fills in a few of the details:

> I started work with some new designers and tried to reinvent the
> brand. We came up with this sort of rock and roll "in-your-face" stuff
> and I think it helped pick it up. We ran with that for about five or six
> years. By the time I left that chair to do other things in the organization,
> we had over 24,000 subscribers. There were some bumps and dips,
> but ultimately we sort of reinvented the ensemble.
>
> A couple of things that we did were to create essentially an
> imperative for all press people to refer to Joan Allen as "Steppenwolf
> ensemble member Joan Allen" and John as "Steppenwolf ensemble
> member John Malkovich" etc. We pounded that, and suddenly we
> saw it in print when these guys were doing something outside of
> Steppenwolf. You still see it to this day, so that was a conditioning that
> somehow worked. Promoting the celebrity of the ensemble coupled

with promoting the "in-your-face" style of theatre that Steppenwolf was known for really helped us at the time.

Gennaro continues:

> The thing that changed everything was the dynamic of the way the organization was run. Martha and I had a seamless relationship. She picked the plays and put the cast together and the directors and everything, but we both had involvement in all the areas of the theatre. She weighed in on marketing. We talked together about development. My goal was to bring some kind of "best practices" into the theatre as a business model.
>
> In my first eighteen months we hired five more people in development. We spent a lot of time upgrading the business mindset of the organization and we had an extraordinary staff. Our board was made up of a lot of entrepreneurs who were very smart about business. Steppenwolf has the best board I have ever worked with, including Bruce Sagan and John Fox, who said at a board meeting, "We're very fortunate that this place is as successful as it is and our job now is to stay out of Martha and Michael's way." People like Bruce Sagan just thought big.
>
> When I got there we had the theatre building and the lot next door, but shortly thereafter, we acquired the parking garage and created The Garage space as a source of revenue due to Bruce's forward thinking. Then it was the building on the corner, which ultimately housed business offices and the Yondorf Rehearsal Hall upstairs. It was a series of really smart moves by really smart people to acquire real estate at a time when that area was not exactly a hot spot where people wanted to be.
>
> It's pretty unique for an arts organization like Steppenwolf to own their real estate. The theatre at 1650 N. Halsted cost about $8.5 million. You could never build that space right now for that kind of money. Part of that money had come from bonding, so after I had been there about two years, Bruce said, "You know what we should do? I bet we can get more money from bonds and pay the same debt service and we'll use that money to buy The Garage and whatever else."

Efforts to energize the building with activities and special events that went beyond the traditional subscription season began to help increase the audience size. Evans:

I presented Michael and Martha with the idea of "Let's do some stuff that's really audience development." We started the *Traffic* series using non-theatrical performers that would come to the theatre. We did all of the *Traffic* shows on Monday nights on the Mainstage. The first two or three years we did the *Traffic* series it was very jazz-heavy. The goal was to have more activity in the theatre. We wanted to bring some non-theatrical audience to the theatre that had never been in the space before. My theory was that if they could find their way to the theatre, they'll come back to see something else, and something theatrical. I think we converted almost 30 percent of the *Traffic* audience, who became regular patrons at Steppenwolf Theatre.

T Bone Burnett came in a couple of times and performed once with Sam Shepard. Sam read him some of his work and T Bone underscored it. Ensemble member Jim True-Frost did an evening of poetry and music. We had award-winning poets, writers like Don DeLillo and Frank McCourt and others. They didn't get paid much, but they got to work on our stage and the Steppenwolf name meant something to them. That was T Bone's thing: "Oh yeah, Steppenwolf's cool. I'll go there." And we had Studs Terkel as well.

In 1998, we got invited to the Clinton White House to receive the Medal of Honor—a very prestigious honor. I was doing press at the time, so I got a chance to do all sorts of national press around the Award, which was great. We had our own little section in *Variety*, a *New York Times* story, and stories from the London press.

The addition of the *Traffic* series, the marketing impact of the Medal of Honor, and other audience development and fundraising efforts helped the theatre through a difficult transition from a business standpoint, laid a foundation for sustained growth of the subscription base, and increased corporate and private donor support. Additionally, the performers in the *Traffic* series furthered the goal of bringing greater diversity to the theatre in both audience and performers. Special event participants during this period included Kahil El'zabar, Ntozake Shange, Mort Sahl, Garrison Keillor, Dr. John, Andrea Marcovicci, Elaine Stritch, Bill Irwin, and others; as well as jazz greats Von Freeman, Franz Jackson, Archie Shepp, Mark Isham, and Delta Blues guitarist Honeyboy Edwards, and the legendary Buddy Guy.

Gennaro's comments powerfully capture the impact of Martha Lavey and her ability to diplomatically and strongly navigate through what had been a difficult moment in Steppenwolf history:

Martha is without question the smartest person I have ever met. With all due respect, there was a tremendous insularity to the company when she and I got there. You had the driving force of Gary, Jeff, and Terry as the so-called "brothers," as we affectionately called them, and Martha broke through that insularity by embracing and engaging outside artists. She was able to expand the reach and the spirit of what Gary, Jeff, and Terry had first created, and she also brought an extreme intelligence to the choice of material and a tremendous rigor in terms of developing directors and writers. Martha nurtured an openness to the Chicago theatre community and became the matriarch of Chicago theatre. Her impact on Steppenwolf and beyond is as big as you can possibly imagine.

Artistically, the theatre continued to present new and exciting work in the late nineties and into the new millennium with many trips to both Broadway and international festivals and venues, which included a Tony Award for Best Revival of a Play for *One Flew Over the Cuckoo's Nest*, directed by Terry Kinney and featuring Gary Sinise and Amy Morton.

The development of the New Plays Lab and particularly the addition to the company of three dynamic female artists, directors Tina Landau and Anna D. Shapiro, and actress-turned-director Amy Morton—coupled with Martha Lavey's increased assertiveness as artistic director—began to change the culture of Steppenwolf. The company went from being exclusively an actor-centered company to one focused on directors as well, while simultaneously putting a strong eye to new play development. Though acting remained the cornerstone of the company's mission, this shift reaped both immediate and long-term benefits to the artistic side of the theatre.[27]

Tina Landau's first production with Steppenwolf, Charles Mee's *Time to Burn*, a reimagined version of Maxim Gorki's classic *The Lower Depths*, in 1997 positioned her as a meaningful force and trendsetter within the ensemble. She followed *Time to Burn* just nine months later

27. This broadening of the Steppenwolf culture separated the company from the fateful path of one of its inspirations, the Group Theatre. Whereas the Group suffered a mass exodus of its ensemble to Hollywood, most significantly playwright Clifford Odets, which ultimately was a death knell for their existence, Steppenwolf's constantly evolving culture and innovation sustained them well beyond the Group's ten-year lifespan.

with *Space*, an original play she wrote and directed. Landau shares a bit about her approach to the creation of a project such as *Space*:

> I'm working at my best when I'm working not only as a creator but also as an editor who collects things, arranges them together and shapes them. It's an odd way—an alternative form of authorship that constructs moments that are put in a series, that form dramatic events, which become part of an overall story. I have the most fun, get the best work out of my collaborators, and find the most unexpected choices when I can create an environment where everyone has a sense of their own possibility and is generating ideas and materials. There's no sense of something being right or wrong or appropriate or not. Anything is possible and it all gets created and laid out and made into a mess on the floor, and then I'm left with, hopefully, a whole range of inspired choices that have come not only from myself but from others and I put it together in some form.

Landau's use of Viewpoints, a theatrical training methodology inspired by choreographer Mary Overlie and created by Anne Bogart and Landau, is a central element of much of her work. The Viewpoints system encourages physical work with the ultimate goal of increasing the actors' openness, awareness and spontaneity. This theoretical and spontaneous approach meshed well with many in the ensemble and led them to some incredible results, as Landau shares:

> Viewpoints provided a way for me to name things that in some form, however unconscious or undeveloped, I was doing and that everyone does. It wasn't about learning something new as much as bringing more into consciousness something that was of our instincts anyway.
>
> On *Time to Burn*, my first show at Steppenwolf, I remember thinking I am headed for disaster. I am going to work at a company that is renowned for its kitchen-sink naturalism, and they are interested in psychology and props and realism, and I am coming in with something that's asking them to listen and express—not with text and not with character—but with their bodies and with time and with space. It's oil and water. I'd heard a story about Rondi Reed who was in a play previously with a director who apparently was asking them to work on gestures. This wasn't Viewpoints-related. It was just some kind of technique of using gestural work. Rondi threw down her script and walked out of a rehearsal declaring, "I don't do gestures." I had simply heard that as lore, so I was walking in with the terror of Rondi looming behind me.

Landau continues with two specific production-based stories that capture the growing allure of the Viewpoints work to the ensemble.

> In *Time to Burn*, I did some work the first couple days and on maybe the third or fourth day we were sitting and talking and Mike Nussbaum raised his hand and said, "I'd like to say something about Viewpoints." I thought, "Oh no, here we go." Even though Mike wasn't an official ensemble member, he is a Chicago legend. He said, "I just want to say in all of my many years of doing theatre, I've never learned so much in two or three days and I am living proof that you can teach an old dog new tricks."
>
> The following year I went through the same terror again when I did *Space*. In an early Viewpoints session I looked around and suddenly Bob Breuler had an orange that he was smashing into his head and Amy Morton was standing about forty feet from a wall and running into it full force and splatting her body against it. I remember those two things happening concurrently and thinking, "They've surrendered." Now the ensemble members across the board have taken to Viewpoints like fish to water. Viewpoints to me is not "the way"; it is "a way." Text table work is a way. Sense memory is a way. Meisner is a way. What Steppenwolf was doing and what Viewpoints brought to the table had exactly the same goals. They were all committed to providing tools for finding truth on stage and spontaneity and boldness and extreme listening.

Landau's 2002 production of William Saroyan's *The Time of Your Life* represented a crowning achievement of her work and established her as a major artistic influence for Steppenwolf. Yasen Peyankov and Tracy Letts, who would also become influential contributors to the ensemble, officially joined the company in 2002. Peyankov would play a role in *The Time of Your Life*, which gained recognition for its ensemble connection and scenic beauty. The staging of Saroyan's masterpiece was emblematic of the expansive work the company was producing with regularity during this very active time in the theatre's history. Michael Phillips's *Chicago Tribune* review from September 27, 2002 captured Landau's special expertise:

> A professor of atmospheric chemistry was among this week's MacArthur Genius Grant recipients. Not to take anything away from the man who got the MacArthur, Steppenwolf Theatre's gorgeously realized revival of the 1939 William Saroyan saloon play *The Time of Your Life* suggests that director Tina Landau is, in the actual terms, a

first-rate chemist herself ... Watching her production is like walking into a Thomas Hart Benton mural, expanded and exploded into three dimensions.

Chris Jones's *Variety* review from October 2, 2002 added more accolades:

Steppenwolf's legendary acting prowess is firing on all cylinders here ... The taciturn (Jeff) Perry; one of the theater's co-founders is simply extraordinary in the lead role of Joe. Amy Morton (of *One Flew Over the Cuckoo's Nest*) is equally powerful in a small role. The show's dreamy sensibility requires an audience with patience willing to ponder quiet truths, but this is Steppenwolf's best production in quite some time—and again demonstrates Landau is at her best when reinvigorating serious American fare.

Jeff Perry gives an insider's take:

The Time of Your Life demonstrated Tina's skill set for creating large ensemble work, and further, a universe that unearthed Saroyan's original intent of creating a jazz rumination on how we might best live. In Tina's hands, a play historically considered overly sentimental, the author's Armenian-American dream reality, naturalism, and melodrama happily commingled into this inner peace that was deeply spiritual and emotional.

Not only was Tina Landau securing her place in the company's ever-changing ethos; simultaneously Amy Morton was doing the same as she began her path to becoming one of Steppenwolf's—and America's—leading directors. Morton's direction of productions such as Jon Robin Baitz's *Mizlansky/Zilinsky or Schmucks* (1999), David Mamet's *Glengarry Glen Ross* (2001), ensemble member Bruce Norris's *We All Went Down to Amsterdam* (2003), Suzan-Lori Parks' *Topdog/Underdog* (2003), Ronald Harwood's *The Dresser* (2004), and others demonstrated her ability to work on wide-ranging material. At the same time, Anna D. Shapiro was carving out her niche and honing her directorial chops in the New Plays Lab. Her emergence from the Garage Theatre to become a Tony Award-winning director, and eventually artistic director of Steppenwolf, rivals the story of Steppenwolf's rise from a church basement.

The New Plays Lab grew to become one of the great examples of the foresight of Steppenwolf leaders and continues to add a sense of strength and longevity to the company's story. The path that the New Plays Lab's origination would follow was unclear and had to be carefully crafted, as former literary manager and dramaturg Michele Volansky reflects:

> By the time I started, the notion of the New Plays Lab had already begun. Anna had not finalized the writers in our initial conversation. My specific role was still developing. Firstly, what was I actually going to be doing in a full-time capacity? Anna and I talked about commissioning, literary management and acquisition, processing and responding to plays, and dramaturgy of the development of plays, and then the research aspect of dramaturgy in the rehearsal room through the course of the season and, secondly, infrastructural and dramaturgical support for Anna for the New Plays Lab. It's pretty safe to say the first couple months were about trying to figure out what the hell we were doing. The constant was Phyllis Schuringa, who had been there with Steve and Randy as casting director. She provided stability.
>
> Anna had come right from Yale and Martha had just stepped into her position, and I had just come from Actors Theatre of Louisville. Plays were coming in from all different angles and we were trying to create a system that allowed the ones that really needed to get to Martha to get to her, and then identify other plays for more emerging writers through the New Plays Lab, while also trying to figure out what the relationship truly was between the New Plays Lab and the regular season.
>
> We wanted to expand the notion of what an ensemble could do beyond simply actors. Steppenwolf hadn't yet figured out how to cultivate writers in the same way that they cultivated actors, and, to a certain extent, directors. The creation of the New Plays Lab and the hiring of a dramaturg or a literary manager represented a concerted expansion of what the company wanted to be. Clearly, the outcomes have been enormous between Bruce Norris and Tracy Letts and so on. Jeff Perry said, "You guys planted the seeds."

Two other noteworthy developments occurred during this time. The first was the establishment of The School at Steppenwolf in 1998 as a means to train students in methods of ensemble development and scene/text study. The intense ten-week summer program auditions students across the country, and offers those who are accepted a variety of training methodologies, admission to all the shows at Steppenwolf, and interactions with ensemble members both in and out of class.[28] Jeff Perry described the School's origins on the web video blog *Gatekeepers* with Isaac Simpson:

> I was on *Nash Bridges*, but I was missing my theatre roots at that moment deeply. I called Martha Lavey, Anna D. Shapiro, and one of Steppenwolf's great mentors, Sheldon Patinkin. I said, "You guys, we all love teaching. Could we impart something authentic about the collegial, communal way of actors helping each other get better through ensemble work that has been at the base of why Steppenwolf exists?" Can we come up with methods, practices, repeatable teachable behavior, so that we could help students to explore the greatest number of possibilities through rigorous text analysis and learn to trust their instincts and live "in the moment"? The core lesson being that present tense communication between two or more people onstage is where the story is most revealed.

The second significant event was the hiring of David Hawkanson as executive director in 2003 as a replacement for Michael Gennaro, who moved on to Goodspeed Musicals in East Haddam, Connecticut. Hawkanson brought a wealth of experience to the business leadership of the theatre, having come from the Guthrie Theatre and the Hartford Stage Company. Hawkanson would prove influential in the moving of productions to New York and other venues, most notably *August: Osage County*.

Steppenwolf's landmark thirtieth anniversary season was the first in the company's long history to feature a schedule of all new plays. The theatre had successfully moved from being an exclusively actor-based theatre to that of a theatre shaped by pioneering directors and, most importantly, new playwrights. The stage was firmly set for something special as Steppenwolf entered their thirty-first season.

Ensemble member Tracy Letts's seminal play, *August: Osage County*, provided Steppenwolf with a piece that coalesced all of the burgeoning elements that the theatre had been developing through the late nineties. *August: Osage County* was an original play, written by a company

28. The School at Steppenwolf continues to thrive in Chicago, and its California incarnation Steppenwolf Classes West, although no longer directly affiliated with the theatre, continues year-round with a variety of individual classes, as well as summer intensives working with the California State University system.

member with the company's actors in mind, that played to the Steppenwolf strength of ensemble performance. Furthermore, it was directed by an ensemble member, Anna D. Shapiro, whose sensibility had been built on the history of Steppenwolf and a deep connection to the process of new play development. *August: Osage County*'s importance as a play stems from the universality of its message about conflicted family dynamics. It recalls great American classics that deal with similar themes such as *Death of a Salesman, The Glass Menagerie, Long Day's Journey into Night,* and countless others. The fact that this play was written relatively near to the events of 9/11 changes the nature of how the play was received by audiences, who were now seeing the world and theatrical work through a lens of heightened intensity. The sometimes chaotic no-holds-barred style of Letts's script captured not only family forces at play, but somehow what audiences were feeling in a much broader context.

Director Anna D. Shapiro shares her impressions upon reading the play for the first time:

> You just kicked up about ten levels working with these people at Steppenwolf. When *August* happened, Tracy sent me the play. It was only the first two acts and a sketch of a third act. It was so thick. I thought, "OK, I'll start reading it and fall asleep and then finish it tomorrow." I started reading it and couldn't put it down. I was astonished. I've known Tracy since we were eighteen years old. I called him and said, "You've written an incredible play and I have no idea who you are. I don't know where this came from." It was so shocking to me. It needed a lot of work, because it was so big. But, obviously we were going to do it.

Amy Morton, who originated the key role of the oldest daughter, Barbara, tells the story of her first encounter with *August: Osage County*:

> Tracy walked into the offices with the play. He's a very neat guy and was shuffling the papers to make them perfectly square because he was about to give this thick play to Martha. Anna got a copy—I got a copy—Martha got a copy and we all went away to our homes. I was thinking, "Great. I'll read this, but it's going to take me a week." One sitting. I was just floored. I've never seen that in a first draft ever.
>
> Working on *August: Osage County* was an experience that any actor in the entire universe would want to have and I got to have it. I remember saying to somebody at the *New York Times* or something

after it became this huge hit, "This is the epitome of my career. It's all downhill after this, but in a good way."

Shapiro speaks about the challenges of casting:

Nobody who did the roles that they did were doing the roles they were originally supposed to do. Tracy wrote the Amy [Morton] part of Barbara for Laurie [Metcalf] and the Sally [Murphy] part for Amy. Laurie said, "I don't want to play that part. I want to play the mom." Laurie is a friend of mine and me having to tell her, "I like you, but you can't play her, she's seventy years old. She should be seventy-five years old." She said, "I can play seventy-five years old." I said, "What, are you crazy?" It was a real watershed moment for me in terms of the kinds of work that I wanted to do versus the kind of work that had inspired me.

I remember having the conversation with Martha about Laurie. She said, "You know she'd be great in it." I said, "Well, yeah, she could play Willie Loman if she wanted to, but that's not the discussion." Martha said, "The theatre is based on this—this is what they did." I said, "They were in a little black box theatre with eighty-seven seats or something when they started. It's not a Christmas pageant at a high school." I remember saying that sentence to Martha. It was the first time I feel like I ever really stood up for myself. I want to say that I think Laurie Metcalf is probably the greatest actor in the world. She's just like from a whole other world. I tell her she's got an acting chip at the base of her skull.

Can you imagine anyone other than Amy? Can you imagine anyone other than Sally? Can you imagine anyone other than Ian [Barford] or Deanna [Dunagan]? Rondi [Reed] said "No" to Mattie Fae about four times. This thing that looked so effortless was not that way in the casting process. We agonized over it.

We did a couple of big workshops of it, and finally, into rehearsal, I've never been more prepared. I had never felt so confident. I was so happy to be in there every day even though by the time it went into production, the third act wasn't right. We would joke in rehearsal about "Would we lose more people between Act One and Act Two or between Act Two and Act Three?" We knew we had a disaster on our hands. The fucking thing was three hours and forty-five minutes at one point. Ian started saying, "I don't know, you guys. I think people are going to come back and see it more than once." He could feel it. Some of us couldn't feel it.

It was complicated for me. I mean I understand its place in the theatre's history. I understand its place in people's experience. I realize that I had participated in making something here that had the impact on other people that the shit they had made before had had on me. That sequencing is really intense when you realize that, but I had a lot of ambivalent feelings about it.

Erica Daniels, casting director adds:

August: Osage County, which people constantly say was such magical casting, was recast about a week before the first rehearsal. We thought we had Chelcie Ross as Beverly and Mike Shannon as Little Charles, but they both got movies, so we had to think very quickly. We went right to the ensemble with Ian for Little Charles. Rondi almost wasn't available for the show. She was in *Wicked* and I had been tracking that, but she said, "I can't get out." Literally the day I was going to somebody else with an offer, she called and had been put on a three-month hiatus. It was one of those magical moments that we got this magical cast, but who knew? Tracy was really excited about the notion of his dad playing Beverly.

Tracy Letts follows up on the "magical moment" with the story of casting his father Dennis as the patriarch Beverly in the show:

Anna and Ian both started talking to me about my dad. I said, "I got to think about that. This play is a big deal. It's a big gesture in my life and it's weird to think about having your father in your work space." I didn't think about it for very long—maybe two days. I sat and pondered the great John Waters quote: "Anybody over the age of thirty still fighting with their parents is an asshole." I really subscribe to that, so I thought, "Yeah, I think I can."

My dad was a great man and I love him dearly, but he also could be difficult in his own ways. I called him and thought there was a chance that Dad might hear the offer and think, "Boy, that's too challenging. I'm seventy-two years old and I'm not up for a challenge like that right now in my life." I said, "Dad, I've written this play." Dad had read the play at that point and I said, "I wonder if you would be interested in coming here to Chicago and playing this part in the play." He said, "Yes." No hesitation. I was a little surprised at how quickly he jumped at it. I was delighted. I have to say it was the right call.

Daniels continues:

> Tracy Letts knows his instincts and his plays and I certainly wasn't
> going to stand in his way if he thought his dad could do it. Dennis
> was just the king of men—the loveliest of men and a wonderful actor.
> It's just one of those weird, random things.
>
> Deanna didn't want to play Violet. We really had to talk her into
> that over three or four weeks. She just knew the role was going to be
> so difficult and challenging. It wasn't that she didn't want to try to
> take it on. It was more like, "Oh my gosh, I don't know if I can do this
> eight performances a week."

Deanna Dunagan responds to Daniels's comments:

> The reason I finally decided to take the role was because I thought, "I
> can do anything for two months." The passage that terrified me was
> the description of the fight between Violet and Barbara at the end of
> Act Two. They roll around. They crash through the French doors,
> rolling around on top of each other. Barbara pulls her hair out and
> I thought, "There's no way in the world I can do that." I also didn't
> know how people on pills acted. I had never been around anybody on
> pills. I had been around stoned people. I had been around drunken
> people. But pills?

Daniels:

> I don't think we thought that we were going to go to Deanna for the
> role and then she did the reading and we felt, "Oh my God. We have
> to go to Deanna." It was like as plain as day after her reading. The role
> of Violet just came alive on her.

Dunagan:

> We did the first reading and between the acts I paced around. People
> were avoiding my gaze and looking at the ground. They weren't really
> talking to me and I was terribly emotionally upset by it. Afterward,
> they asked if I would stay and discuss it. I said, "I've got another show
> and this is my only day off and I just can't." It was true, but it was also
> true I didn't want to talk about it because I found it so disturbing, so
> vicious. I walked downstairs and Anna was at the bottom and said,
> "You're a rock star." It was very gratifying. So then I thought with
> great trepidation, "Oh great. I'm excited." There was never a thought

when we started rehearsing that it was going to do anything but close at the end of the summer and that it would be just another Steppenwolf season show.

The first time I ever heard the Tony Award mentioned was from a friend of mine named Tracy Arnold. It had already been decided we were going to Broadway. After seeing the show, Tracy hugged me and whispered in my ear, "You're going to win the Tony." And that was the first time I'd ever heard it mentioned. The first time I'd ever even dreamed it.

Despite her reservations, Dunagan would go to New York where she did indeed garner the 2008 Tony Award for Best Actress for her portrayal of the family matriarch Violet, competing against her onstage daughter Amy Morton.

The cast for *August: Osage County* was filled out with the greatest percentage of ensemble members and cumulative experience ever assembled in a Steppenwolf-produced show: Morton, Rondi Reed, Francis Guinan, Jeff Perry, Ian Barford, Sally Murphy, Mariann Mayberry, and Rick Snyder. Although Dunagan was not an official member of the company, her résumé included many shows with Steppenwolf, which made her something of a surrogate ensemble member. Dennis Letts had his unique connection, and Kimberly Guerrero, a wonderful Native American actress, brought a certain Oklahoman sensibility to the crucial role of Johnna. Non-ensemble members filled two other smaller roles, but this group brought years of shared experience to the development of the play, which paid particular dividends in the rehearsal room. Tracy Letts recalls Shapiro's reflection on the impact of his father and Guerrero:

Anna said a very smart thing about the beginning of the play: "This play isn't set in Chicago; it's set in Oklahoma. The beautiful thing about this prologue is that we get to start with your dad and Kimberly Guerrero, who grew up thirty miles away from you and your family in southeastern Oklahoma. We showed that to our Chicago audience and that was their window into this world. And then we open that up and start bringing in Rondi (Reed) and Fran (Guinan) and the people they know, and we see them now inhabiting the world that your father and Kim have established." That's the way it worked. It was really beautiful.

My dad was not a writer, but he was a great editor. So to have him working on my play, not only as an actor, but also as a sort of literary advisor, was huge. He played a big part in certain lines, by just coming up and sort of whispering in my ear, and saying, "I think maybe you'd be better served if you cut this line; or this turn of phrase doesn't sound quite right." He had a lot to do with honing the material; however, once when he was just about to do his scene, he stopped at the desk where I was sitting with Anna and said, "Right here where it says 'children,' I'm going to say 'girls,' all right?" I said, "No, actually, it's not all right." Dad turned around and says, "Oh, oh." Kind of like, "Oh, here's the young man standing up to me." He goes up and does it the way I said. About a week or two weeks later, he came back to me and said, "You were right about that." It was a great father–son moment.

While rehearsals were progressing, Shapiro's Yale School of Drama classmate, scenic designer Todd Rosenthal, was hard at work creating the set for *August: Osage County*. Legendary director Mike Nichols, when asked about Joseph Mielziner's famous set for the original production of Arthur Miller's *Death of a Salesman*, commented, "The set is intimately connected with the way the play develops. It's everything and nothing." Rosenthal's setting for *August: Osage County* had much the same type of "selective realism" in its styling, as the following story indicates, and once again providence played a role in what would be his Tony Award-winning scenic design:

The thing about *August: Osage County* was that it was still in process. Tracy wanted to wait until the workshop to really solidify how the set functioned and originally he wanted a full nine-room house that you just pull away the side and look into. We needed to give audience access to those rooms, which is why we eventually just spewed the rooms out in front of the house. The problem with that whole process was that the workshop was two weeks before we had to submit the final drawings. So, we cranked that show out in a very short time. It was one of the fastest design processes I've ever had. But, sometimes when you crank something out, you don't think about it. You just do it. My assistant at the time Kevin Depinet and I pretty much co-designed the show, because I would say, "Listen, you go ahead and do this model based on this sketch. You bring it back to me. I'll look at it and we'll talk about it."

This exchange offers an example of the trust necessary between artists that can happen not only on the performance side, but also in technical deliberations in a collaborative process.[29] Rosenthal continues:

29. This recalls the moment during *The Grapes of Wrath* when Sinise and Kinney suggested something similar to playwright Galati during the extensive cutting process that occurred.

We finally got the design to where we liked it, but Martha thought it was way overdone. Initially, I agreed with her instincts, because I had thought that the scale of the event was not to the scale of the house. It felt like a small domestic play to me at first, but I ultimately realized that wasn't true. When you saw it on Broadway, it filled the theatre.

We designed this house and brought it to the shop and the response was, "No way—This is way over budget." We had to start building on Monday and this was Friday, so I just started pulling pieces of the model away and ripping walls away. And, all of the sudden, I'm looking at this skeleton of a house, that looked a lot more interesting. The impetus for simplifying it was budgetary, but by removing all these pieces, it became this kind of white skeleton of a house which had the Gothic elements which I thought were important. It also felt like a dolls' house, which had this kind of juxtaposition of the gothic and the whimsical. So that's how that happened.

Anna came to the shop when the set was half built, and she's looking at the model, and said, "I can't do the show on this set." The TD [technical director] kind of looked down at the ground and I said, "Well, you have to do it. We don't have a choice." And we did. That's what is great about Anna. Anna just deals with it. She just goes with it.

The quality of Letts's writing and the ensemble's acting performed on Rosenthal's Tony Award-winning set prompted this opinion from Ian Barford about Act Two:

I would put the second act of *August: Osage County* up against any American play of all time. It's an extraordinary piece of writing. We started with that and knew we were in great hands with Tracy and Anna.

The dinner scene that develops slowly and then builds to a fever-pitched conclusion at the end of Act Two, which beautifully sets up the denouement at the end of Act Three, is one of the most compelling scenes in the play and, again, we see designer Rosenthal and director Shapiro working together to realize her vision:

One of the ideas that we had, which was a little bit strange for a show that eventually goes to New York, is that we said, "We don't want the actors to configure themselves around a table in a way that shows that they are in a play. The scene should play in complete reality of the situation. We want to have all the people around the table and you see what you see, and if someone is blocked, so be it." Anna's idea of "It's like you looking in through someone's home and filming them and they're just going about their business."

The set and other technical elements quickly came together in readiness for opening. Rehearsals progressed, and the culling of Letts's script by Shapiro and the cast to mine all potential beats and moments remained a constant focus. Barford shares his recollections of *August: Osage County* in terms of the playwright/director collaboration and how the powerful text allowed him easy access to his emotions:

> I've worked on many original productions over the years. The anxiety that writers can have about their play as it begins to interact with a director and then, ultimately, a cast can be very uncomfortable. There can be conflicting opinions and energies in the room, which can serve to dissipate or somehow corrupt the flourishing of creative collaboration, but Tracy and Anna had such a remarkable connection on the show; such a graceful, mutually respectful way of working together that was so harmonious. Anna had an ability to figure out some of the challenges in the third act, which originally was not quite complete, and she kept us all in that sweet spot of delivering what was required technically.
>
> My first scene was with Fran on the porch and I had to cry within five seconds of being onstage. I never once felt like I had to manufacture. Just go out onstage and there's your scene partner. There's the person in front of you. It's not turned out to the audience. You're acting with your partner. They're observing that. And that dynamic was so alive in that production. It's fair to say for all of us involved, *August: Osage County* genuinely changed our lives. Things shifted in such a great and joyous way.

In advance of the official opening and throughout previews, the company was still somewhat unaware of the phenomenon in which they were participants. Steppenwolf has historically held a Veterans' Night for all shows just prior to the preview run. This free night of theatre, which includes a free meal and is now sponsored by the Gary Sinise Foundation, was initiated as a tribute to veterans during the 1984 run of *Tracers*, a play created and originally performed by playwright John DiFusco and other Vietnam War veterans. These nights have always provided a wonderful example of Steppenwolf's community engagement, but also one of the first looks by an audience at the play being produced. Designer Todd Rosenthal remembers the event around *August: Osage County*:

> During Veterans' Night I was thinking that there's no way that these guys are going to like this three-and-a-half-hour play about this dysfunctional family in Oklahoma. After the play, this vet came up to me and says, "You know what? That was screeching tires. That was smoking. I really enjoyed that."

These heartfelt comments provided a glimpse of what was to come. Amy Morton remembers the moment when she realized that the show was something bigger than she had imagined:

> At the end of the second act at the first preview, when I scream bloody murder at mom and the lights go down—it all of the sudden erupted into a hockey game out in the house—that's how it sounded in that blackout. We all kind of walked offstage and thought, "What the fuck? What was that?" I remember Tracy saying that he and Anna were sitting in the audience with everybody erupting and them thinking, "Holy shit." Nobody expected that at all.

August: Osage County premiered on July 8, 2007 and the response from both critics and audience was passionate and positive, as Ian Barford remembers:

> I had been in many shows that I would describe as successful, but *August: Osage County* hit people in a way that I've never experienced before. It just manifested what people sort of talk about as the "Steppenwolf style." It was about family. There was eccentric behavior. There was chaos. There was danger. There was humor. There was a marriage of simultaneous moments of profound tragedy and absolute hilarity. People just went crazy for it. One morning, we had a meeting just before the box office opened and there was a line all the way down Halsted to try to get tickets. We'd never seen that. Then we came to New York and there were no stars in the show and it was three and a half hours long—and it just exploded.

Barford's reference to the "Steppenwolf style" echoes Malkovich's words at the top of this chapter—"The ensemble in full attack mode." *August: Osage County* captured the essence of the early Steppenwolf "in-your-face" style that had originally gained them notoriety in productions like *Balm in Gilead, True West*, and others. Chris Jones's enthusiastic *Chicago Tribune* review captured this sentiment:

> With this staggeringly ambitious—and, for my money, staggeringly successful—three-act domestic opus for the Steppenwolf Theatre Company, Letts has penned a major, not-to-be-missed new American work ...
>
> *August* is like an Oklahoman *Long Day's Journey Into Night* shoved into a blender with Quentin Tarantino (with added Lillian Hellman and Jonathan Franzen syrups). Remarkably, the strangely sweet resultant milkshake re-energizes the great American tradition of the pseudo-memoir about growing up among the parental crazies, because it flavors its recognizable home truths with enough sin, lies and black comedy to keep your eyes popped out on stalks for nearly 3½ hours ... This remarkable show, more than any other production at this theater in quite some time, powerfully energizes and centers the acting ensemble.

Longtime Chicago critic Hedy Weiss's opening paragraph of her *Chicago Sun-Times* review is equally effusive in its praise:

> In his massive, multigenerational drama *August: Osage County*, now in a blisteringly acted world premiere at the Steppenwolf Theatre, playwright Tracy Letts has channeled Eugene O'Neill's masterwork, *Long Day's Journey Into Night* to devise a startling three-act, 3½-hour version to call his own.

The dual comparisons in these reviews to Eugene O'Neill's American masterpiece put Letts into rarified air and clearly set the play up for a longer future than a Chicago run. Despite the difficult logistics of moving the show, the New York producers quickly came calling. Dunagan shares her apprehensions at the time:

> None of us wanted to go. We had company meetings. We had votes. Nobody wanted to go to New York. We live in Chicago—we like it here—that's why we live here.

The posters for *August: Osage* County used the phrase "There's No Place Like Home" as a tag to tease audiences. But the hidden truth of that simple statement is accurate to the majority of Steppenwolf ensemble members. Dunagan's comment supports the notion that Chicago is Steppenwolf's one and only true home. Taking a show to New York is not an easy proposition either from a personal or a company perspective; however, the ensemble's strong desire to share this particular work trumped all personal feelings. Dunagan's insight further reveals the changing face of the marketplace that for years had held up New York as sole centerpiece of the American theatre. "Making it in New York" was important, but only inasmuch as it would bring greater recognition to what the ensemble felt was an extraordinarily meaningful piece. Executive director David Hawkanson captures the interest of the New York producers:

> We had four offers to transfer the show after it opened in Chicago. We had to decide whether we would go under a regional theatre banner in New York, or whether we'd go under a Broadway producer's banner. That decision we left to the ensemble. They debated it for weeks. We explained to them that if we transferred the production under a commercial banner, it would mean they would have to make a significant commitment of time, which they were not very excited about.

Amy Morton talks about the meeting where the decision was made:

> The company was involved in pretty much every step of the process. David was very forthright about the pros and cons of our choices. We all voted on how we wanted to do this. I remember some people said we should go to MTC [Manhattan Theatre Club], because it was a known audience and had a subscription base, so there was less risk economically. Tracy, who loves to gamble said, "OK, but my vote is I want to go for gold. I want to take the big fat risk. I want to do it on Broadway and just fucking do it." And, of course, we all said, "You're right. Let's fucking do it."

Hawkanson finishes:

> In the end, they decided they didn't want any other theatre's name above Steppenwolf's and that they would go under a commercial transfer versus a set run in a non-profit house. Who would become the producer was Martha's and my decision. It was fascinating stuff, because you'd keep saying to the producers, "This is not that important. They're proud of the show and they want it to get

recognition, but being in New York is not attractive to this company of actors."

Amy Morton recalls a few unexpected bumps before the New York opening and how vital the support of the producer and her fellow company members were to the final realization of the New York run:

> We got there and the stagehand strike happened, which sucked. We got there in October to what was supposed to be one week of rehearsal, one week of previews, and then opening. The strike happened and we were sitting there as a company not working, not getting paid, for weeks. To producer Jeffrey Richards's credit, he is truly is a man of the theatre; they kept giving us our housing stipends because they knew if we started to go back home it would be incredibly hard to get us back. Still, we were like, "Man, how do we stay in this town not working and not spending money?" When the strike ended after three or four weeks, Jeffrey Richards said, "The sooner we open this, the sooner we're going to recoup any losses." So we opened it two or three days later. We were chomping at the bit. The opening was just insane.
>
> I think the delay and the anxiety fueled the show in some way. I remember turning to Mariann (Mayberry) and saying, "I'm so glad I am going through this with you guys. I'm not alone. I'm not just some actor in the company. This truly is a family and we're sharing this all together."

August: Osage County finally opened and met with a ferocity of passionate support as Charles Isherwood captured for the *New York Times* on December 5, 2008:

> *August: Osage County* ... is flat-out, no asterisks, and without qualifications, the most exciting new American play Broadway has seen in years. Fiercely funny and bitingly sad, this turbo-charged tragicomedy—which spans three acts and more than three blissful hours—doesn't just jump-start the fall theater season, recently stalled when the stagehands went on strike. *August* throws it instantaneously into high gear ...
>
> In *August: Osage County* can be heard echoes of other classic dramas about the strangling grip of blood ties—from Eugene O'Neill's *Long Day's Journey Into Night* to Sam Shepard's *Buried Child*— but Mr. Letts infuses his dark drama with potent energies derived from two more populist forms of American entertainment. The play has the

zip and zingy humor of classic television situation comedy and the absorbing narrative propulsion of a juicy soap opera, too.

Clive Barnes in the *New York Post*:

> *August: Osage County*, which originated, like so much of the best in the American theatre, from Chicago's Steppenwolf troupe—is in the grand tradition of American family shenanigans, such as Lillian Hellman's melodrama *The Little Foxes* …
>
> The immaculate staging is by Anna D. Shapiro, and the ensemble acting by the whole cast (most of whom, like Shapiro and Letts, are members of the Steppenwolf Theatre Company) is simply beautiful.

And finally, David Rooney writing for *Variety*:

> Ferociously entertaining *August: Osage County*, the American dysfunctional family drama comes roaring into the 21st century with eyes blazing, nostrils flaring and fangs bared, laced with corrosive humor and so darkly delicious and ghastly that you're squirming in your seat even as you're doubled over in laughing.

Morton gives a more candid memory of the direct response that came from the audience in which she captures how different *August: Osage County* was from the typical star-driven vehicles that were ever-present at the time on Broadway:

> The response to the show—I don't just mean people standing and cheering and stomping their feet—I mean going out the stage door night after night and people were waiting—not because there are any stars in the show—because the show was so meaningful to them that they want to talk to you about it. We heard so many times, "Oh my God, you're just like my mother." Or, "I'm Barbara." The audience related to it so intensely and personally that they would be very emotional. Sometimes, it would be like, "Do you need a hug?" because they would be shaking. It was amazing to be in something that so affected people; they were really transfixed by the artistry and they didn't give a shit if you have had a "name" or not.

The New York run of the show had been preceded by something else unforeseen, a dose of shattering reality: the news that Dennis Letts was dying of cancer. His son Tracy Letts shares his recollections:

What happened with Dad being diagnosed between the run here in Chicago and our run in New York was horrible. It was unimaginable. It was a terrible time in my life and made all the more terrible by how great this other part of my life was—just the extremes of it all. My dad was diagnosed with stage IV cancer just after we closed the show in Chicago in August and before we went to New York in October. I called the producers and told them. They said, "We love your dad in the show. We want him to come if he wants to come. We'll get him a good understudy. We'll help in any way we can." They were really great about it. We did the show in New York and Dad was great.

The stagehand strike was particularly tough because my dad didn't have a lot of time and we didn't know how long it was going to go on. If I'd known it was going to be three weeks, it would have been no big deal, but at the time, we were hearing suggestions that it might go on for six months to a year. I thought, "My dad's not going to get a chance to do this." So it was a really terrible time.

Losing him during the run of the show was just unimaginable. I won the Pulitzer Price six weeks after my dad died. You would hope that something like that would just be purely joyful, but it was just devastating. A lot of people at the time were saying, "How lucky you are that you got to have this experience with your dad. Isn't it great that he died doing something that he loved? Doing his son's play on Broadway?" I can see that now. I feel that now, but, at the time, I couldn't hear it. It was just like, "You're telling me how great all this is and I'm not feeling it." The people, the theatre, they were great with my dad and he had a great time.

The loss of Dennis Letts added to the already stressful work of doing the show. The moments leading up to and including his death were ever-present for everybody involved, and occasionally played out on stage, as Amy Morton remembers:

There were some times after Dennis's death when I would be on stage and I would be so filled with emotion that I would just start crying. I would have to remind myself that my character, Barbara, would not be crying at this particular moment and I would have to force myself to stop. Dennis was a father to all of us and not only in the play. A play, I might add, that deals with the death of the father—the part Dennis played. It was intense to say the least.

Mariann Mayberry adds her thoughts related to her own personal tragedy, which further makes clear the extent to which the cast of

August: Osage County were deeply and personally connected to one another:

> So much happened during the run of that play. Good and bad. Dennis Letts's passing was one of those extreme events that we all mourned and that almost took us all down. Tracy was always with us in New York until that day—and then he was gone. Period. We all experienced Dennis's decline and death. He was a huge heart at the center of the play. He became our father onstage and off. He would sit in that green room every night chatting with everyone. You could talk to him about anything. He was interested in you. We felt lost without him. Thank God we had Kimberly Guerrero—a big heart in the play. She is Native American and played Johnna. She ushered us through a couple of ceremonies and created moments where we could work through that loss. She was a buoy for all of us in a number of ways.
>
> So much life happens when you're in a long run of a play. You can't help but get very close. During *August*, I lost my brother. When I got back from his funeral I went straight into a two-show day. I remember during the matinee I exited after my last scene and was starting up the stairs to my dressing room when I ran into Ian coming down the stairs. He said something to me, I don't even remember what, but I burst into tears. He stopped and hugged me until he had to go on stage. I will never forget that moment. He had my back and I will always have his. Can you imagine? An ensemble with so many unavoidable shared life experiences. So much time spent together. You know each other, you know each other's rhythms, tendencies, energy. That's alchemy. That's the Steppenwolf family. That's why none of us will ever leave.

The show was successful beyond expectation. For many, it was the pinnacle moment in their careers, but the harsh reality of life and a lengthy run of such an emotionally demanding show took its toll as well. Deanna Dunagan shares her deeply personal recollections about the day-to-day life she led during the run:

> When the show was running, I did nothing but go for groceries, eat, lie on the sofa, not talk at all, and do the show. I couldn't go out for lunch. I couldn't go out to museums. I couldn't do anything. I lived like a nun.
>
> I was going to hire a woman, a very famous vocal coach who had worked with my friend Raúl Esparza. My voice had become the main thing. I asked her if she would come see a show and then I could

work with her to help me save my voice. I was in horrible pain from my knees and back, but I was still managing to crawl up the stairs and to do the fight in the show. But, if you lose your voice, you can't do the show. She met me after the show, and said, "You're doing opera eight times a week. There's nothing I can say or do for you." I just rested my body. The producers paid for me to have acupuncture once a week and I usually went twice a week for the pain.

I could never go out. I couldn't drink. Sunday night I would have one, maybe two glasses of wine. If people came to town and they wanted to take me out after the show, I could not do it. I couldn't go out between shows to have a bite with the cast, or anything, I had to just shut up. Just to be by myself. I was a bit of a recluse and that's not my nature. I really loved those guys. They were like my family.

Amy Morton adds another perspective to this underbelly of success:

Productions have a shelf life for a reason. Eight shows a week is the death of art. To do that play, eight shows a week, was torture at times. It's so long. For the most part, all of us walk on stage in a very bad place and it only gets worse. We all got a low-grade depression throughout the entire run even though we were in this enormous hit. It was super high and super low. I wouldn't get out of bed until about noon or 1:00, and then I'd go about my day and, about 4:00, that pall just kind of started to come over me. Part of it is, "Oh no, I have to do a show," but part of it is also your psyche getting ready for what you have to fucking do. It's just really grueling.

Actors are giant carpal tunnels. You're going through the same physical motions eight times a week—things your body does when it's upset—but your body doesn't know you're lying, so it still affects you. There's a lot of screaming, crying, gnashing of teeth and when you do that physically—when you scream or cry—you thrust your head forward, it's what your body does and to do that over a run, let alone a career, is really hard.

During a run like *August: Osage County*, I eat whatever the hell I want because I burn so many calories on stage. I sleep really late. I don't watch violence on TV. I don't watch the news. I go for long walks. I would come down from *August: Osage County* after a Sunday matinee because I knew I had from then until Tuesday night. There would be this lightness in everybody. I'd turn to Mariann, Sally (Murphy), or Kristina, one of the understudies, whoever, and I'd say, "Where are we going to go eat? We're going to spend as much money as we want and we're going to eat whatever we want." You have to treat yourself. It's really important.

When it came time to renew contracts for what was an extended run, the cast began to change. Dunagan recalls how quickly it happened for some:

In New York, the tradition is, if you take a show, you sign to a six-month contract. After the success, the producers asked us all to stay through eight months because of the Tony Awards, and the day after the Tonys, five of us left the cast.

For Amy Morton, the choice was not quite so simple:

I was scheduled to direct Tracy's next play, *Superior Donuts* at Steppenwolf in 2008. I said to Tracy, "What do you want me to do? Direct *Superior Donuts* or stay with *August*?" He said, "I want you to stay with *August*." I said, "Great, but just so you know if they don't come up with my price I'm going to come back to Chicago and direct *Superior Donuts*." It was a win–win situation, to be able to say to your agent, here's the price, there's no negotiating, they either pay me my price or I walk. I don't think the producers realized that I was actually serious and so they kept coming back with different offers and my agent kept saying, "No, I don't think you understand that she's not negotiating." They finally came up with it at the eleventh hour.

People treat actors like shit. I don't think actors realize that the biggest power they have is the ability to say "No." It's the only power you have as an actor. You have to be willing to walk away. I've walked away a lot of times and for the most part never regretted it.

Estelle Parsons took over the role of Violet from Dunagan, but not before Dunagan would claim the 2008 Tony Award for Best Leading Actress in a Play. Obviously, her hard work, personal toil, and dedication paid off. Her comments at the Tony Award ceremony captured the spirit of camaraderie as she recounts the incredible journey while paying tribute to her cast mate and fellow nominee Morton:

This whole year has been entirely unexpected and astonishing. When we started rehearsals in Chicago a year ago on *August: Osage County* none of us dreamed we would be here. I certainly didn't. After

thirty-four years in regional theatre, I never even thought about it. I
watched on TV like everybody else. But Tracy Letts wrote a brilliant
new American play. Anna D. Shapiro brilliantly directed. Steppenwolf
mounted it. The Chicago theatregoers ate it up, made us a hit, which
interested the New York producers. We came to New York and New
York has embraced us so enthusiastically and with hearts full. I
can't get over the reception we've had here. I have to recognize my
follow nominees and especially my stage daughter, Amy Morton. The
astounding Amy Morton. Who should, at the very least, be standing
up here with me, and who can do things on stage I cannot do. And I
want you to know that, ever since I was a little girl, all I ever wanted
to do was get people together and put on plays. And now I get to do
it on Broadway. Thank you so much.

The play received seven Tony nominations that night and won five
awards including Dunagan's and Best Set Design (Todd Rosenthal),
Best Lighting Design (Ann G. Wrightson), Best Featured Actress in
a Play (Rondi Reed), and Best Play. In accepting the award for Best
Play, Letts shared his gratitude with all the folks at Steppenwolf,
and particularly the Chicago theatre community, acknowledging the
undying sense of commitment and pride that each have in a reciprocal
relationship to each other. The sense of ownership that the city of
Chicago feels towards Steppenwolf has been a major factor in the
company's ability able to sustain itself for the last forty years.

   August: Osage County would run for 648 performances in New
York. While the run continued on Broadway, many of the original cast
rejoined the show for a ten-week run at the National Theatre in London
commencing in November of 2008, which was the first show since *The
Grapes of Wrath* to make that special journey. Pádraig Cusack, associate
producer at the National Theatre and head of planning at the time of
August: Osage County, recounts the story of how that project took hold:

> I'd read the play and thought it was sensational, and it felt
> quintessentially American. There was a producer in the West End
> who'd seen it in Chicago and was thinking of doing the play in
> London but with local British actors. We at the National had a
> conversation and said, "Actually, this is so American it's got to be done
> with American actors." There are lots of wonderful British actors who
> can do a fantastic imitation, but there was something unique about
> both the writing and the style of the production that Steppenwolf

had created, so we thought, "The clever thing is to bring over the original company to London."

Steppenwolf is the kind of king of American home-produced theatre. I don't think anyone really matches that, so we began the conversation—David Hawkanson and I—about finding a way of bringing this huge company, at massive expense, and to get them to London for a ten-week run in our season.

David is a creative producer. He's an executive director who's good with money and negotiations and contracts, but he has a great empathy with what a director is trying to achieve, which I think is quite unusual to find in those people who are running theatre companies. David was brilliant as he did some really deft negotiations because, by the time we brought it to London, it had already been to Broadway and union terms on Broadway are prohibitive in terms of bringing your show to London. So, together, we figured it out and made it possible.

It was such a major event in London. Anyone who had the vaguest interest in theatre wanted to see this play. There was such a human element to the play that it had this massive resonance for audiences. In Britain there is a reserve where you don't really delve down in the way that family did in *August: Osage County*. It was just something really special. The audiences just adored it. In New York, everybody stands up if it's half-decent, but in London, we don't. It's a real effort to get people to stand, but for this play, they were on their feet, because they knew this was something unique and special in every sense. *August: Osage County* had such fine quality and finesse to it that it was just a joy to watch. We were very privileged and slightly smug that we had managed to get Steppenwolf back to the National after twenty years.

Much like the Shuberts with *The Grapes of Wrath*, where they produced the show for a greater purpose than economic reward, so was the case with *August: Osage County* at the National, as Cusack describes.

The great thing about working for the National is that we look at the economics globally. We look at the year and if we "wash our face" by the end of the year, it's a successful year. *August* did great business for us. It was never going to make a profit because it was an expensive show, but it cost us less than we anticipated. It sold out every performance, so, in that respect, it was a huge triumph.

Subsequent to the success in London came a national tour and collaboration in 2010 with Australia's Sydney Theatre Company, which was headed at the time by co-artistic directors Cate Blanchett and her husband Andrew Upton, which furthered Steppenwolf's reputation in the national and international theatre community.

The fact that *August: Osage County* was written by a Steppenwolf ensemble member, Tracy Letts, and further, that it was also directed by an ensemble member, Anna D. Shapiro, both of who were relative newcomers, symbolically made an important statement, as Shapiro described in 2015:

> It became a kind of generational shot across the bow. It was really good that this thing happened for us, because when you're a member of a company with the very people who made you want to do theatre, you could be hamstrung a little by that. It was good to make our own history with the company—the younger people. It's hysterical that I'm calling us the younger people, because we're not anymore, but we were then.

Jeff Perry's personal note to Tracy Letts on opening night in Chicago, prior to the heralding of *August: Osage County* as an American masterpiece, captures the deep level of emotion and excitement that the play brought not only to Steppenwolf, but to audiences from Chicago, to New York, to London, to Sydney, and beyond:

> *on the occasion of opening night of august: osage county sunday july 8, 2007*
>
> *Tracy,*
>
> *when the gang and i were kids, our outside inspirations were pretty much from film and tv—bergman, cassavetes, altman, monty python, saturday night live, sctv ...*
>
> *a few of us like me were geekier and motivated by theatre history and had an awed awareness of the moscow art theatre and the group theatre ... we longingly knew they had something we couldn't touch, even with all the gifts of talent and orneryness we had lucked into—they had chekhov and odets to give their ensembles their truest, deepest, most homegrown expression.*
>
> *with the birth of osage, after thirty years of theatrical blood and sweat, steppenwolf, blessedly has you ...*

to be included in this moment just makes me cry with gratitude, but i'll spare ya that ... that you are a gifted actor who can write like this, well it's just pushing the boundaries of greedy good fortune for this house that actors built ... to witness what this means to a place and people that i have loved for decades is one of the deepest joys i've ever felt ...

congratulations don't begin to cut it trace, but a thousand congrats ...

you have created something from your soul that is so beautifully true and universal that i'm certain it will live long past our efforts here ...

... we will never forget that we got to go on it's first amazing ride ...

with love,

jeff

Figure 46. *August: Osage County*, 2007 © Michael Brosilow.

Floor: Fawn Johnstin

Table: Kimberly Guerrero

Couch: Rondi Reed, Ian Barford, Francis Guinan

First Landing: Rick Snyder, Mariann Mayberry

Second Landing: Deanna Dunagan, Sally Murphy

Non-ensemble: Fawn Johnstin, Kimberly Guerrero, Deanna Dunagan

Figure 47. Mariann Mayberry, Jeff Perry, Amy Morton, Francis Guinan, *August: Osage County*, 2007 © Ian Barford.

Figure 48. Amy Morton, Jeff Perry, *August: Osage County*, 2007 © Michael Brosilow.

Figure 49. Sally Murphy, Ian Barford, *August: Osage County*, 2007 © Michael Brosilow.

Figure 50. Dennis Letts, Deanna Dunagan, Kimberly Guerrero, *August: Osage County*, 2007 © Michael Brosilow.

Non-ensemble: Dennis Letts, Deanna Dunagan, Kimberly Guerrero

Figure 51. Francis Guinan, Rondi Reed, *August: Osage County*, 2007 © Michael Brosilow.

Figure 52. John Mahoney, Tracy Letts, *The Dresser*, 2004 © Michael Brosilow.

Figure 53. Kate Arrington, Tracy Letts, *The Pain and the Itch*, 2005 © Michael Brosilow.

Figure 54. Tracy Letts, Mariann Mayberry, *Last of the Boys*, 2005 © Michael Brosilow.

Figure 55. Mariann Mayberry, Robert Breuler, *Wendall Greene*, 2002 © Michael Brosilow.

Figure 56. Laurie Metcalf, Yasen Peyankov, *Frankie and Johnny in the Clair de Lune*, 2004 © Michael Brosilow.

Figure 57. Mariann Mayberry, Amy Morton, Sally Murphy, 2007 © Francis Guinan.

Figure 58. Robert Breuler, Yasen Peyankov, Amy Morton, *The Time of Your Life*, 2002 © Michael Brosilow.

Figure 59. Francis Guinan, Molly Regan, *Love Song*, 2006 © Michael Brosilow.

Figure 60. Mariann Mayberry, Ian Barford, *Love Song*, 2006 © Michael Brosilow.

Figure 61. John Malkovich, Yasen Peyankov, *Lost Land*, 2005 © Michael Brosilow.

IN THEIR OWN WORDS: THE ESSENCE OF STEPPENWOLF

Joan Allen:
In *The Wheel*, there was a trench in the center of the stage that was full of mud and we had to climb through it. The first time that it was there—I thought, "Yeah. It's time to get in the mud." That's what you do. That's Steppenwolf. You get in the mud, and you're happy to be in there.

H.E. Baccus:
If I read a review of a play that says "wonderful ensemble acting," it drives me berserk, because every play should be ensemble acting. Ensemble to me means more than that. It means people who are intimately familiar with each other; who work over a long period of time together; who trust, love, and respect one another. Intimacy is important as well because there are subtleties in your personal life—tones and attitudes that you can pick up from a person only after you have known them awhile. Steppenwolf actors know those slight differences, those inflections, and that makes a difference to their work. Ensemble then becomes the ability to react more sharply and truthfully to what you're given from the other actor.

Gary Sinise:
We started off with a focus on ensemble and having many solid performances all in one piece. We also had an emphasis on having a visceral connection to the written material. We believed that everybody had to contribute fully and equally at the same time. That philosophy applies today as well as it did forty years ago and has carried us through so many changes through the decades.

Rondi Reed:
The Steppenwolf style demands the truth. It may be loud, brash, ugly and fearless, or soft, deeply still and shattering in its simplicity. It can crack open a window to the soul, kick down the door of pain, exhilarate, titillate, and yank the audience along for the ride. It is like nothing else I know. I am completely addicted—a fool for love. I have learned to risk, to fail, to dare to fail, to try again, to trust, to work and then to work harder.

Amy Morton:
We all know each other so well at Steppenwolf that there is a shorthand. We can cut to the chase much more quickly than a room full of strangers. There is also a certain amount of freedom to being brutally honest about what is and what is not working. Steppenwolf is my life and these people mean as much to me as my own family. I would not be where I am without them. I don't think any of us would be where we are without the collective consciousness of Steppenwolf. The stars aligned. It's a profoundly meaningful place. We all have the same work ethic as well. It's a Midwestern pragmatism. It's a very practical approach that is all about entertaining each other. The worst thing you can be in Steppenwolf is boring.

John Mahoney:
I remember John Malkovich saying that he'd gotten a great review in something, and other people weren't mentioned, and he said, "I hate that, I hate that. We're a company. Why don't they just say we do a good play? They don't need to single people out." I knew what he was saying was true and that this was a dominant tenet of the company. People get much greater joy out of seeing a production praised than they do from individual praise, especially when it is at the expense of somebody else not getting it.

Rondi Reed:
We were like-minded individuals, sort of "fearless to the point of stupidity," as Jeff Perry has said on more than one occasion. We all feel that "the work" is always the most important thing.

William Petersen:
These are seriously the most talented group of actors I've ever encountered in one place. The things that Laurie (Metcalf) can do while she's doing something else are remarkable. She can be thinking about something completely different, but what she's doing in the moment is spot-on brilliant. John (Malkovich) does things that are probably a little like Brando in that, "What is he doing? I've never seen that." Joan (Allen) is like a flower that grew into sunflower status reaching the sun with her face. Everyone. It is a remarkable band of unbelievable talent. I don't think a collection like this will ever be duplicated. What makes Steppenwolf unique is that I don't think there could ever be a time when this much talent could arrive in one place at one time.

Al Wilder:
The best actors are always a combination of the internal preparation and the external. It really depends on the part. I like to strip down and "unprepare." Early on, when we were trying to make a company, we had an army of nine instead of 500 soldiers, and this army of nine had to be specialists. Somebody is demolition and somebody is a martial artist, and at the beginning my task became, and it stuck with me even after we expanded the company, that of the character actor, which forced a distancing from my personal experience in terms of dialect and physicality.

Naturally, that kind of character work takes a different kind of preparation. I wouldn't trade that type of experience for the world because it is like being trained to be a brain surgeon. Being trained to be an actor allowed me to do the things that I have done and not just be myself. As a result, I have been in more shows than any ensemble member—over sixty since we began.

Martha Lavey:
What I saw right away and felt kind of singular was the hunger that was in all of these people here to make it better. There was never good enough. There was always this pushing forward. It's a wild combination of both camaraderie, but also very competitive. This is an ambitious group of people with a huge appetite for excellence and that feels like the forward movement of this company.

This manifests itself in very practical ways, for instance, like never feeling like we're done rehearsing, and having huge ambition for the company, and now in things like wanting to get really good writers. We have always been each other's best audience and want to be good in the evaluation of the other company members. It's great to get accolades from the world, but this feeling that our best critics were each other— those are the people in whose eyes we want to shine.

Francis Guinan:
You can have selfish actors that kind of hide out. I've seen it onstage, where people literally vanish onstage. One of the important things in the early exercises that Sheldon Patinkin shared with us is that you give it away. You give the scene away. You take focus not because it's your turn, but because you have responsibility for the focus. The thrust of the play was always more important than the individual egos of the performers in that moment.

Alana Arenas:
Every single show that I've done at Steppenwolf has been a gift, because I'm always working with people who have a high standard for their work. I always feel like I learn something. The theatre has gifted me with the opportunity to be able to stretch as an actor. I've had the opportunities to play characters that nobody else would have given me the opportunity to play. For example, I played Miranda in *The Tempest*, I played Mary Warren in *The Crucible*, and I played Marie Antoinette. Where else could I play Marie Antoinette? I think that's the gift of being an ensemble member. They are your artistic family and they're committed to you as an artist.

Tim Hopper:
During the run of *The Night Alive* by Conor McPherson, the power went out on the theatre's side of the block. We were about fifteen minutes from the end of the show and the lights just went out in the middle of a scene. There was a pause, "What are we doing? What's going on?" The next thing you hear is the stage manager saying, "Sorry, but it looks like power is out on the block. We're seeing if we can fix something right now. Hang with us." A few minutes later they came back and said, "We're not going to have power back. I'm sorry. You can exchange your tickets and come back to another performance." Somebody in the audience said, "Finish the play." Our crew came out with flashlights, because we couldn't do it on the main part of this set because there was this huge lip and you could drop off into the orchestra, but we went over to a stage right platform area in front of the proscenium at audience level. We all looked at each other and thought, "Alright, yeah, let's do this." We went out there and finished the play in flashlight. We tried to do as much of our blocking as we could on this little eight by ten space. It's the Steppenwolf thing because you're just looking at the eyes of somebody and that is all. You're just listening to them and telling the story.

Mariann Mayberry:
I remember Randy Arney saying, "Steppenwolf has a healthy disregard for the audience." We have to. No performing, no turning out, or playing to the audience. You turn your back to the audience because that's reality. You can't be worried about the audience seeing or hearing everyone in every single moment—no spoon feeding. Audiences are smarter than that. If there are audience members walking out that's good too—means we've got them riled up.

Molly Regan:
We're so relaxed with each other. I go out there with Fran (Guinan) in Rory Kinnear's *The Herd* and that's my third marriage to him on stage. We know each other's ticks. We can read each other like an old married couple, because we've known each other for thirty years. You get into rehearsals and there's no pressure of "Does my scene partner think I'm any good?" or "Am I going to be fired?" We've had all these years and start with that and you don't get to start with that anyplace else. Just walking into the rehearsal room, you start with thirty years of shared history.

James Vincent Meredith:
When I was in *The Crucible* being amongst all these actors who I had held with such admiration, it was kind of an all-hands-on-deck sort of thing. I remember thinking, "I got to fake it till I make it, because they are all extremely strong actors." There were no egos in those rooms. It was just filled with strong actors that wanted to make sure that the story was told. We all shared a desire to be faithful to the story. I've done a lot of theatre over the years, but that was the first time that I felt that warm cocoon feeling.

Kate Erbe:
Terry, Gary, and Jeff are three parts of a whole. Their personalities are very different but all of them were driven by a common vision. They wanted to do what the music and films of that time did, but they wanted to do it on stage. Jeff is sort of more mild mannered and softer spoken, but very driven; Terry is incredibly articulate and literary, but also incredibly driven; Gary is sort of muscular and driven. They are all willing to call a spade a spade and say, "No, that's not good enough. Be better."

Tracy Letts:
I came here to Chicago to work and learn my craft in the theatre. I love the ethic about the work here in Chicago and at Steppenwolf. People who were here doing this work weren't here to get famous. They weren't here to break into the big time. They were here because they loved the theatre and because they were surrounded by like minds and there was a real rigor about the work.

Laurie Metcalf:
We always knew that it was collaborative, because that's a given. It's not a given everywhere you go to do theatre. You can step on people's toes if

you assume that. A lot of people don't want to work that way. I have to bite my tongue sometimes when I go somewhere else. I go back to Chicago mostly to do plays for the audiences that have subscribed to the plays because they're the ones that enabled us to become what we are. I want a Steppenwolf audience to have the best time possible in a theatre. I think they deserve it.

I hope Steppenwolf will always be a group of artists, designers, actors, directors, playwrights and staff giving 150 percent. Every production is not going to work, but you want to know that the heart was there. We always want to challenge ourselves and give the audience a ride that they maybe won't forget—maybe that will move them—maybe do whatever art does to people. It's "Go big or go home," and that attitude we all unconsciously understood.

Frank Galati:
I don't think one can overstate the sort of coincidental historical context of the educational theatre movement in the United States, particularly in the Midwest, where high-school programs and college programs in theatre like Illinois State were doing great work in the 1970s. It was sort of in the atmosphere. It was true at Northwestern too, where we had some giant teachers like Alvina Krause, who was as tough as it gets, just like your mentor Barbara Patterson from Highland Park High School. Teachers like them laid the foundation for the Steppenwolf aesthetic. The never-ending striving towards total honesty, committing oneself, and taking risks and being brave has been at the heart of what makes Steppenwolf Steppenwolf.

Chapter 5

NOW AND INTO THE FUTURE

Steppenwolf's original members were extremely dynamic and successful. A comet shot through the atmosphere. We're all still creating in the wake of that comet.

—Ian Barford

What sets Steppenwolf apart right now in August of 2015 is that we have the opportunity to reintroduce ourselves to the theatre community and be a vital contributor to the American theatre experience. I don't think that because those guys forty years ago miraculously found each other and created this theatre that we can lean back into that because none of us are those guys. It's like living off your parents' inheritance. It's different to take on somebody's belief system and live by that belief system. I'd like us to get clearer in our belief system. We need to stop patting ourselves on the back for things we didn't have anything to do with, but were just fortunate enough to inherit. I think we have a nice big push on our hands.

—Anna D. Shapiro

In 2007, as Tracy Letts's *August: Osage County* was beginning its Chicago run and its journey towards international recognition for Steppenwolf as a leader in homegrown American theatre, there were events occurring in Chicago that were a harbinger of things to come. The addition of six new ensemble members—Kate Arrington, Alana Arenas, James Vincent Meredith, Jon Michael Hill, Ian Barford, and Ora Jones—and just a few years later the award-winning playwrights Tarell Alvin McCraney and Bruce Norris, evidenced the company's intentions to generate significant new plays, such as Tracy Letts's opus. It had become clear that the company would aggressively pursue filling the theatre with plays and events that reflect a myriad of voices and cultures.

The past was not forgotten. In fact, it was just the opposite, as ensemble members from the earliest days of the theatre continued to be significant contributors to the company on all fronts. Symbolic in some ways of the link to the past, William Petersen, a longtime contributor from the early days of the company, was finally made an official member of the ensemble in 2008, after his lengthy hiatus and successful TV career. The vitality of Steppenwolf's history—its unrelenting commitment to truth onstage— would continue to provide a secure base from which to launch new initiatives and approaches as the company moved forward.

The ensemble members universally understand the importance of adapting to new ways, while keeping true to the company's roots, as Yasen Peyankov expresses:

> Steppenwolf is an ensemble that has been evolving through the years while at the same time adding really talented artists. You have the original group, Jeff Perry, John Malkovich, Terry Kinney, Gary Sinise, Laurie Metcalf, Al Wilder, and they produce *True West, Balm in Gilead*, then it's Frank Galati and Tony-winning *The Grapes of Wrath*; then you bring in Tracy Letts, Anna D. Shapiro and the theatre gets another Tony with *August: Osage County* for a play that's actually written by an ensemble member and directed by an ensemble member. Now you have Tarell Alvin McCraney and Bruce Norris. The group just seems to keep getting stronger and stronger. All of these new artists have that thing that the original group had and nobody can really put their finger on it, but it's a little bit of craziness, a little oddness that somehow makes them all fit. In a strange way, Steppenwolf is like a broken toy that is always a source of imagination that leads to work that is really magical.

Jon Michael Hill furthers Peyankov's thoughts:

> Steppenwolf is a very raw manifestation of artistic drive to work with other people towards a common goal and accomplish something special. The way the founders went about it ended up making the theatre unique because they were so fearless. If we lose that fearless spirit, that is when it could fall apart, but the people that are running the place now still have that fearlessness inside of them. It's got to be inside of all of us and we have to be committed to it. It's going to be risky and it won't get easier. This business is very tough, but as long as we all want to get together and continue to surprise each other, we're going to be alright.

Hill and Peyankov, both more recent ensemble additions, are emblematic of the newer generation of artists that comprise the Steppenwolf ensemble. Their obvious awareness of and respect for the company's history, coupled with their individually distinctive cultural perspectives, represent the new voices that will help shape the collective consciousness of the company. The element of surprise to which Hill alludes will be key to keeping the work fresh and vibrant.

The Steppenwolf for Young Audiences (SYA) program is one example of an earlier initiative that continues to surprise. The SYA production of *The Bluest Eye* in 2005 and reprised in 2006 was written by Lydia Diamond and was based on the novel by Nobel Prize winner Toni Morrison. *The Bluest Eye* tells the tale of a young African-American girl's coming of age in the 1940s and her desire to go to extreme lengths to gain acceptance. Although a simple and sweet story, the play proved controversial, as director Hallie Gordon described:

> In *The Bluest Eye*, the main character Pecola played by Alana Arenas gets raped by her father and becomes pregnant. She then goes to a pedophile preacher and tells him she wants blues eyes. She thinks this will save her. There were people from the Chicago Public Schools who felt that the preacher was blasphemous. There was concern about the rape and how that was going to be portrayed on stage. It was not. We directly took it from Toni Morrison's words. We invited all teachers to come to the first rehearsal and reading of the play. They all loved it.

The Bluest Eye typified the excellent work at all levels and further demonstrated the company's commitment to community engagement, stories that reach new audiences, and compelling educational experiences. Although not a subscription series production, *The Bluest Eye* proved so successful under SYA artistic director Gordon's direction and featuring ensemble member Alana Arenas in her first work with the theatre that the play moved to New York's Duke Theater on 42nd Street in association with the New Victory Theater. Arenas recalled the excitement and meaning of the show:

> Adult audiences were lining up to see that show on the weekends and this was a more diverse audience for Steppenwolf. I think it was an eye-opening experience for the theatre to realize that engaging different content will get different audiences to appear. The show was significant for me because it firmly established my relationship with Steppenwolf. I was very interested in the dialogue that I was able to have with my community through that show and it felt like I was

doing work that meant something beyond just entertaining people. *The Bluest Eye* met my goals in terms of what artistry can and should be. The talkbacks with the young audiences after the show were some of the most meaningful and rewarding experiences I have ever had with an audience.

James Vincent Meredith, another of the new generation of ensemble members, also participated in the Chicago restaging in 2006 and the New York incarnation. A move to New York was nothing new to Steppenwolf, but the fact that it gained this level of recognition for a teen-focused production proved Steppenwolf's voice was getting stronger with teen audiences while further cementing the company's brand in a national context.

The Steppenwolf for Young Audiences mission is to bring theatre experiences to high-school-age audiences and particularly under-served populations. In addition to the productions that SYA does bi-annually, the program also oversees a Young Adults Council that provides further opportunities for young people to learn about the collaborative nature of the theatre process and how those principles apply to decision making in everyday life. The lessons learned through the implementation of a variety of Steppenwolf's educational programming has proven to be transformative for many of its participants.

The year 2015 proved to be the beginning of another moment of major transition in the company's history. Artistic director Martha Lavey, the longest-standing artistic director in Steppenwolf's history at nineteen years, and executive director David Hawkanson both moved on to new horizons, and newly installed artistic director Anna D. Shapiro was charged with leading the theatre into its next chapter. Former board chairman Bruce Sagan, speaking of this moment and Shapiro's ascension, said:

> An absolutely magical thing occurred. You have new leadership in which the artistic office is going to be run by Anna D. Shapiro, who's probably the hottest American director in the country and is a person who has strong ideas about where American theatre should go. She's going to be running this theatre. Anna is a person who, in her youth, followed this theatre, so even though she's of a new generation, she knows intimately the history of the theatre and has been a witness to it. What more could you ask for?

This shift in leadership, as Sagan intimates, represents a literal and figurative changing of the guard. While the artistic advisory board, made up of founders Sinise, Perry, and Kinney, continues to provide overall guidance, and Lavey and Hawkanson's stewardship established a strong business and artistic platform and staff, Shapiro's artistic directorship provides a younger generation the opportunity to further the company's evolving mission. To add to this picture, new to the management leadership of the theatre is David Schmitz, managing director. Schmitz, like Shapiro, has a long history with Steppenwolf, and not only understands Steppenwolf's historic culture, but also recognizes the changes that are occurring in the Chicago, national, and international theatre communities. The challenge these new leaders face as the company grows will be to successfully blend the historic traditions of the theatre; the company's new diversity and youth; and the emerging trends in playwriting, theatre technology, and audience development though new media. Schmitz, a protégé in many ways of his predecessor David Hawkanson, in a Steppenwolf-produced video, enthusiastically describes what he sees as important elements of his job and why this is a vital time in the history of Steppenwolf:

> The thing that I am most passionate and interested in is thinking about diversity and equity in this theatre company and thinking about how to create a company that is more reflective of the community in which we live, and that includes staff, board, ensemble, and audience—all four of those areas. We are going to do things in the next ten years that nobody has any clue are even possible from this institution. Because we are an ensemble-based company, it is about the ambition of forty-four people—not one person—not two people—it's forty-four plus myself plus the whole staff, our board, and our audience. There are a lot of people working to make this place amazing and that's why this is an exciting place and this is an exciting time.

Shapiro talks about the future from a larger perspective:

> You're lucky if you're at a theatre where a lot of the people don't have to be there. They choose to be there. I don't have to have this job. I'm here because I believe in this place. I want to acknowledge what it's given me. I believe in what it can become, and, that it has several chapters of greatness ahead.

In taking the job as Steppenwolf's artistic director, Shapiro relinquished her role as Director of the MFA Directing Program at Northwestern

University. But with that experience, Shapiro brings not only the artistic background necessary for the job, but also the administrative skills that are essential to her new role. The sense of optimism and belief in the power of ensemble inherent in the comments of both Shapiro and Schmitz reaffirm the principles on which the company was originally formed forty years ago.

Ian Barford shares his feelings about the skills that he feels will help Shapiro succeed:

It's hard for me to talk about Anna because it might appear biased because obviously I love her and I'm married to her. Anna has a very unique combination of talents that make her very well suited for the job of artistic director. First of all, you have to have a person who understands the ethos of Steppenwolf and who knows the types of people who shaped this place. Anna was taken to Steppenwolf shows starting at about the age of twelve, so she grew up a student of, and a fan of, those actors and shows and how they did their work.

Because of her work with the New Plays Lab, she's got an extraordinary understanding of how to fully realize new work on stage: understanding the role of the writer; understanding the role of the director; understanding the role of the designers; understanding the role of the actors. Her work with Northwestern gave her experience working with administrations and fund raising.

She's been in the trenches with some big theatre producers. She's worked with celebrities and stars—people who've never been in a play before. Most importantly, because of all this work she's done on new plays, she understands how to diagnose a problem with a show. To have an artistic director who can come in during your last week in the rehearsal room or maybe in your first week of previews and understand where the problems are and be able to articulate how to approach solving those problems is a tremendous asset.

People have different kinds of careers, so people want different things. The theatre wants to make itself attractive to people who don't need to work here—people who have very big careers and who can do whatever they want. John (Malkovich), Gary (Sinise), Laurie (Metcalf); the list goes on and on. I don't feel like any of them have turned their back on the theatre. They're all interested in what's going on. They want to come back, which is great, but that's easier said than done. The challenges are many, but Anna is up to that challenge.

The artistic directors throughout Steppenwolf's history have proven vital in establishing the company culture and a blueprint for growth and forward momentum; each has brought their own unique perspective and style to the position. Through both immense skill and large portions of luck, these artistic directors have proven to be the right people in the right place at the right time. This includes H.E. Baccus back in 1976, who provided the young fledgling company with a sense of maturity, ease, and stability that balanced the original ensemble's youthful impulsiveness and fire; the ambitious and intuitive nature of Gary Sinise in his first tenure as artistic director, who laid a foundation for expansion beyond the comfortable confines of Steppenwolf's Chicago home; the brief but essential leadership of the deeply reflective Jeff Perry, who provided a calming force in the aftermath of a particularly rough transition that had threatened to break the company apart; Sinise's second tenure, where his energy and zealousness helped to revitalize the company's commitment during a period of rapidly expanding recognition and financial responsibility; the pragmatic and multi-talented Randy Arney, who oversaw the development of both the beginnings of homegrown theatre and the creation of a company-owned facility; to the brilliant and visionary Martha Lavey, who envisioned a theatre that would be intimately connected to its neighborhood through the development of original work and stronger programs specific to the needs of the community; and finally, the emerging and Sinise-like passionate leadership of Anna D. Shapiro, who brings a composite of many of the qualities of her predecessors to the theatre at another moment of significant redevelopment and redefinition. All of these artistic leaders are interconnected by a shared purpose to tell truthful stories in a bold and dynamic way through the ensemble principles that have been the backbone of Steppenwolf from its earliest rumblings.

National Theatre's Pádraig Cusack puts into perspective Steppenwolf's status in the international theatre community:

> Steppenwolf in the English-speaking world is one of the major companies. Chicago is the home of theatre-making in America. Broadway's a great place for pizzazz and excitement, but Chicago is the cutting edge of American-produced theatre and Steppenwolf is at the top of that. Steppenwolf has this extraordinary reputation and British actors always talk about Steppenwolf actors and their style, their discipline, and their commitment. Many of the Steppenwolf actors of the last twenty years have gone on to these extraordinary careers and yet they keep going back to Steppenwolf—that actually speaks volumes.

In a quiet way there's a kind of envy on this side of the Atlantic that Steppenwolf created this world and this ethos and this respect and kind of magnetism for their ensemble members that makes them keep on wanting to try something new and experiment. When you become a star, the experiment is scary because you can only fall. You've risen up. You got the Oscar or the Golden Globe or whatever and then you go back and do a brand new play with Steppenwolf and you could just fall flat on your face—and yet they keep on doing it. It's so easy for an established company to sit back on its laurels and just do the tried and tested, but they never do that. They keep on pushing those boundaries and taking those risks. Steppenwolf sets the standard. They are the paradigm in a way, so if they keep on pushing forward, that gives the rest of us the impetus to do the same.

Barford shares an experience with similar sentiments to Cusack:

We were in London doing *August: Osage County* at the National Theatre and we were fortunate to share the backstage area with an Irish company and a couple of English companies that were also there. We were talking about the spirit of the companies. Several of the people that I talked to said that they consider Steppenwolf to be the National Theatre for the United States.

There is no National Theatre for the United States, but Barford's experience clearly reflects the reverential impression of Steppenwolf on an international stage. Important, though, is the fact that the Steppenwolf leadership, ensemble members, and staff still consider the most meaningful function of the theatre is to stay connected to their immediate community—Chicago. Interestingly, committing locally to their mission through the company's decades of work is the very thing that has brought them into the international spotlight. The tenet of hard and disciplined work on which Steppenwolf was established is summed up by Frank Galati, and says a great deal about the cause and effect suggested in Cusack's impressions and those shared in Barford's story:

Chicago is the "city of big shoulders" and all that, but there's a lot about the kind of working-class ethic that makes up the audience as well as the kind of acting, the so-called "Chicago acting style," but it can be as much on a Midwestern farm as it is in the city. In the kind of rural regions that produced John Malkovich, Randy Arney, Joan Allen, and others, there was a working-class ethic and an uncompromising commitment to the value of honest labor. This was an informing principle and continues to be a nourishing resource to this day for the work that's done at Steppenwolf.

Steppenwolf's dedication to creating a more diverse voice is implicit in Galati's comments about the ethic of both ensemble members and the audience, and extends well beyond the rural and suburban roots of the early members of the theatre. Reaching out with this wider perspective will more fully connect the company with the Chicago community it works in.

Adding the worldview of a playwright of the caliber of Tarell Alvin McCraney to the ensemble is a demonstrative step towards giving voice to a new generation of ensemble members who will bring forth stories to new audience members in a way that had not been a strong component of the theatre's early history. McCraney believes in the power of the living, breathing theatre, which has become something of a mantra for Steppenwolf as evidenced by his quote:

> You can blast a television show into every house around the world pretty much, but you can't do that with theatre; they have to come to you. So when they come to you, how open do you make the play so that they can be a part of it? How much do you say, "Yes, you belong here" and that this is a conversation—not a monologue but a dialogue between the audience and the play, and you need to be here in order for this play to exist. Just as the actors have to be there; if one or the other isn't there it doesn't exist, it doesn't happen ... and that has always been important to me, to preserve that opening to preserve that back and forth.

McCraney's plays have been produced on a variety of international stages; at Steppenwolf, *The Brother/Sister Plays* and *Head of Passes*, both directed by ensemble member Tina Landau, have sent a strong signal that the culture of Steppenwolf is changing. McCraney is a 2013 recipient of a prestigious MacArthur Fellowship Genius Grant, but perhaps more telling has been the great respect and admiration that comes from his fellow ensemble members, including Jon Michael Hill:

> Tarell studied under August Wilson at Yale and he studied with the Royal Shakespeare Company. He's got an incredible mind. He has experienced so much of the world's theatre and dance, and I think he's going to be very important and vital to the company moving

forward into the future. I would like to be at his side as much as I can, learning and putting my two cents in when I can.

Hill's immense respect for the artistry of McCraney, combined with the work of Pulitzer Prize winners Bruce Norris and Tracy Letts, will continue to foster Steppenwolf's ongoing commitment to new plays, as former literary manager Michele Volansky summarizes:

> If Steppenwolf's vision had not expanded to include the writers, I don't know what the theatre would be right now. The effort towards the larger landscape of theatre is just what Steppenwolf did, and its added breadth and depth as opposed to focusing on one aspect like in the earliest days of the theatre.

The fortieth season, which was selected before the artistic transition from Martha Lavey to Anna D. Shapiro, embodies the essential importance of presenting original works: it includes *East of Eden*, adapted for the stage by Frank Galati; *Domesticated* by Bruce Norris; *The Flick*, the Pulitzer Prize-winning play by Annie Baker; *Mary Page Marlowe* by Tracy Letts; and *Between Riverside and Crazy* by Stephen Adly Guirgis.

Galati's *East of Eden* is his second adaptation of a Steinbeck work and comes close to twenty years after his epic *The Grapes of Wrath*, which was chronicled in Chapter 3. The artistic longevity of the company shines through with Galati's continued presence, Terry Kinney's direction, and a cast that features a large contingent of ensemble members both old and new. Ensemble member Bruce Norris's *Domesticated* is his ninth play to be produced at Steppenwolf and features another Steppenwolf veteran, Tom Irwin. *Mary Page Marlowe*, a play in its world premiere by Tracy Letts, is the first collaboration between him and director Anna D. Shapiro since *August: Osage County*. And, finally, the addition of plays by two of America's most dynamic playwrights, Annie Baker and Stephen Adly Guirgis, rounds out a season that captures many of the new directions that the company seeks to follow.

Changes are being discussed with regards to how plays are scheduled, and whether or not the traditional subscription season format that is utilized by just about every major regional theatre in America, including Steppenwolf, can be modified to encourage the ongoing involvement of ensemble members whose personal schedules do not necessarily fit with the time requirements of a standard season format. While Steppenwolf aims to develop seasons that are both exciting for audiences and engaging for the ensemble members, can the company re-envision the way in which plays are delivered in order to meet the desires of both groups? Anna D. Shapiro contemplates this question:

> We have a lot of the same challenges that any kind of entrepreneurial business has. You start with an idea and then the idea goes crazy and it's very successful. You manage it up to a point and then you change and then you manage that up to a point. Where we are right now is that we are finding ourselves as Steppenwolf Theatre a bit confounded by the subscription model, and not for any abstract reasons, but for very practical reasons. We have a very high percentage of our company that works a lot. Many of them work on television, and the way that television schedules work versus the way that a very limited five-show subscription series works is like oil and water. It couldn't be more of a hostile contradiction.
>
> For David Schmitz and me the question is, "Since when does Steppenwolf go along with the model? Why do we have to go along with this model if it's not working for us?" The goal that we have (and he and I share it) is that we have to get as many ensemble members in this building making art as is humanly possible. Our energy is moving toward that and I foresee a lot of change happening. We need more avenues of communication with our public. We need more programming streams. We need a more agile, responsive, supple way to program. It's about becoming more responsive, so that our artists are able to act on their impulses.

Managing director Schmitz puts Shapiro's comments in a more earthy and emotional perspective:

> In some moments it feels thrilling and exhilarating, like you're jumping onto a well-oiled machine that's just rumbling between your legs and you just can't wait to let it go. Then other moments it's completely terrifying and all you can think is, "We got to make sure this keeps going." It's a lot of responsibility, but part of it is to have fun and keep this crazy experiment moving forward.
>
> It's an interesting place that Anna and I are in. We are trying to figure out the answer to the questions, "Where do we go from here? What's the next step? How does this company keep growing? Does it keep growing? Does it want to stay where it is? Is the ensemble growing, and if so, how do we support that growth? And, how do we support them if they don't want to grow (in numbers)?"

In response to those questions, the company is working to increase the versatility of the physical space of the theatre facility, or "the campus" as many ensemble and staff members refer to it. Their intention, currently in the planning stages, is to provide ample space to pursue the new goals of quick response and a more malleable performance-scheduling approach. Within the ensemble there is a degree of trepidation as the organization anticipates this dramatic change. Shapiro shares some emotional feelings that recall one of the most difficult transitions in the company's early life, the move of *True West* to New York:

> I do know that some concerns have to do with my commercial life. It kind of lines me right up with Gary (Sinise) and so I feel OK. I don't have a problem with having ambition. But my personal ambition has nothing to do with my ambition for the theatre, because luckily I don't need to use the theatre to advance my own agenda. I can make whatever decision I need to make and it doesn't affect the theatre.
>
> A lot of people think that we're having this conversation for the first time. Gary, Jeff, and Terry know we're not having this conversation for the first time. We're having this conversation for the hundredth time between people who have certain feelings about people who are afraid or ashamed of ambition—people who define success in different ways. Those are the conversations.
>
> We're a world-class organization. I want the most people possible to see us. I'm not going to sell state secrets in order to do that, but I'm not going to not try. It's like Gary says, "You don't want to go to New York, don't go. You don't want to move the show, don't move it. You don't have to go." I think we're in that spot again.

The company is poised to once again challenge established patterns, but, unlike the move of *True West* in 1982, when there were only about fifteen ensemble members and a very small staff, this time, circa 2015, there are forty-four ensemble and eighty-nine full-time staff members to consider in the decisions being made. Shapiro realizes the dependence of this large group of people on the theatre, but also provides a cautionary word:

> I would always rather the theatre be inhabited by somebody who is fluid like mercury—that's what our ensemble members are. The challenge is how to function responsibly because so many people depend on Steppenwolf, but to do this and not become so institutional that we're too afraid to try shit.

Bruce Norris, the newest ensemble member, builds on Shapiro's words, pointing out the complexities inherent in a company filled with a myriad of personalities:

> I was having a conversation with Joan Allen and we were discussing a current debate within the company about whether or not we should be producing plays that are already owned by commercial producers. Those producers would then have partial subsidiary rights to the plays. Joan said, "All we want to do is good work." I said, "There's no longer one definition at Steppenwolf about what good work is. It's become a multifaceted thing." If good work is just the kind of work that Steppenwolf used to do, how does that address the needs of Jon Michael Hill, or K. Todd, or Tina Landau who doesn't want to direct that kind of stuff and wants to direct large things on an epic canvas. "Good work" isn't just a simple term anymore.

Steppenwolf, in moving forward on a mission to tell a wider range of stories, faces a tableau of circumstances unlike earlier times in the company's history. Now the individual voices that contribute to the discussion are greater in number and also come from a far more wide-ranging set of experiences with a different palette of perspectives. History suggests that Steppenwolf will continue to thrive. Amy Morton captures what is at the heart of the Steppenwolf ethos, and how it plays out on stage and makes the theatre vibrant:

> You have to have a really large imagination and not go for the safe thing or not go for the usual thing around this theatre. Limits are always being stretched, which is what makes it so fun. None of us are particularly "precious" about our work. It's sort of "run and gun." You never hear a company member say something like, "It would be better if you move over there because I am so used to doing it this way."
>
> When working with Jeff Perry on *August: Osage County*, he would change the blocking in our scenes because he likes to shake things up. He gets bored and he'll just start moving wherever he wants, and I was like, "Cool! Let's go. Go wherever you want. I'm with you. I'll catch the ball." That's sort of been the approach by everybody. The thing that worked last night, don't hold on to that, because then you are just going to get stale and stuck and "perform" and horrible, and you will be shunned out of the company. That is what I mean by not being "precious." We are very in-the-moment. There is

something unsentimental and extremely practical and humble in the way we work.

We don't do "uppity." That is one of the reasons Chicago theatre is successful as it is. Chicago has turned out some really great actors, but if you get high and mighty, Chicago will turn its back on you. You keep it very real and humble and you don't puff yourself up. We are extremely family-oriented, so you do your work. You don't shirk your work.

The transformation of an inspired group of twenty-year-olds into a world-class theatre organization is the stuff of legend. It wasn't planned, but it didn't just happen. Forces growing from the interacting dynamics of the group, the character of the city they inhabited, and the historical moment in time in which they matured, created a whole that was far greater than the sum of its parts. The Steppenwolf ensemble, whose earliest members were products of the "sex, drugs, and rock and roll" era, created an electrifying brand of theatre in response to the beliefs and attitudes their generation had instilled in them. Over the years, ensemble members of culturally and ethnically diverse backgrounds were added, and smart leaders allowed those new voices to help determine the directions of Steppenwolf as the company has grown into an institution that has far exceeded the dreams of its founders. In terms of the Chicago theatre, their impact has been incalculable, as evidenced by the number of new theatres that continually attempt to be the "next Steppenwolf," or by the direct amount of national exposure that has come to the city's theatre as a result of the company's efforts. The number of companies that their special style has helped spawn and the extent of their influence on a national and international level will only be clearly defined by history.

It is no small coincidence that the earliest members of the Steppenwolf ensemble came from small and mid-sized Illinois towns, rural and suburban; the relative stability and rootedness of their Midwestern origins laid a community-oriented foundation that has helped sustain Steppenwolf through both lean and abundant times. The sense of family that Morton speaks of, developed over decades, helped to create an individualized language, verbal and non-verbal, that has allowed the ensemble members to connect efficiently and deeply with one another. Ensemble member Ora Jones spoke about the virtues of being an ensemble member while on the road in the national tour of the musical *Matilda*:

This tour and the time away from Steppenwolf and Chicago has been an eye-opening experience. It has given me a chance to think about how I can better serve the Steppenwolf community—my friends and associates. A question that gets asked every time I do a show at Steppenwolf, every time I go to a meeting, every time we go to the gala, anytime I participate in any aspect of Steppenwolf is "What is my voice? How is my voice going to serve the community?" Right now being on the road feels like I have put myself in a position to be paid to go on a fact-finding mission. I have in the past, like many people in the ensemble, put forth projects that I thought would be interesting. They will read anything you give them. The door is always open. You are never alone in Steppenwolf unless you really want to be.

The unrelenting focus of the Steppenwolf ensemble on "the work" has pushed the company to fully realize the moments in each play they produce, and further, to take full advantage of business opportunities that presented themselves through the years. The joy of "the work" is what makes Steppenwolf special. This is a company that finds as much, if not more pleasure in the rehearsal process as it does in the final performances. The relentless zeal to improve the work didn't necessarily stop when rehearsal ended. Robert Falls, the longtime artistic of the Goodman Theatre and a person who grew up in the Chicago theatre right alongside his Steppenwolf colleagues, said of Steppenwolf:

> As individuals and as a company, they have been committed to excellence; they have weathered enormous transitions; they established the iconic recognition of Chicago as a source for grittiness and vitality in performance; and above all, they have continued to make clear to young theatre artists everywhere that "If we can start in a basement and achieve great things then you can do it too." Their impact has been immeasurable and it has been a joy to witness their journey from the very beginning.

The passionate sports environment in Chicago is part of the fiber of the city. The way Chicagoans embrace their sports teams carries over to the way they support "their" theatres like The Second City, the Goodman, Steppenwolf, and others. Chicagoans take great pride in homegrown talents and, as a result, have a certain sense of ownership of their teams and institutions. Chicago has been called "the biggest little city in America," because of the shared love of the city by its people. The sense of pride that defines the relationship between Chicago and

Steppenwolf Theatre Company has helped to sustain the company's existence.

Many of the patrons who have supported Steppenwolf from the beginning, and even those new to the company, develop over time a sense of ownership in the theatre's existence. The leadership of Steppenwolf works equally hard to give that same sense of ownership to all of its staff members by inviting them to readings of all season plays, as well as the final rehearsal before a show moves into the actual theatre space where it will be performed. Ensemble member James Vincent Meredith shares what those moments are like:

> There's this thing that happens at the beginning of every rehearsal process where we all go into that same room in Yondorf Rehearsal Hall where we rehearse. It's kind of a meet-and-greet at the very beginning and then we all get together and we get into this huge circle of people and it's everyone who works on the show; from the front of the house to the carpenters to electricians, to company managers, to ticket agents, to actors, to the director, it's got to be about sixty people in that circle and we all introduce ourselves and we say what we do and it's a way to center the whole project into the fact that we're all working together. We're all a part of this circle. It's not the actor and the director and then the crew. It's all of us. We're all in this circle together.

Through this practice, the staff members not only develop a sense of ownership and pride but also are put in an informed position to share the theatre's current work with potential patrons with whom they might come in contact. The inclusiveness of this Steppenwolf custom breeds an abiding connection to the theatre and to the members of the ensemble for the staff, and is reciprocated by the ensemble members through their appreciation of the staff's efforts behind the scenes. Everybody from top to bottom in the organizational structure has a purpose that supports the whole. This was the principle of Steppenwolf at its nexus, and despite their exponential growth, remains the driving force in the company's culture.

Each year theatres start anew with hopes of great distinction and audience acceptance, while just as many others close their doors, beaten down by the reality of the business of running a theatre. The odds of building and sustaining a theatre company are staggeringly low, but over the last forty years, Steppenwolf Theatre Company has not only managed to survive, but has literally redefined contemporary American theatre as we know it.

During the writing of this book, I discovered this quote, written on a wall in a hotel in Turin, Italy: "The perfect journey is a circle." And this reminded me of one of the credos I learned as a student of Del Close at Second City: "You know you are at the end when you are back at the beginning." So, with those thoughts in mind, I will repeat "in my own words" the story of my friend Gary Sinise passing around a hubcap during performances of *Grease* soliciting donations to fund a dream he shared with his high-school classmate Jeff Perry. He raised so much money that he was able to seed the next production under the Steppenwolf banner, *Rosencrantz and Guildenstern are Dead*, where he came back together with Jeff and Jeff's newfound college friend Terry Kinney. Together the three would start a progression of events that would ultimately change the face of the American theatre.

Figure 62. New Ensemble Members 2007 © Michael Brosilow.

Front Row: James Vincent Meredith, Ora Jones

Back row: Jon Michael Hill, Ian Barford, Kate Arrington, Alana Arenas

Figure 63. Martha Lavey © Michael Brosilow.

Figure 64. Anna Shapiro © Michael Brosilow.

Figure 65. Alana Arenas, K. Todd Freeman, *The Bluest Eye*, 2005 © Michael Brosilow.

Figure 66. James Vincent Meredith, *The Bluest Eye*, 2005 © Michael Brosilow.

Figure 67. Frank Galati, Jon Michael Hill, *The Tempest*, 2009 © Michael Brosilow.

Figure 68. K. Todd Freeman, Yasen Peyankov, Tim Hopper, *The Tempest*, 2009 © Michael Brosilow.

Figure 69. James Vincent Meredith, Alana Arenas, *The Crucible*, 2007 © Michael Brosilow.

Figure 70. Alana Arenas, James Vincent Meredith, *The Hot L Baltimore*, 2011 © Michael Brosilow.

Figure 71. Robert Breuler, Laurie Metcalf, Ian Barford, *Detroit*, 2010 © Michael Brosilow.

Figure 72. Laurie Metcalf, Kate Arrington, Kevin Anderson, *Detroit*, 2010 © Michael Brosilow.

Figure 73. Martha Lavey, Francis Guinan, *Endgame*, 2010 © Michael Brosilow.

Figure 74. William Petersen, Ian Barford, *Endgame*, 2010 © Michael Brosilow.

Figure 75. Francis Guinan, Tracy Letts, *American Buffalo*, 2009 © Michael Brosilow.

Figure 76. John Mahoney, Alan Wilder, Francis Guinan, Randall Newsome, Tom Irwin, *The Seafarer*, 2008 © Michael Brosilow.

Non-ensemble: Randall Newsome

Figure 77. Tracy Letts, Amy Morton, *Betrayal*, 2007 © Michael Brosilow.

Figure 78. Tracy Letts, Amy Morton, *Who's Afraid of Virginia Woolf*, 2010 © Michael Brosilow.

Figure 79. Kate Arrington, Francis Guinan, *Fake*, 2009 © Michael Brosilow.

Figure 80. Alana Arenas, Tim Hopper, *Marie Antoinette* rehearsal, 2015 © Joel Moorman.

Figure 81. Tina Landau, Tracy Letts, *Superior Donuts* rehearsal, 2008 © Joel Moorman.

Figure 82. Amy Morton, Bruce Norris, *Clybourne Park* rehearsal, 2011 © Joel Moorman.

Figure 83. Yasen Peyankov, Mariann Mayberry, *Grand Concourse* rehearsal, 2015 © Joel Moorman.

Figure 84. Austin Pendleton © Francis Guinan.

Figure 85. Eric Simonson, K. Todd Freeman, *Carter's Way* rehearsal © Jay Geneske.

Figure 86. Tina Landau, Tarell Alvin McCraney, *Head of Passes* rehearsal, 2013 © Joel Moorman.

Figure 87. Ora Jones, *The Unmentionables*, 2006 © Michael Brosilow.

Figure 88. Alana Arenas, *Marie Antoinette* rehearsal, 2015 © Joel Moorman.

Figure 89. Tim Hopper, *Grand Concourse*, 2015 © Joel Moorman.

Figure 90. Alan Wilder, Alana Arenas, *Marie Antoinette* rehearsal, 2015 © Joel Moorman.

Figure 91. Molly Regan © Francis Guinan.

Figure 92. Tarell Alvin McCraney © Mark Campbell.

Figure 93. Joan Allen, *The Wheel*, 2013 © Michael Brosilow.

Figure 94. Tom Irwin, Kate Arrington, *A Parallelogram* rehearsal, 2010 © Michael Brosilow.

Figure 95. Alan Wilder, *East of Eden*, 2015 © Joel Moorman.

Figure 96. Ora Jones, *In The Red and Brown Water* from *The Brother/Sister Play*, 2010 © Joel Moorman.

Figure 97. Kate Arrington © Francis Guinan.

Figure 98. Tina Landau © Francis Guinan.

IN THEIR OWN WORDS: A SHORT TRIBUTE

On January 26, 2015, four months after his death, a memorial celebration was held for longtime mentor, director, and friend to Steppenwolf Sheldon Patinkin. The standing-room-only crowd that packed the Northlight Theatre in Skokie that night honored Sheldon, one the most prolific supporters of theatre in Chicago in the twentieth century. Remembrances were shared of a man who influenced countless young Chicago theatre artists in his role as Chairman of the Theatre Department at Columbia College in his hometown of Chicago and who was one of the earliest supporters of the young Steppenwolf Company in the late 1970s.

Jeff Perry shared the following a few years before Sheldon's passing when Sheldon was honored for lifetime achievement by the League of Chicago Theatres and it will stand here as a tribute to Sheldon and the following people who in some way, shape, or form were part of the Steppenwolf story, but who are no longer with us: Nathan Davis, Joseph and Headman Shabalala, Billie Williams, Dennis Farina, Molly Glynn, Guy Adkins, Bernie Sahlins, Joyce Sloane, Del Close, Susan Raab Simonson, Dennis Letts, and others.

> For me, Sheldon's teaching and directing springs from a beautiful combination of insight and modesty. He reminds me of Chekhov, one of his favorites, because he possesses the mind and heart to capture the essence of a play or to impart an indelible lesson, all the while rendering his own footprints invisible. There is wisdom and craft and empathy abounding in his work, but no apparent ego. It is no coincidence that this ability to disappear into the work is also the realm of our best actors. It has led to a profound kinship Sheldon has had with performers, and they with him, his whole life.
>
> For Steppenwolf, Sheldon has been an invaluable director, a revered tribal elder, a master teacher who co-founded our school, and a ridiculously generous friend who kept us from starving in the early days. The gifts and generosity those roles entail have been repeated by him in unique variations for literally dozens of theatres and thousands of artists and students throughout his career.
>
> I have to bear witness to one of the many hats Sheldon wears so well—from the time we met him in the Highland Park basement, we

at Steppenwolf have trusted no one as we have trusted Sheldon to "please, I'm begging you, please come give notes" ... as most of you know and have benefited from, Sheldon is a world champion note giver. His process is gorgeous; like movements in a symphony or rules of comedy, it comes in "threes"—first are the Socratic questions that lead you to this pleasantly shocked re-understanding of your intent; then he continues with a great, blunt, non-judgmental articulation of what he saw *compared* to what you intended; and finally, as you launch into a spin cycle of anxiety and self-justification about all the obstacles sabotaging your genius, he has the knack of being able to steer you, like a shrink, bartender, and rabbi rolled into one, into the belief that the fixes are easy, they are absolutely in your reach, and there's plenty of time to work them in—and God bless him, even if the work in question was doomed, it didn't matter, he has always known how to calm you down so you can actually understand your task and resume your work.

In our business, these attributes of mentorship and collaboration, practiced at Sheldon's level, are downright precious and exceedingly rare. They go all the way back to his roots, attributes he shared with, and learned from, his crazily talented peers at the University of Chicago like Paul Sills and Mike Nichols. They are gifts often overshadowed by artists who are more "personality" driven, but all great directors and teachers who have a reputation for engendering great work among their fellow artists share them. They are values that, like Sheldon, are sublimely "Chicagoan"—fame and fortune are nice, but for him and for the theatre town he loves, it is the love of the work that keeps the home fires lit.

My friend, you have always insisted the spotlight be thrown on the work, not on yourself. But tonight you'll have to put up with some praise ... because your way of living a life in this art, your talent, passion, discernment, and love for this art we share, and last, but far from least, your absolutely singular generosity of spirit, has touched more of us than you can imagine. Congratulations Sheldon. It is with thanks, love, and deep respect that we throw the light on you tonight.

APPENDIX: MUSIC PLAYLIST

Do a YouTube search for **Steppenwolf Theatre Company of Chicago: In Their Own Words** to access the link to the playlist:

INDEX